THE NORTON ANTHOLOGY OF SHORT FICTION

SECOND EDITION

INSTRUCTOR'S HANDBOOK

THE NORTON ANTHOLOGY OF SHORT FICTION
SECOND EDITION

INSTRUCTOR'S HANDBOOK
For the Complete and Shorter Editions

R. V. CASSILL

W. W. Norton & Company
New York   London

W. W. Norton & Company, Inc.   500 Fifth Avenue,
New York, N.Y. 10110

W. W. Norton & Company Ltd. 37 Great Russell Street,
London WC1B 3NU

Contents

Preface ix

Stories for Teaching Fictional Techniques:
A List x

Stories for Teaching Fictional Techniques:
A List for the Shorter Edition xii

Stories as Examples of Modes, Themes, and
Subjects: A List xiv

Stories as Examples of Modes, Themes, and
Subjects: A List for the Shorter Edition xvii

General Questions for All the Stories xix

*WOODY ALLEN *A Giant Step for Mankind* 1

SHERWOOD ANDERSON *The Egg* 2

I Want to Know Why 6

Questions for Comparing the Author's Stories 8

JAMES BALDWIN *Sonny's Blues* 8

*HONORÉ DE BALZAC *A Passion in the Desert* 11

DONALD BARTHELME *The Indian Uprising* 12

*SAUL BELLOW *Leaving the Yellow House* 15

AMBROSE BIERCE *An Occurrence at Owl Creek Bridge* 18

*JORGE LUIS BORGES *Pierre Menard, Author of the
Quixote* 20

RAY BRADBURY *The Veldt* 22

MORLEY CALLAGHAN *Let Me Promise You* 24

*R. V. CASSILL *The Biggest Band* 25

*WILLA CATHER *Paul's Case* 26

The Old Beauty 29

Questions for Comparing the Author's Stories 32

JOHN CHEEVER *The Enormous Radio* 32

The Fourth Alarm 34

Questions for Comparing the Author's Stories 37

ANTON CHEKHOV *The Lady with the Pet Dog* 37

A Visit to Friends 39

The Darling 41

Questions for Comparing the Author's Stories 43

KATE CHOPIN *Désirée's Baby* 44

*ARTHUR C. CLARKE *The Star* 45

SAMUEL CLEMENS (Mark Twain) *The Notorious
Jumping Frog of Calaveras County* 46

JOSEPH CONRAD *Heart of Darkness* 49

ROBERT COOVER *The Babysitter* 55

*MARK COSTELLO *Murphy's Xmas* 58

---

*Appears only in the Complete Edition.

v

STEPHEN CRANE   *The Open Boat*   60
    The Blue Hotel   63
    Questions for Comparing the Author's Stories   65
*ISAK DINESEN   *Sorrow-Acre*   65
*ARTHUR CONAN DOYLE   *A Scandal in Bohemia*   68
 RALPH ELLISON   *King of the Bingo Game*   69
 WILLIAM FAULKNER   *A Rose for Emily*   71
    That Evening Sun   74
    Barn Burning   76
    Questions for Comparing the Author's Stories   80
 F. SCOTT FITZGERALD   *Babylon Revisited*   80
*GUSTAVE FLAUBERT   *The Legend of Saint Julian
    the Hospitaller*   83
*E. M. FORSTER   *The Road from Colonus*   86
*MARY E. WILKINS FREEMAN   *The Revolt of "Mother"*   89
*MAVIS GALLANT   *Acceptance of Their Ways*   91
 GABRIEL GARCÍA MÁRQUEZ   *The Handsomest Drowned
    Man in the World*   92
*MAXIM GORKY   *The Hermit*   94
*JAMES B. HALL   *A View of the Beach*   96
 NATHANIEL HAWTHORNE   *Young Goodman Brown*   98
    The Birthmark   100
    Questions for Comparing the Author's Stories   103
 ERNEST HEMINGWAY   *Hills Like White Elephants*   103
 SHIRLEY JACKSON   *The Lottery*   105
*W. W. JACOBS   *The Monkey's Paw*   106
 HENRY JAMES   *The Tree of Knowledge*   108
    The Jolly Corner   110
    Questions for Comparing the Author's Stories   113
*SARAH ORNE JEWETT   *The Flight of Betsey Lane*   113
 JAMES JOYCE   *Araby*   115
    A Little Cloud   117
    The Dead   118
    Questions for Comparing the Author's Stories   125
 FRANZ KAFKA   *The Metamorphosis*   125
    A Hunger Artist   130
    Questions for Comparing the Author's Stories   132
*RING LARDNER   *Haircut*   132
*MARGARET LAURENCE   *The Loons*   134
 D. H. LAWRENCE   *Tickets, Please*   135
    The Horse Dealer's Daughter   137
    The Rocking-Horse Winner   140
    Questions for Comparing the Author's Stories   143
*STEPHEN LEACOCK   *The Marine Excursion of the
    Knights of Pythias*   143

*Appears only in the Complete Edition.

URSULA K. LE GUIN   *The Ones Who Walk Away from Omelas*   145
DORIS LESSING   *To Room Nineteen*   147
CARSON McCULLERS   *The Jockey*   150
*JAMES ALAN McPHERSON   *Gold Coast*   151
BERNARD MALAMUD   *The Jewbird*   153
THOMAS MANN   *Disorder and Early Sorrow*   154
*KATHERINE MANSFIELD   *The Garden-Party*   156
*W. SOMERSET MAUGHAM   *The Outstation*   158
GUY DE MAUPASSANT   *The Necklace*   160
HERMAN MELVILLE   *Bartleby the Scrivener*   162
*YUKIO MISHIMA   *Patriotism*   165
ALICE MUNRO   *Royal Beatings*   167
VLADIMIR NABOKOV   *Signs and Symbols*   169
JOYCE CAROL OATES   *How I Contemplated the World from the Detroit House of Correction and Began My Life Over Again*   171
FLANNERY O'CONNOR   *A Good Man Is Hard to Find*   174
    Everything that Rises Must Converge   177
    **Parker's Back*   180
    Questions for Comparing the Author's Stories   183
FRANK O'CONNOR   *Guests of the Nation*   184
    **My Oedipus Complex*   187
    Questions for Comparing the Author's Stories   190
*TILLIE OLSEN   *Tell Me a Riddle*   190
*GRACE PALEY   *The Used-Boy Raisers*   193
*DOROTHY PARKER   *Big Blonde*   194
*WILLIAM PEDEN   *A Boone County Parable*   195
*JAYNE ANNE PHILLIPS   *Souvenir*   196
EDGAR ALLAN POE   *The Fall of the House of Usher*   198
    **The Purloined Letter*   200
    Questions for Comparing the Author's Stories   202
KATHERINE ANNE PORTER   *Theft*   203
    Flowering Judas   205
    Questions for Comparing the Author's Stories   207
J. F. POWERS   *The Valiant Woman*   207
*PHILIP ROTH   *The Conversion of the Jews*   209
SAKI (H. H. Munro)   *The Open Window*   211
*MAX SCHOTT   *The Horsebreaker*   212
*IRWIN SHAW   *The Girls in Their Summer Dresses*   214
*ISAAC BASHEVIS SINGER   *The Spinoza of Market Street*   215
*JEAN STAFFORD   *In the Zoo*   216
*JOHN STEINBECK   *The Chrysanthemums*   219
*PETER TAYLOR   *Dean of Men*   221

---

*Appears only in the Complete Edition.

JAMES THURBER   *The Secret Life of Walter Mitty*   224
LEO TOLSTOY   *God Sees the Truth, but Waits*   226
    The Death of Ivan Ilych   227
    Questions for Comparing the Author's Stories   230
JOHN UPDIKE   *A & P*   230
ALICE WALKER   *Everyday Use*   232
EUDORA WELTY   *Powerhouse*   234
    A Worn Path   236
    Questions for Comparing the Author's Stories   237
EDITH WHARTON   *The Muse's Tragedy*   238
*RICHARD WILBUR   *A Game of Catch*   240
WILLIAM CARLOS WILLIAMS   *The Use of Force*   241
VIRGINIA WOOLF   *Kew Gardens*   243
RICHARD WRIGHT   *The Man Who Was Almost a Man*   244

*Appears only in the Complete Edition.

PREFACE

At every step of preparing the *Norton Anthology of Short Fiction*, my enthusiasms and hopes were those of a teacher of fiction as well as an editor trying to make stories I cared about accessible. I wanted to be a collaborator with other teachers as well as, in some sense, with the authors themselves, for the enterprise of literary education involves us all in turn with the creative process. It seemed to me that just as a storyteller might spoil his effects by an untimely or digressive explanation of what is truly at stake in the conflict of his characters, so the editor preparing footnotes or other interpretive apparatus might intrude on the gradual revelations by which fiction works its magic.

Editorial tact suggested that the stories in the main text be left relatively free of interpretive labels, while those that might on some occasions be necessary for classroom exploitation should be available in this supplemental handbook. As you continue to use the *Norton Anthology of Short Fiction* you will probably become increasingly aware of the very many pedagogical concerns reconciled in settling finally on the table of contents, and the following pages should explicate some of the strategies for meeting these concerns.

Lists will direct you quickly and conveniently to examples of techniques, modes, and themes. There are generalized blocks of questions on the main elements of fiction—questions that might be asked of any story in the text. In some cases these will overlap the particular questions appended to stories and reprinted here after my commentaries. In other cases the questions will lead into extensive concentrations when a teacher finds reasons for lingering on a favorite story or rewarding example.

My commentaries on the stories are in no way offered as exhaustive or definitive critical examinations. Rather they might be thought of as one reader's (one teacher's) response to the problems and pleasures of short fiction. The comment is not systematically keyed to the questions. In some cases it will suggest an alternative or complementary approach.

Finally, the bibliographic references supplied for some of the best-known stories will direct student and teacher to more extensive and detailed types of criticism. The use of all this apparatus or none of it thus remains at the discretion of the teacher while untrammeled encounter with the stories is left open to the user of the text itself.

R. V. Cassill

ix

Stories for Teaching Fictional Techniques
A List

The stories listed here are the most clear-cut examples of each technique. In general, the stories mos
useful in demonstrating the form will appear at the t
of the list.

First-person Narration (in which the pronoun I or, i
rare cases, we designates the teller of the tale)

Narrator as Central Character
James Joyce, *Araby* (p. 690)
William Carlos Williams, *The Use of Force* (p. 14£
Frank O'Connor, *Guests of the Nation* (p. 1119)
Sherwood Anderson, *I Want to Know Why* (p. 14)
James B. Hall, *A View of the Beach* (p. 583)

Narrator as Secondary Character
Maxim Gorky, *The Hermit* (p. 561)
Arthur Conan Doyle, *A Scandal in Bohemia* (p. 42£
Edgar Allan Poe, *The Purloined Letter* (p. 1222)
James Baldwin, *Sonny's Blues* (p. 22)

The "Unreliable" Narrator (whose report is inter
to be taken with a grain of salt)
Ring Lardner, *Haircut* (p. 786)
Samuel Clemens, *The Notorious Jumping Frog of
Calaveras County* (p. 246)

Narrator Speaking for a Group of Observers
William Faulkner, *A Rose for Emily* (p. 451)

Third-person Narration

Omniscient Narrator (the author takes the priv
of invading the awareness of any or all charac
or of explaining things done to them)
Sarah Orne Jewett, *The Flight of Betsey Lane* (
Kate Chopin, *Désirée's Baby* (p. 235)
Willa Cather, *Paul' Case* (p. 139)
D. H. Lawrence, *The Horse Dealer's Daughter* (
Shirley Jackson, *The Lottery* (p. 617)
Bernard Malamud, *The Jewbird* (p. 912)
Isak Dinesen, *Sorrow-Acre* (p. 399)
Yukio Mishima, *Patriotism* (p. 1021)
Somerset Maugham, *The Outstation* (p. 958)

Narration Limited to Point of View of Major Character

James Joyce, *A Little Cloud* (p. 695)
Ralph Ellison, *King of the Bingo Game* (p. 443)
Alice Munro, *Royal Beatings* (p. 1041)
Jayne Anne Phillips, *Souvenir* (p. 1193)
Saul Bellow, *Leaving the Yellow House* (p. 65)
John Steinbeck, *The Chrysanthemums* (p. 1326)
Richard Wilbur, *A Game of Catch* (p. 1458)

Story in an Envelope (the principal story is enclosed within an external setting; the narrator is introduced objectively before he begins his narration)

Honoré de Balzac, *A Passion in the Desert* (p. 48)
Joseph Conrad, *Heart of Darkness* (p. 251)

Present-tense Narration

Katherine Anne Porter, *Flowering Judas* (p. 1243)
Thomas Mann, *Disorder and Early Sorrow* (p. 920)

Experimental Forms (conventional technical devices are reshaped or abandoned)

Jorge Luis Borges, *Pierre Menard, Author of the Quixote* (p. 100)
Joyce Carol Oates, *How I Contemplated the World from the Detroit House of Correction and Began My Life Over Again* (p. 1064)
Mark Costello, *Murphy's Xmas* (p. 344)
Robert Coover, *The Babysitter* (p. 322)
Virginia Woolf, *Kew Gardens* (p. 1465)

STORIES FOR TEACHING FICTIONAL TECHNIQUES: A LIST FOR THE SHORTER EDITION

The stories listed here are the most clear-cut examples of each technique. In general, the stories most useful in demonstrating the form will appear at the top of the list.

First-person Narration (in which the pronoun I or, in rare cases, we designates the teller of the tale)

Narrator as Central Character
James Joyce, *Araby* (p. 313)
Frank O'Connor, *Guests of the Nation* (p. 535)

Narrator as Secondary Character
James Baldwin, *Sonny's Blues* (p. 9)
Edgar Allan Poe, *The Fall of the House of Usher* (p. 545)

The "Unreliable" Narrator (whose report is intended to be taken with a grain of salt)
Samuel Clemens, *The Notorious Jumping Frog of Calaveras County* (p. 108)

Narrator Speaking for a Group of Observers
William Faulkner, *A Rose for Emily* (p. 233)

Third-person Narration

Omniscient Narrator (the author takes the privilege of invading the awareness of any or all characters, or of explaining things done to them)
Kate Chopin, *Désirée's Baby* (p. 103)
D. H. Lawrence, *The Horse Dealer's Daughter* (p. 337)
Shirley Jackson, *The Lottery* (p. 294)
Bernard Malamud, *The Jewbird* (p. 402)

Narration Limited to Point of View of Major Character
James Joyce, *A Little Cloud* (p. 318)
Ralph Ellison, *King of the Bingo Game* (p. 225)
Alice Munro, *Royal Beatings* (p. 473)

Present-tense Narration
Katherine Anne Porter, *Flowering Judas* (p. 565)
Thomas Mann, *Disorder and Early Sorrow* (p. 409)

Experimental Forms (conventional technical devices are reshaped or abandoned)

Joyce Carol Oates, *How I Contemplated the World from the Detroit House of Correction and Began My Life Over Again* (p. 497)

Robert Coover, *The Babysitter* (p. 184)

Virginia Woolf, *Kew Gardens* (p. 673)

Stories as Examples of Modes, Themes, and Subjects: A List

Allegory
Nathaniel Hawthorne, *Young Goodman Brown* (p. 589)
Nathaniel Hawthorne, *The Birthmark* (p. 600)
Shirley Jackson, *The Lottery* (p. 617)
Franz Kafka, *A Hunger Artist* (p. 779)
D. H. Lawrence, *The Rocking-Horse Winner* (p. 829)
Gabriel García Márquez, *The Handsomest Drowned Man in the World* (p. 556)

Artists and Art
Edith Wharton, *The Muse's Tragedy* (p. 1446)
Jorge Luis Borges, *Pierre Menard, Author of the Quixote* (p. 100)
Henry James, *The Tree of Knowledge* (p. 634)
Franz Kafka, *A Hunger Artist* (p. 779)
Eudora Welty, *Powerhouse* (p. 1429)

Class Conflict
Guy de Maupassant, *The Necklace* (p. 983)
Katherine Mansfield, *The Garden-Party* (p. 946)

Comedy
John Cheever, *The Fourth Alarm* (p. 192)
James Thurber, *The Secret Life of Walter Mitty* (p. 1359)
Samuel Clemens, *The Notorious Jumping Frog of Calaveras County* (p. 246)
Grace Paley, *The Used-Boy Raisers* (p. 1168)
Philip Roth, *The Conversion of the Jews* (p. 1261)
Woody Allen, *A Giant Step for Mankind* (p. 1)
Robert Coover, *The Babysitter* (p. 322)
Henry James, *The Tree of Knowledge* (p. 634)

Detective Story
Edgar Allan Poe, *The Purloined Letter* (p. 1222)
Arthur Conan Doyle, *A Scandal in Bohemia* (p. 425)

Fantasy and Science Fiction
Honoré de Balzac, *A Passion in the Desert* (p. 48)
Arthur C. Clarke, *The Star* (p. 240)
Ursula Le Guin, *The Ones Who Walk Away from Omelas* (p. 856)
E. M. Forster, *The Road from Colonus* (p. 526)
Flannery O'Connor, *A Good Man Is Hard to Find* (p. 1077)
Edgar Allan Poe, *The Fall of the House of Usher* (p. 1206)
Ray Bradbury, *The Veldt* (p. 109)

Generation Gap and Changing Times
Willa Cather, *The Old Beauty* (p. 156)
William Faulkner, *Barn Burning* (p. 473)
Alice Walker, *Everyday Use* (p. 1421)
Thomas Mann, *Disorder and Early Sorrow* (p. 920)
Flannery O'Connor, *Everything that Rises Must Converge*
                    (p. 1090)

Ghost Story
Henry James, *The Jolly Corner* (p. 646)

Horror
W. W. Jacobs, *The Monkey's Paw* (p. 625)

Initiation
John Updike, *A & P* (p. 1416)
Sherwood Anderson, *The Egg* (p. 6)
Sherwood Anderson, *I Want to Know Why* (p. 14)
R. V. Cassill, *The Biggest Band* (p. 125)
Katherine Mansfield, *The Garden-Party* (p. 946)
Jean Stafford, *In the Zoo* (p. 1309)
James Joyce, *Araby* (p. 690)

Justice
Stephen Crane, *The Blue Hotel* (p. 376)
Leo Tolstoy, *God Sees the Truth, but Waits* (p. 1364)
Isak Dinesen, *Sorrow-Acre* (p. 399)
William Faulkner, *Barn Burning* (p. 473)
Peter Taylor, *Dean of Men* (p. 1335)

Personal Alienation
James Baldwin, *Sonny's Blues* (p. 22)
F. Scott Fitzgerald, *Babylon Revisited* (p. 489)
Herman Melville, *Bartleby the Scrivener* (p. 991)
Vladimir Nabokov, *Signs and Symbols* (p. 1059)
James Joyce, *A Little Cloud* (p. 695)

Race Relations
Flannery O'Connor, *Everything that Rises Must Converge*
                    (p. 1090)
Kate Chopin, *Désirée's Baby* (p. 235)
Bernard Malamud, *The Jewbird* (p. 912)
Eudora Welty, *A Worn Path* (p. 1439)

Religion
Maxim Gorky, *The Hermit* (p. 561)
Leo Tolstoy, *God Sees the Truth, but Waits* (p. 1364)
Leo Tolstoy, *The Death of Ivan Ilych* (p. 1370)
Philip Roth, *The Conversion of the Jews* (p. 1261)

Satire

John Cheever, *The Fourth Alarm* (p. 192)
Samuel Clemens, *The Notorious Jumping Frog of Calaveras County* (p. 246)
Woody Allen, *A Giant Step for Mankind* (p. 1)

Strife Between the Sexes

Ernest Hemingway, *Hills Like White Elephants* (p. 613)
Irwin Shaw, *The Girls in Their Summer Dresses* (p. 1290)
D. H. Lawrence, *Tickets, Please* (p. 804)
Dorothy Parker, *Big Blonde* (p. 1173)
Anton Chekov, *The Darling* (p. 225)
John Steinbeck, *The Chrysanthemums* (p. 1326)
Mark Costello, *Murphy's Xmas* (p. 344)
Morley Callaghan, *Let Me Promise You* (p. 121)

Women in Search

Sarah Orne Jewett, *The Flight of Betsey Lane* (p. 673)
Edith Wharton, *The Muse's Tragedy* (p. 1446)
Mary E. Wilkins Freeman, *The Revolt of "Mother"* (p. 536)
Doris Lessing, *To Room Nineteen* (p. 862)
Margaret Laurence, *The Loons* (p. 796)
Alice Munro, *Royal Beatings* (p. 1041)
Jayne Anne Phillips, *Souvenir* (p. 1193)

Stories as Examples of Modes, Themes, and Subjects: A List for the Shorter Edition

Allegory
Nathaniel Hawthorne, *Young Goodman Brown* (p. 279)
Shirley Jackson, *The Lottery* (p. 294)
Franz Kafka, *A Hunger Artist* (p. 329)
D. H. Lawrence, *The Rocking-Horse Winner* (p. 351)
Gabriel García Márquez, *The Handsomest Drowned Man in the World* (p. 275)

Artists and Art
Edith Wharton, *The Muse's Tragedy* (p. 658)
Henry James, *The Tree of Knowledge* (p. 301)
Franz Kafka, *A Hunger Artist* (p. 329)

Class Conflict
Guy de Maupassant, *The Necklace* (p. 436)

Comedy
John Cheever, *The Fourth Alarm* (p. 74)
James Thurber, *The Secret Life of Walter Mitty* (p. 587)
Samuel Clemens, *The Notorious Jumping Frog of Calaveras County* (p. 108)
Robert Coover, *The Babysitter* (p. 184)

Fantasy
Ursula Le Guin, *The Ones Who Walk Away from Omelas* (p. 364)
Flannery O'Connor, *A Good Man Is Hard to Find* (p. 509)
Edgar Allan Poe, *The Fall of the House of Usher* (p. 545)
Ray Bradbury, *The Veldt* (p. 49)

Generation Gap and Changing Times
William Faulkner, *Barn Burning* (p. 241)
Alice Walker, *Everyday Use* (p. 643)
Thomas Mann, *Disorder and Early Sorrow* (p. 409)
Flannery O'Connor, *Everything that Rises Must Converge* (p. 522)

Initiation
John Updike, *A & P* (p. 637)
Sherwood Anderson, *The Egg* (p. 1)
James Joyce, *Araby* (p. 313)

Justice
William Faulkner, *Barn Burning* (p. 241)

Personal Alienation

James Baldwin, *Sonny's Blues* (p. 9)
F. Scott Fitzgerald, *Babylon Revisited* (p. 256)
Herman Melville, *Bartleby the Scrivener* (p. 443)
Vladimir Nabokov, *Signs and Symbols* (p. 492)
James Joyce, *A Little Cloud* (p. 319)

Race Relations

Flannery O'Connor, *Everything that Rises Must Converge*
(p. 522)
Kate Chopin, *Désirée's Baby* (p. 103)
Bernard Malamud, *The Jewbird* (p. 402)

Religion

Leo Tolstoy, *The Death of Ivan Ilych* (p. 591)

Satire

John Cheever, *The Fourth Alarm* (p. 74)
Samuel Clemens, *The Notorious Jumping Frog of Calavera
County* (p. 108)

Strife Between the Sexes

Ernest Hemingway, *Hills Like White Elephants* (p. 290)
Anton Chekhov, *The Darling* (p. 93)
D. H. Lawrence, *The Rocking-Horse Winner* (p. 351)
Morley Callaghan, *Let Me Promise You* (p. 61)

Women in Search

Edith Wharton, *The Muse's Tragedy* (p. 658)
Doris Lessing, *To Room Nineteen* (p. 320)
Alice Munro, *Royal Beatings* (p. 473)

General Questions for All the Stories

Exposition and Setting

1. How and when has the author introduced the main characters?

2. How much background information or history has the author provided for them? At what point in the story, and by what means, is this background information brought in? What makes such backgrounding necessary or (in cases in which it is scanty or lacking altogether) unnecessary? Are the characters made quickly comprehensible by representing them as familiar types?

3. What means provide us with an understanding of the situation prevailing before the action, properly speaking, begins? To what extent is a prevailing and pre-existing conflict used as a jumping-off place for the present action of the story.

4. What is there of special interest or significance in the setting of the story? By what means are we informed about the details of the setting? At what point in the story? How is its relation to the significance of the action expressed?

5. Is the setting vividly represented or merely implied by the way in which events unfold? Has the author assumed that readers would be familiar with the significant qualities to be found in this setting?

6. How is the setting exploited to enhance or control the mood of the story? How does it help to bring out the feelings or emotions experienced by the characters?

7. In stories told in the first person, do we learn essential things about the narrator by the feelings or attention the narrator devotes to the setting?

8. Could the action take place meaningfully in another setting? That is—has the setting been chosen arbitrarily, for its own sake, or because it has an integral connection with the action?

Plot

1. Are the meaning and emotional impact of this story heavily dependent on the working out of the plot? Or is the plot—if it is noticeable at all—subordinate to other elements?

2. To what extent does the action of the plot emerge from the kinds of characters depicted in the story and their relation to each other?

3. Are there any major breaks or omissions in the chain of causality that links the events or episodes of the plot? Is the outcome of the plot consistent with the actions that initiated it? If there is a surprise ending, does it emerge from some unforeseen but plausible change in direction of the plot line?

4. How is the plot related to the chronology of the story? That is, have some decisive actions, necessary to the plot, taken place before the narration begins? Is the narration halted with an implication of some event still to come that will round out the plot?

5. Test the plot for meaning and credibility by imagining alternative events which, at any point, might have made for a different outcome.

6. What motivations in the characters are necessary to move the plot along?

Character and Conflict

1. Who is the central character? (Or, who are the central characters?) What are his or her distinguishing qualities? What means has the author used to demonstrate these qualities? To what extent is the character defined by contrast with minor characters?

2. Do we understand the characters as types or as individuals? By their actions? Their speech? Their thoughts? (It may be useful for you to pick a single instance of action, speech, or thought and ask in what ways it represents the character to whom it is attributed.)

3. Which characters are active and which passive within the pattern of the story?

4. Does the story show growth or change of character? How much of the story's meaning depends on such growth or change?

5. How much of the conflict in the story rises from an opposition between the central character and his or her environment?

6. Is the conflict inherent in the personality of the characters assembled by the author or in the backgrounds they represent?

7. How has the author worked to involve the reader's sympathies for certain characters, and how does this contribute to the reader's assessment of the issues of the conflict?

8. How much are the characters (or their representation) conditioned by their time and place?

Point of View and Person of Narration

1. Has the author confined the narration to a single point of view? Taking into account the nature of the material in the story, what apparent advantages lie in telling about it from the point of view actually chosen?

2. What potentially interesting aspects of the subject matter have been subordinated or omitted by choice of point of view?

3. In first-person narration, to what extent does the author appear to have identified himself with the narrator? What has the author gained by keeping a distinction between himself and the personality of the narrator?

4. What would be gained or lost by changing the narration from first to third person, or vice versa? (Class exercises in rewriting parts of stories may be useful in support of this question.)

5. How is the point of view complemented by disciplines of style and diction? How do self-imposed limits of diction reinforce the emotional impact of a story or focus its meaning?

6. Is an illusion of reality enhanced by choice of point of view? A sense of immediacy?

Theme

1. Does the story make a general statement about life or experience? Can it be stated in the form of a maxim? (The effort to reduce the meaning of any piece of fiction to a short, aphoristic summary can stumble all too readily into simplistic errors. The teacher should point out that summary of any theme is less than a complete understanding of the story from which it comes.)

2. Is the thematic statement accomplished chiefly by the outcome of the action? What qualifications and shadings are given to it by the awareness of the characters of what has happened to them?

3. What values and ideas have been put into the conflict from which the thematic statement comes?

4. Is the theme a traditional one? Has the story given a new twist to traditional wisdom? Where else—in literature, history, or religion—have you encountered a similar theme? Can you recall a poem or another story which makes a comparable thematic statement?

Description, Representation, and Symbol

1. Pick out some examples of language used by the author to stimulate and control the reader's visualization of the scene. Consider not only individual words and phrases but the accumulations and combinations of nouns, verbs, and their modifiers in paragraph structures.

2. How have the details chosen by the author given the essential appearance of characters or scene? Is the story fully presented to your senses? Comment on the adequacy of the description.

3. Has the author relied on your familiarity with certain scenes, characters, and situations to fill in what has been omitted from the actual text of the story?

4. How has the objectively rendered action of the story helped you to understand the thoughts, emotions, and motivations of the characters? Can you fill in the thought processes of those characters whose thoughts are not described?

5. What objects, acts, or situations have a symbolic meaning? Are the characters aware of these symbolic meanings? Has the author used symbols as a means of communicating to the reader some meanings not implicit in the action and not understood by any character in the story?

Mode (as it applies)

1. What devices or instances has the author relied on to heighten the comic (pathetic, tragic, satiric, elegiac) effect of the story?

2. What exaggerations or distortions of reality do you find used to shape the material of the story to a particular purpose? Could the same material serve another purpose? (I.e., in the case of comedy, could the material have been treated in a way that would produce a tragic effect?)

3. To what extent has the author manipulated the tone of the story to give a special flavor to the material?

4. With what views of life does this story fit best?

5. What satiric or ironic elements can you distinguish in ths story? Do these dominate the whole story? Are they consistent with the overall quality of the story, or do they provide tension, variety, and suspense as you wait to learn what the author is really driving at?

6. Does the story appeal chiefly to a romantic or realistic sensibility? Does it tend to stir up pity, contempt, amusement, awe, dismay, admiration, or a desire that life should be different than it is?

THE NORTON ANTHOLOGY OF SHORT FICTION

SECOND EDITION

INSTRUCTOR'S HANDBOOK

Very few things are more difficult to discuss in the classroom than delightful farce. Students feel—correctly—that laughter must be spontaneous, and their deep-seated feeling is offended when the inevitable format of analytical discussion begins to slide into the sticky explication of the mechanisms of humor in any piece intended primarily as entertainment.

Surely the approach to wit as nimble as Allen's requires a light touch. In the understandable fear of bogging down and spoiling the operation of this wit, the course of wisdom is probably to skirt the kind of examination which works successfully in stories of more serious substance or plain sobriety. Perhaps, though, the teacher can find advantage in the strategy of appealing to the common desire to sharpen the cutting edge of mockery by emulating its deft practitioners. How does Allen manage to keep twisting the knife after the first insertion? The question to raise is not what is funny about the piece as a whole but how has the author managed to prolong the entertainment far beyond the time span of the ordinary joke, which depends on a quick buildup to a single punch line. You might well point out that any fool can provoke laughter, but only the skilled comedian can keep 'em laughing.

It may seem a long stretch of Keats' dictum that poets should "load every vein with ore" to find it the first principle of successful farce, but that is just what a detailed examination will discover here. Note, to begin, the profusion of names in the first paragraph—and their incongruous, surprising exploitation. That the choking man should turn blue is a commonplace. The commonplace is made laughable by the ludicrous specification that the particular shade of blue is one "associated" with the paintings of that genteel portrait and landscape painter, Thomas Gainsborough.

Of course, there are sentences lacking comparable twists. But not so many, at that. Incongruous or ludicrous nouns, verbs, modifiers provide a constant sparkle to the entire surface of a piece which has a minimal, though comic, substructure. While it would be counterproductively tedious to labor through the

whole text to point out how each sentence is loaded
with barbs and extravagances, calling attention to
several should be useful in pointing out the author's
dependence on a constantly shimmering surface. Among
these are the ones introducing Shulamith Arnolfini,
whose hair is "skun in a, bun," the entry of "January
7," and the observation at Marcello's Villa in the
entry of March 18. (In the latter, note the offhand
allusion to the "gentleman well placed in the cement
and contracting <u>community</u>." My underlining emphasizes
a slyness in the choice of a noun. The allusion, of
course, is to a tough mobster, and mobs are not
soberly denominated "communities.")

This is the kind of fiction that depends for success almost exclusively on its devices rather than on
any profundity of revelation about the human condition, either comic or tragic. From the beginning to
the end of his absurd caricature of scientists at
work, the author skates on thin ice. The real trick
is the way the ice has been reinforced by wordplay to
keep the skater from falling through before he has
finished his turn.

Questions

1. Are the mind and character of the narrator essentially the same as those of the author of the diary?
2. What familiar aspects of the scientific mind
and professorial character are parodied here?
3. Does the story have any point beyond pure
entertainment? Discuss its value as lampoon or satire.
4. What is being parodied by the outcome of the
action?
5. What is the difference between this story of
moderate length and the ordinary joke?

Sherwood Anderson   *The Egg* (p. 6)
                     (Shorter Edition, p. 1)

In very few stories will the narrator appear so
prominently and visibly in his storyteller's role as
in *The Egg*. The vocabulary, the digressions, and the
whole air of the presentation conjure up an image of

a loquacious entertainer sitting in front of us as he
piles up embellishments and watches for the response
of his audience while he calculates which tack to take
next. The storyteller, that is, occupies the foreground so completely that for a considerable time the
story of his father's pathetic bid for success seems
only one among many of the themes strewn before us.
That story is, of course, the axis on which everything
else revolves, the vehicle for the central theme. The
narrator, whose imagination flies so far out from the
circumstances of his childhood, knows himself to be
"the son of my father" and the father's cyclic spins
through hope and despair are the cycles through which
his son's life and thought must return.

The mother instigates the move from the farm to
town—a move emblematic of a general evolution in
American society. "For herself she wanted nothing. For
father and myself she was incurably ambitious." Her
ambition is the egg from which the migration emerges.
The move is made in stages, first to a chicken farm
where things go badly and then into a place called
Pickleville, which was at least adjacent to the small
town of Bidwell. The plans for the family to open a
restaurant are an extravagant mixture of cunning, desperation, and naiveté. The skimpy measure of their
success up to this point is registered by the recollection of the storyteller that he was "glad to be
away from the farm" but still superstitiously "afraid
of being seen in my gay mood" for fear that present
gains might at any moment be swept away.

Looking back from our times, we can admit that it
is cunning of the father to foresee that entertainment would be the wave of the future. But he has no
talents as an entertainer. Worse, he is so poorly
tuned to the mood of townspeople that he is quite
mistaken about what would entertain them. Because
eggs are interesting to him, he supposes that everyone
must be interested in them. His first valiant attempt
to prove his theory is a disaster.

The most striking formal feature of the story is
that this disastrous episode is, in fact, told twice.
First we get it as it was actually experienced by the
storyteller when it happened. He was upstairs in bed
when he heard the commotion downstairs and then saw
his father come up, trembling, from below with an egg
in his hand. "He bgan to cry like a boy, and I, carried away by his grief, cried with him" Testifying
from his present view on the matter, the storyteller

says, "I remember only my own grief and fright and the
shiny path over father's head glowing in the lamplight
as he knelt by the bed." The second telling of the
episode is a growth of sympathetic imagination sprung
from this small egg of literal memory.

It can also be likened—as a narrative device—to
the familiar instant replay of a segment of a sporting
event reported on television. In such replays the
observer is able to sort out the details that gave
significance to what he has just witnessed. Knowing
the outcome, he can concentrate on the pattern of
forces in action that brought it about.

But it is most important to stress that Anderson
here insists on the primacy of the imagination in
coming at the truth of events, for which the unaided
senses are always an inadequate witness. "For some
unexplainable reason I know the story as well as
though I had been witness. . . ." The reason is not
explained in so many words, but we may infer it hand-
ily. The author is implying that stories are known
best when they are assembled in retrospect by sympathy
and analogy to a range of other experiences. The
imagined scene has a concreteness and objectivity that
the hypothetically real present (in which the story is
being told) has not. There is direct dialogue and dramatic interaction between the father and Joe Kane of a
sort unmatched by anything before or after it. The invented, or imagined, scene also has the comic force
required to prepare the reader for the pathos to come.
Showing a hungry customer the unappetizing monsters
bottled on the shelf approximates farce.

It is, nevertheless, the farce and buffoonery of a
small-town Quixote, the mistake of a man willing to
risk humiliation in his pursuit of an ideal. (The
ideal itself may be a shabby derivative of the American
dream of success; no matter—the devotion remains.)
The final irony is that the egg itself, in its unpredictable resistance to human intentions, frustrates
the man just as he imagines he is going to triumph.
Naturally Joe Kane laughs.

The larger irony, however, emerges from the storyteller's imaginative speculation on the relatively
trivial event. Recalling how his father came up the
stairs with an egg in his hand, he says, "I imagine he
had some idea of destroying it, of destroying all eggs,
and that he intended to let mother and me see him begin." But by now the expanded imagination has seized
on the "egg" as a symbol of a principle that cannot be

destroyed. The egg of the father's despair produces the chick of family sympathy, which in its turn will produce eggs, and so on forever. The egg of an event in time has produced a problem that "remains unsolved in my mind. And that, I conclude, is but another evidence of the complete and final triumph of the egg. . . ." The triumph of the creative principle, eternally destroying to bring forth new growth.

Questions

1. The narrator calls himself a "gloomy man." What evidence is there for or against such a characterization?

2. What has the story to say about the American dream of upward mobility and success?

3. How does the narrator know what happened between his father and Joe Kane? Is the scene in which these two appear together more or less credible than the other parts of the story? How is the chronology of the story affected by the repetition of the moment when the father brings the egg upstairs?

4. What is meant by the comment, "Most philosophers must have been raised on chicken farms"? Are we to take it seriously?

5. What does the egg symbolize? In what ways does it obtain a "complete and final triumph"?

See also "Questions for Comparing the Author's Stories," p. 8 of this *Handbook*.

Further Reading

Anderson, David D. *Sherwood Anderson: An Introduction and Interpretation*. New York: Holt, Rinehart and Winston, 1967, pp. 64-65, 66, 75, 78, 164.

Gerhard, Joseph. "The American Triumph of the Egg: Anderson's 'The Egg' and Fitzgerald's 'The Great Gatsby,'" *Criticism*, VII (Spring 1965), 131-140.

West, Michael D. "Sherwood Anderson's Triumph: 'The Egg,'" *American Quarterly*, XX (Winter 1968), 675-693.

Sherwood Anderson   *I Want to Know Why* (p. 14)

The story begins and builds momentum as a celebration of nature and the natural goodness in men. The sights, sounds and smells of the racetracks in the morning all come to the boy's senses not only as pleasures in themselves but as promises of what life can be when he comes into full possession of it. Everything opens for him into broader and broader horizons. Running away to go to the races at Saratoga is an entry into the world of grown-ups and a break from the confinements of childhood. And what happens at Saratoga is, up to a point, a confirmation of all the expectations that have been built up in the boy by his earlier observations and the enthusiasm they have fed.

In his numerous visits to the horse farms around Beckersville, the boy has been enchanted by the undeniable beauty of the thoroughbreds. "There isn't anything so lovely and clean and full of spunk and honest and everything as some race horses." In Saratoga he sees all these wonderful virtues concentrated in the horse Sunstreak. By seeing them thus embodied he seems to understand that he, too, as a part of nature, shares these qualities that nature has bestowed on the splendid animal. And at that point in the story there is no reason for him to suspect that anything but good can come from such endowments.

Before Sunstreak's great race the boy looks at him and believes "he was just a raging torrent inside. He was like the water in the river at Niagara Falls just before it goes plunk down." Clearly, the boy feels this potential in himself as he stands on the verge of manhood. Further, his perception of uncomplicated natural goodness seems to be shared and confirmed by Jerry Tillford. The boy is confident that Tillford not only shares his perception but also is an embodiment of the goodness they both see in the horse.

In recapitulating and trying to come to terms with the whole experience in Saratoga, the boy says, "Now I know [Sunstreak was] better than Jerry." But in the moment of exhilaration before the race, that distinction did not have to be made. Man, boy and horse share the same gifts from nature, and it hardly matters which has the greater share. Still caught up in the euphoria of his vision after the race, the boy recognizes that the trainer is more important to him than his natural father. Tillford is a teacher who has taught the colt "to run and be patient and when to let himself out and not to quit, never." Clearly these things are what the boy has wanted to be taught in order to fulfill the potentials of his own nature.

But then, in the complication of the story, we understand—even if the narrator protests that he does not—how the same natural gifts that bring men to their high moments of victory can overshoot the mark and carry them to ugliness and degradation. It is the sporting impulse in men that moves Jerry Tillford to his devotion to Sunstreak. It is the same impulse, turned ugly, that carries him on in the aftermath of the race to visit the sporting house full of bad women. It is the exultation of victory that carries him on to lie and brag "like a fool" and that makes his eyes shine in the presence of the whore "just as they did when he looked at me and at Sunstreak in the paddocks at the track in the afternoon."

What the boy has seen—though he can not bring himself to admit it—is that the promises of nature are more equivocal than we can, mostly, bear to believe, that there is as much potential for evil as for good in the beautiful gifts of our natural existence. What is also implicit in his discovery is that this ambivalence in nature presents a snare and a dilemma for humans which it does not for horses. While we may see in the animal world a mirrored image of all that is good in ourselves, the distinguishing gift of a moral consciousness burdens us with a knowledge of evil that the rest of nature will never share. Why? Since we are natural creatures, why can't we be as simple as the rest of nature? The boy says that the knowledge that we cannot "spoils . . . everything." The implication of the title and of the final passages in the story is that all of us—not just this heart-stricken fifteen-year-old—want to know why mankind carries this extraordinary burden of the knowledge of good and evil.

Questions

1. What kinship with nature does the boy feel and how is this expressed by the choice of details and language in the story?

2. Why is the boy's discovery about Tillford so acute at his age?

3. What does the boy want his own life to be like? Does he lose faith that it can be as he wants it?

4. What elements in his own nature does the boy see embodied in the horse Sunstreak? Does Jerry Tillford possess the same characteristics?

5. Has Tillford betrayed the boy's trust? Or taught him a good and useful lesson? Discuss Tillford's role as teacher.

See also "Questions for Comparing the Author's Stories," below.

Further Reading

Lawry, Jon S. "Love and Betrayal in Sherwood Anderson's 'I Want to Know Why,'" *Shenandoah*, Spring 1962, 46-54.

Ringe, Donald. "Point of View and Theme in 'I Want to Know Why,'" *Critique: Studies in Modern Fiction*, Spring-Fall 1959, 24-25.

Sherwood Anderson—
Questions for Comparing the Author's Stories

1. What differences in the author's attitude toward nature are discernible in the two stories?

2. Discuss different uses of the first-person narrator in the stories, noting that both deal essentially with childhood quandaries.

3. How does innocence figure as an essential ingredient in the stories?

4. Account for all differences in tone you note in comparing the stories. In each case, is the tone consistent with subject and theme?

James Baldwin   *Sonny's Blues* (p. 22)
              (Shorter Edition, p. 9)

In the last two pages of this story we find a strong and relatively clear statement of what the whole thing is about. After all, the narrator is wise, sympathetic, and articulate—quite able to sum up the meaning of Sonny's struggles and the way Sonny saves himself by abandoning himself to his music and the life

of a musician. What the musician (the artist) must do
is "leave the shoreline and strike out for deep water,"
for "deep water and drowning were not the same thing."
The tale told by the artist (or by the blues) is "not
about anything very new" but it must be kept new at all
costs "to find new ways to make us listen. For, while
the tale of how we suffer and how we are delighted, and
how we may triumph is never new, it always must be
heard, it's the only light we've got. . . ." In this
we find a paraphrase of Ezra Pound's admonition to artists—"Make it new"—and an echo of Walt Whitman, who
told us to steer always for deep water if we hope to
possess our souls. The traditional idea that the artist continues an apostolic succession thus emerges as
the revelation toward which the whole story has been
moving.

It began with the narrator taking an outside view
of his brother's career and its risks. Understandably
he does not want Sonny to suffer or destroy himself.
Sonny's "privacy" seems a flaw—at least an obstacle to
communicating the common sense in which his brother
reposes trust. The different orientation of the
brothers appears early when the older remonstrates:
". . .you know people can't always do exactly what they
<u>want</u> to do—" and Sonny responds, "<u>No</u>, I don't know
that. . . . I think people <u>ought</u> to do what they want
to do, what else are they alive for?" After Sonny has
served time in prison, his brother is "dying to hear
him tell me he was safe." The common sense view is
that he would be "safe" if he had learned to count the
cost of doing what he wanted to do.

The death of the narrator's little girl functions
in the progress of the story by bringing the brothers'
viewpoints closer together. "My trouble made his
real." The child's death surely demonstrates that a
life lived by the rules of common sense is not guar-
anteed to be safe. But even though sympathy grows
toward understanding, the older brother cannot abandon
his role as guardian. He must honor not only his own
impulse to watch over someone precious to him—he must
honor their mother's command to "hold on to your
brother."

He will never be let off his promise to do so.
Nevertheless, we note a slight, crucial difference
between what he rashly promises ("I won't let nothing
happen to Sonny.") and what their mother actually

asked. From experience she knows, "You may not be
able to stop nothing from happening. But you got to
let him know you's there."

There, in such a context, is a word that must seem
completely ambiguous to the rational, common sense
mind. Its significance is quite simple and apparent
in the context of emotional sympathies woven by the
story as a whole. It means standing by with love and
faith, knowing there may be no practical remedies for
trouble, believing that one's brother may save his life
by losing it.

There is where we find the older brother in the
climactic scene in the nightclub. He has not abandoned
his common sense concerns. But he has suspended them,
or they have been superceded by a larger wisdom.
Guided in part by the example of the musician called
Creole, the elder brother is now able to wish Sonny
"Godspeed" and listen to Sonny speak for himself without anxiety. ". . . the man who creates the music is
dealing with the roar rising from the void and imposing
order on it as it hits the air." Now the narrator can
admit this, and though he will not change his character
or his life, because he cannot, his brotherhood has
been confirmed by what he is able to hear in Sonny's
music.

Questions

1. What views of life and its meaning are in conflict in this story? Does one appear to triumph over
the other?

2. What does the "privacy" of Sonny's character
come from and what are its results?

3. What relationship does the author see between
art and religion?

4. What does the narrator reveal when he says, "My
trouble made his real"? What does the story say about
living a "safe" life?

5. What does the mother contribute to the older
brother's knowledge of Sonny? What does she mean when
she says, "Let him know you's there"?

6. Interpret this passage and relate it to the
theme of the story: "For, while the tale of how we
suffer and how we are delighted and how we may triumph
is never new, it must always be heard."

Further Reading

Ognibene, Elaine R. "Black Literature Revisited:
    'Sonny's Blues,'" *English Journal,* 60 (January
    1971), 36-37.

Honoré de Balzac   *A Passion in the Desert* (p.48)

Stories of beast marriages—sexual love between a
human and an animal—are abundant in folklore, ballads,
and mythology. Their full psychological significance
can never, perhaps, be thoroughly expounded, but part
of their fascination surely comes from the fact that
animals are metaphorical equivalents of some aspects
of human nature. (Not only are people seen to be foxy
or sheepish; they badger and buffalo one another. We
go about our daily business among jackals, lions, apes.
We marry gazelles and tigers, according to common
metaphor.)

So, in a fantastic story like this, we are strongly
prompted to feel we are reading about a "great passion"
between a man and a woman even while the rational part
of our mind accepts the language that declares the
participants to be a man and a panther.

The soldier names the panther after his first
sweetheart—presumably because he has recognized a
fundamental similarity. He addresses the beast as
"Mademoiselle." "Solitude revealed to him all her
secrets and enveloped him in her delights." Such a
sentence inevitably—and no doubt intentionally—
invokes the developments of a honeymoon. The moral-
istic summary near the end of the story generalizes
with obvious reference to human love affairs.

One of the joys of reading the story is to observe
how cunningly Balzac exploits this ambiguous double
image of human and animal. The ambiguity permits him
to make observations on the immense and dangerous differences between male and female—on the immeasurable
difficulties inherent in their efforts to live peace-
ably together. The device is like that of a cartoonist
simplifying basic traits to make sweeping observations
with a force and clarity impossible in a more realistic
and detailed approach.

At the same time the author profits from the sheer strangeness, the exoticism, of the circumstance he has to tell about. By attributing the tale to an old soldier, Balzac makes allowance for the possibility that the romance is only a tall tale. By setting it in the uninhabited and inhospitable wastes of the desert, he severs its connections with the world where passion and action are inhibited by civilized restraints. The main action thus takes place as it might in a dream, free of the restraints of ordinary morals and rational consciousness.

The last line of the story is an aphorism that may be hard for most students to interpret. A sufficient paraphrase would be: In God—or in the desert—all possibilities exist, while in the world ruled by human conventions many imaginable things are agreed to be impossible.

Questions

1. The main events of the story are reported by a stranger encountered in a menagerie (though they are narrated in the third person). Are they more or less credible than if Balzac had narrated them on his own authority? Are they credible at all?
2. Interpret the story as an allegory of human love.
3. Is it sheer coincidence that the soldier is rescued just after he has killed his beloved panther?
4. What effect is obtained by making the love object both beautiful and frightening?
5. What is the meaning of the soldier's last line?
6. Compare the qualities of this story with those of modern fantasy and science fiction.

Donald Barthelme   *The Indian Uprising* (p.60)
(Shorter Edition, p.36)

This is an excellent story to use in class discussions of the expressive values of distortion, and it might be well to begin by pointing out to students that they are very familiar with the distortions commonly used by graphic cartoonists today. As a side note it

might also be pointed out that Barthelme is a graphic
artist of distinction whose comic collages are similar
in technique and effect to several of his stories.

The cartoonist exaggerates certain features of his
subject and suppresses others. Retaining only the
features that can be manipulated into novel, incongruous, surprising and enlightening combinations to obtain his meaning or effect, the cartoonist must, nevertheless, hold on to enough recognizable ingredients of
a familiar situation and familiar personages to keep
identities stable or his point will be lost in sheer
confusion. The basic and familiar premise retained by
Barthelme here is that the impoverished minorities of
our world are in a perpetually seething revolt against
the established (and perhaps decadent) centers of
wealth, which are loosely identified with our cities.
If we hold on to the premise that in our time the
cities are under siege by the dispossessed, the most
fanciful of Barthelme's distortions will fall into
place sufficiently well to make sense of the whole
design.

In all his fugues and incoherent allusions, the
narrator appears as an incarnation of the modern
decadent. His overrefined intelligence leads him to
analyze the composition of the barricades erected to
block the invasion instead of putting the barricades
to effective use. The composition of these barricades has been distorted beyond the realms of conceivable probability for comic and satiric purposes.
The "window dummies, silk, thoughtfully planned job
descriptions," etc., of which the barricades are composed, are the accoutrements of what is considered normal life in a modern city; at the same time, their
doubtful utility in stopping a military assault is
highlighted by the list being confined to a variety of
physically flimsy consumer goods. The point of this
section of Barthelme's parable is simply that affluence
as we know it cannot provide security in times of
revolution.

Nor does the narrator have any inner security to
call upon in the crisis. Miss R is identified as a
"teacher." This extraordinary epithet has to be defined
to mean she is a type of psychic counselor sought out
by those extreme decadents among us who have become so
rarified in their requirements that even ordinary psychiatry no longer reaches their needs.

By various allusions we learn that the narrator has
had numerous liaisons with women. It appears he has

gotten on well with them because he readily shares the
tastes and habits he likes to believe are feminine.
But part of the point of the story is that his adaptation has engendered no loyalty on the part of any of
the women.

In a word, the narrator has nothing to protect him
but the mechanized defenses provided by the state.
The helicopters and rockets of the collective defense
effort kill "a great many," but it is significant that
the dead are not identified as the attackers—they are
merely "children," utterly irrelevant to the balance of
contending forces.

Most of the distortions that distinguish the story
from a conventional firsthand account of battle will be
apparent line by line to the student reader. Some are
easier than others to translate back into the common-
places of such reportage. "Dusky warriors padded with
their forest tread into the mouth of the mayor" can be
translated fairly easily if we think of the mayor as
spokesman, mouthpiece or "mouth" of the decadent city
dwellers. The inarticulate or subliterate invaders
have shut him up; his sounding off is no longer relevant. There will probably be no doubt that the story
ends with the abject and unconditional surrender of the
helpless narrator.

Questions

1. In what ways does the situation of the story offer
a recognizable caricature of our contemporary political
situation?

2. What sort of relations with women has the narrator
cultivated?

3. What is the function of Miss R? Does she provide
any help to the narrator?

4. What familiar patterns of city life do you recognize? How have they been distorted or exaggerated?

5. What do the Indians represent in allegorical or
symbolic terms?

6. How does the story imitate the transformation of
familiar objects and situations as we experience this
in dreams?

Further Reading

Gillem, Francis. "Donald Barthelme's City: A Guide," *Twentieth Century Literature*, 18 (1972), 38-39.
Tanner, Tony. *City of Words: American Fiction, 1950-1970*. New York: Harper & Row, 1971, pp. 405-406.

Saul Bellow *Leaving the Yellow House* (p. 65)

The leisurely, easygoing pace of Bellow's narrative enables him to build a densely particularized portrait of Hattie in her setting. The setting and minor characters are important chiefly because Hattie, in her old age, has adapted herself to them like some animal putting on protective coloration. She wants "to be thought a rough, experienced woman of the West," and though she is not quite that, in ordinary times she gets along. She manages largely because she has no real purpose left except survival. She has outlived ambitions and real passions, coming to the point where convenience and comfort are of more importance. Before her accident she has—barely—what she needs to sustain her fundamental requirements.

The first phase of the accident exposes pretty shockingly how little margin of sustenance she would have if her routine should be forcibly altered. While the car is sitting immobile on the railroad tracks, she admits with understandable panic that if it should be demolished her life in this community would be finished. Even if the axle or oil pan were damaged she would be hard put to salvage the routines she must depend on. And there is nowhere else in the world for her to go. By this Bellow establishes the precariousness of existence for people circumstanced as she is and clears the way for showing--as the rest of the story will show—that extraordinary heroism is required merely to go on living when one's resources are so inflexibly narrow. This demonstration—and the discovery of nobility and beauty of character in an unexpected quarter—are what the story is mostly about.

The impact of Hattie's accident is, of course, compounded by the injury she received in the course of the drunken, bungling attempts to get her car off the tracks before a train demolishes it. When she returns

to the lake after her hospitalization it seems that
"she had triumphed again," As far as practical matters go, the triumph is illusory enough. She is not
only dependent as never before—on the Rolfes, for
instance, who have nothing to gain from supporting her
as India had—but she is dependent on expectations
that are bound to collapse and progressively give way.
Her health and the good intentions of her friends are
irreversibly dissolving. Only the yellow house which
India gave her remains to her, a common material symbol of the sort that people cling to when they sense
that their lives are finished.

The richest part of the story begins now as Hattie
tries to make her ownership of the house suffice as a
substitute for all she has lost to increasing age and
bodily decrepitude. She rises to a noble indignation
in refusing Pace's offer, and he, unable to understand
what is going on in the depths of her psyche, accuses
her of being drunk again. There is no other explanation, he thinks, for her refusal. Drunk . . ." and so
she was, but she was more than that. . . ." She is not
only drunk on cheap booze, she is intoxicated with the
dawning sense that the house is, somehow, the life raft
that will keep her from sinking completely.

The beauty of the story lies in the way it uncovers
layers of resilience in a human being when, for all
practical purposes, all hope is gone. After rejecting
Pace's offer for the house, Hattie becomes more and
more unreasonable, but it is just in her unreasoning
rebellion against things as they are that her salvation
lies.

She begins to write her will in a fit of indignation
—not only against Pace but against all practical considerations and indeed against the reality of the human
condition. "She was still angry. Her heart was
knocking within. . . ." We begin to realize that it is
her anger that will save her—not only because nothing
else can, but because it can consolidate her life and
give it an integrity that time and practical circumstances would only dissipate. As she writes she
thinks: *"I was never one single thing anyway. Never
my own. I was only loaned to myself."* She has,
indeed, a philosophical revelation of the doubleness
of the self—the self known by common experience and
experiential awareness and the true self that emerges
when the meaning of experience proves inadequate.

If such philosophic distinctions prove to be hard
to deal with in classroom discussion of this story or

any story in the collection, it must still be realized
that literature leads us to the point where no other
distinctions will be adequate to its interpretation.
Students have trouble admitting anything beyond the
world of experience. It is good for them to learn
that literature has dimensions beyond those encountered in a first and tentative reading.

Hattie's rebellion against what has befallen her
opens up her past so that she can, in a figurative
sense, see her life as the continuous film that she
has vaguely fantasized. She sees her relationship
with the men in her life with a clarity that has previously been beyond her grasp. In her drunkenness she
recollects the text: *"Have ye eyes and see not?
Sleepers awake."*

She has, in a strange way, awakened. And if it is
to an appalling strangeness that she has awakened,
that strangeness is at least closer to the realities
of her nature than any of the opinions of herself and
her life that she has tried to live by earlier.

This apparently realistic study of a social eccentric has led us into quandaries of a mystic kind. If
it is funny that Hattie should, in the end, will the
house to herself, this is the sort of funniness that
translates out into recognition of the vast mysteries
of being human in a world that conforms awkwardly to
our human expectations.

Questions

1. Discuss the importance of the setting in its relation to Hattie's problems and whatever solution she
finds for them.

2. What does the story say about the resources of a
human being faced with extinction? About dying with
dignity?

3. What does Hattie's pride have to do with the
outcome of the action?

4. How do the attitudes and actions of the minor
characters contribute to our understanding of Hattie?

5. How is the point of view related to the development of the theme? To what extent has the author used
his main character as a witness testifying to the
world around her?

Ambrose Bierce   *An Occurrence at Owl Creek Bridge*
                  (p. 92)
                  (Shorter Edition, p. 41)

There is a great deal of fine craftsmanship in this celebrated story, and not all of it is expended just to produce a surprise at the end. As the line of action moves toward that end we get a meticulous picture of a segment of military life during the Civil War, some tart and savage irony about the nature of war in any age, and a moving speculation on time, consciousness, and reality.

The details of the setting in section I are objectively presented but are interrupted and, as it were, painted with sinister significance by the author's intrusion in such comments as "The liberal military code makes provision for hanging many kinds of people, and gentlemen are not excluded." There is a gradual modulation from the visual and objective rendition of the bridge and the makeshift trap from which the man will be dropped to an intense and distorted subjectivism as Farquhar hears the loud, slow percussion—which is merely the ticking of his watch. This distortion of time and perception serves as preparation and foreshadowing for the hallucination to come.

Section II functions to give us the essential specifications of the character of the man to be hanged and drive home the merciless irony of warfare. There is no sensible reason why the Federal scout should have entrapped Farquhar and brought him to the point of being hanged.

What follows thereafter is a carefully controlled medley of (1) those sensations which we can accept as the credible consequences of dropping from a bridge with a noose around one's neck, (2) the slightly less credible events and actions leading to Farquhar's escape into the woods, and (3) the hallucinatory walk through the forest at night and his arrival at the gate of his own home. Note that in respect to element (2) of this mixture, the author has pushed very hard to authenticate his picture of a man who has actually plunged into the water beneath the bridge. Before he can free his arms and neck from the ropes, Farquhar feels intense pain— and the temptation to avert it by dying. "'Put it back, put it back!' He thought he shouted these words to his hands, for the undoing of the noose had been succeeded by the direst pang which he had yet experienced." The hypersensitivity to the ticking of his watch is paralleled by his perception of the fish—"he heard the rush of its body parting the water." This gives a continuity between the present passage and the previous one in which he was, in fact, alive.

The illusion of continuity is maintained <u>until</u> we read of his walking on a road with no fields bordering it. The stars above his head are "unfamiliar and grouped in strange constellations."

By such signs the author modulates his story toward the barren factuality of the last paragraph. We are apprised that something passing strange is taking place, but the author still veils his revelation by references to the "circle of black where the rope had bruised it" on Farquhar's neck.

The next to last paragraph is, of course, a virtuoso play of language, images, and time signals. There is a shift into the present tense—abruptly repudiated by evidence that the hallucination of meeting his wife in a radiant, idealized form <u>preceded</u> the instant when the rope broke his neck. Oddly, what might have passed as a reunion in heaven is terminated with brutal swiftness by the arrival of death—a real twist on the sequence approved by conventional sentimentality.

We have to grant at the end that the story leaves us with little verifiable truth about the experience of the dying. Since there is no verifiable truth about that particular experience, this need not be taken as a positive fault. Bierce sets his stage at the borderline where psychology and metaphysics give up.

Questions

1. If the story is not, in your view, intended as realism, what purpose is served by the realistic details and description?

2. Why does the disguised Federal scout suggest to Farquhar that he should burn the bridge?

3. Account for Farquhar's intense sensitivity to his surroundings after his "escape."

4. At what point in the story do you get the first hint that the escape is an hallucination? At what point are you sure?

5. What bits of information are supplied by the departures from Farquhar's point of view?

Further Reading

Bahr, Howard W. "Ambrose Bierce and Realism,"
    Southern Quarterly, 1 (July 1963), 309-331.
Crane, John Kenny, "Crossing the Bar Twice: Post-
    Mortem Consciousness in Bierce, Hemingway, and
    Golding," *Studies in Short Fiction*, VI (Summer
    1969), 361-376; *passim*.
Woodruff, Stuart C. *The Short Stories of Ambrose
    Bierce: A Study in Polarity*. Pittsburgh:
    University of Pittsburgh Press, 1964,
    pp. 153-163.

Jorge Luis Borges   *Pierre Menard, Author of the*
                 Quixote (p. 100)

We have already stumbled into the labyrinth of
enigmas and paradoxes prepared for us by the author
when we call this a story and place it in an anthology
among other stories. For it (deliberately) excludes
nearly all of the elements and formal devices exploited by storytellers. We could call it an "anti-
story" if we wanted to give it a fashionable label--
or we can enjoy its absurd contrariness to greater or
lesser degree without worrying too much about the con-
fusions the author has set out to compound.

In form, it is an obvious parody of a scholarly
comment, fictional at least in the sense that Menard is
a fictional writer (or antiwriter) though a very great
number of references are made to actual persons. The
footnotes are an integral part of the parody.

For our purposes, it may be enough to comment on
the central concept--which in itself is enigmatic.
Menard proposed to write *Don Quixote*. How could he
write it when it had already been written in the
seventeenth century by Cervantes? The task, then, is
impossible. The riddle Borges presents is this: How
can a man do the impossible? Or: How can the impossible be done? Or: How can we conceive the possibility of doing the impossible? Again the questions

build, one on another, in the direction of infinity.
Or into absurdity.

At any rate, Menard rejects the idea of mechanically copying *Don Quixote*. To copy is not the same
thing as to create, to write a novel. He even rejects
the method of being Cervantes in order to write what
he proposes. Rejects it not, as "my reader will say,"
on the ground that it is impossible for one man to be
another, but on the ground that "of all the impossible
ways of carrying it out, this was the least interesting."

But, after sufficiently establishing the impossibility of the task, the author asserts that it was
indeed accomplished. Menard not only wrote *Don
Quixote*, his *Don Quixote* is superior in ambiguity and
therefore in richness to the one written by Cervantes.
No evidence of the accomplishment can be given because
the text of the latter work is indistinguishable from
a copy of the original. The two excerpts given appear
to be identical. The words on the page are the same.
But they are not identical. Menard's achievement is
invisible. It--and its distinction from what
Cervantes wrote--can only be perceived by an exercise
of pure intellect--which, as Plato pointed out, is the
only means by which humans can come at the truth.

Call this, if you wish, a matter of the Emperor's
New Clothes. The small boy, looking through innocent
eyes, will perceive that the Emperor is naked.

The small boy may be right. For all practical purposes he is. But the human mind is not governed or
limited by practical purposes. The pure intellect,
contemplating the Emperor, may conclude that he has
glorious new clothes and that the evidence of the
senses is a deception. In the same way the pure intellect might conclude that Menard did accomplish the
impossible task of creating what had already been
created.

It is impossible to predict what students (or anyone else) will make or want to make of such an exercise
in the absurd. Perhaps it is enough to get them into
the midst of the deep water and leave them to sink or
swim.

Questions

1. Is Menard's self-appointed task of rewriting
Don Quixote an absurdity or a meaningful literary
undertaking?

2. To what extent does the personality of the narrator color the story? What does his enthusiasm for Menard's "impossible" undertaking tell us about his own values and literary aims?

3. To what extent is the story a satire on scholarly methods?

4. What does the story say about the value of tangible evidence of productivity in an intellectual enterprise?

5. Is Menard's work a hoax? Is Borges' story about it a hoax? Is the fabrication of a hoax a legitimate, entertaining, and enlightening form of literary activity?

Ray Bradbury   *The Veldt* (p. 109)
                (Shorter Edition, p. 49)

One of the great traditions of science fiction is that by an exaggeration or conceivable extension of contemporary technologies it becomes a vehicle for satire--satire aimed at exposing the quirks and abnormalities inherent in manners or lifestyles we take for granted. Here one notes readily that the "Happylife Home" George and Lydia Hadley have provided for their children is a parody of the contemporary American home. The house with its manifold appliances has mechanically usurped some of the family members' personal opportunities and obligations, as it has relieved them of certain arduous chores that previously went with housekeeping. Beyond even feeding, clothing, playing and singing to parents and children alike, the house "was good to them." The nursery of this almost familiar fantasy house is recognizable as an exaggeration of the room where the television set babysits with American children, bringing them images of exotic violence and, perhaps, inciting them to murderous rebellion against parents who try to limit the unleashed frenzies and appetites brought into the house by the Tube.

In terms of the story Bradbury has constructed, the images from the nursery walls (or television screen) become real enough to attack and devour the parents. The lions which entertained the children with their suggestions of ferocity actually materialize in a three-dimensional world to act out the passions roused

in the children by the threat of frustration from their
parents. This exaggeration of fantasy provides the entertaining surface of the story. Surprise at the mate-
rialization of insubstantial moving pictures is one of
the devices exploited by the author to entertain and
amuse the reader. It is funny to think that the images
which engage our emotions on the screen of the television or in a movie theater might move into reality
to act out what we fear or hope as we watch.

But in this case that initial manipulation by the
author is immediately linked to a suspicion that in this
pattern of bloody fantasy there is buried a realization
of common homicidal impulses felt by children against
parents who have spoiled them out of ill-advised affection. "'Nothing's too good for our children,'" George
Hadley says when he acquires the nursery. And there
is humor (of a grisly sort) in the irony that turns
this mushy sentiment into the instrument for his own
destruction.

In fact, the main cargo of humor here is grisly--
so horrifying in its implications that one is moved to
laughter as a defense against confronting them seriously.
Freud and others have eloquently analyzed laughter as
a defense against ideas we are not stong enough to contemplate soberly. And the idea that, through the television sets American parents buy to keep their children
safely entertained at home, the children make parricidal
alliances with lions is not one that either parents or
children can comfortably entertain. Even the "normal"
hostilities of children toward their parents are hard
for most minds to entertain without disguising them in
some neutralizing fable.

There are probably no childish fantasies more
heavily tabooed and more consistently disguised in the
literary and television fare of children than the fantasies of murdering parents in some gory fashion.
Bradbury here tickles those fantasies, rousing them
enough so defensive laughter will be triggered from most
readers. Then he complicates this primal response by
diverting it through an astonishing comic exaggeration
and by reconstructing it as a socially valuable lesson
on the perils of handing over the means of destruction
to spoiled children. On top of everything else we are
moved to approving laughter at the author's nimble
cleverness in whisking past a forbidden subject.

Questions

1. In what ways are the Hadleys a typical American family?

2. What is the significance of the change of program in the nursery, from innocent fairy tales to the appearance of the lions?

3. Why does the psychologist recommend tearing down the nursery? Does his appearance in the story have any bearing on the theme of the story?

4. What explains the hatred the children feel for their parents?

5. Can the story be considered humorous, since it is constructed of superficial horror and underlying pessimism about parents and children?

Morley Callaghan   *Let Me Promise You*   (p. 121)
                   (Shorter Edition, p. 61)

The discipline of this story confines it to an almost cinematic objectivity except for a few comments on the quality of emotion experienced by the two characters as they enact the single scene. What we know about their past relationships with each other, their social backgrounds and involvements, their earlier expectations, etc., must be inferred from hints in the dialogue or a few very general allusions to what they have experienced together or apart. We understand that the occasion represented is an attempt on Alice's part to resurrect an affair that seems to have dwindled drastically from its peak of intensity. We are told that Georgie has known Alice for a long time, that she has been only one of several girls he had on the string, and that he has felt sure he could leave her at any time.

But clearly, such information is so minimal that the story seems almost a pure example of the "slice of life" type of fiction. The limits on our understanding are almost the same as they would be if we could observe and eavesdrop for an hour or so on the behavior and conversation of total strangers. Our understanding of the significance of this brief encounter in relation to past and future depends on how we feel about the characters and on the pattern we can discern as the action progresses. What happens within this short span of time must serve as the guide to inferences we make about the larger dimensions of the characters' future life.

As the action begins Alice seems to be in a position with few advantages. Whatever she gives Georgie must be given without any real hope of return. Her gifts establish no credit with him. She is dealing from weakness. But the turn in the story appears when the sheer impotence of her maneuvers awes him and overcomes his indifference. The weaker of the two emerges as the victor. If this pattern is prophetic of the future, she will continue to dominate him. But the second twist of irony may be that her dominance will require a steady series of exorbitant sacrifices on her part. She may win . . . but leave herself nothing.

Questions

1. Who or what is to blame for the painful stress of the situation?
2. How does the breaking of the watch change the vision each has of the other?
3. Who has the upper hand at the conclusion of the story? How was it gained?
4. How well can you understand the pattern of the past relationship between these two? Is it possible to predict their future?

R. V. Cassill   *The Biggest Band*   (p. 125)

There is a double journey in this story--the journey of a boy out of his small-town environment to the big city and the journey from adulthood back to boyhood when the trip to Chicago is remembered. The first trip is an excursion from seductive illusions into the harsh disillusionment of experience. What happens in Chicago is frustrating and humiliating. Instead of looking on the glamorous nakedness of the fan dancer, the boy sees his own gullibility. Instead of inspiring awe among the fair-goers, the Biggest Band in the World inspires derision, when it is not ignored altogether. But in the return journey of memory, another kind of romance is created to take the place of smashed illusions. The narrator comes to realize, after all, how the trip mingled his destiny with that of "the biggest band"--the bank of ordinary humanity. From the perspective of recollection the whole story might be told for Mrs. Packer (that is, for the ideal listener) not as a blunder or a defeat, but as a victory.

At the time of the trip the narrator was a bundle of grotesque and unsorted wishes. He lied to Mr. Packard unscrupulously in an attempt to wheedle money out of the old man. But the shabby wishes, the scrambled and sneaky eroticism that drives boys to peepshows and pornography, are ripened, by simple processes of living and remembering, into a conception of the ideal feminine listener.

Questions

1. What is the prevailing tone of the story? What elements of circumstance and narration combine to produce it?

2. Why is Mrs. Packer of any importance? What is her relation to the figure of the mother?

3. Is the boy any more honest with himself than he is with the other characters? What is the source and meaning of his misrepresentations?

4. In what ways is the "Midwest Concert" the climax of the story? Is the boy mistaken about what happened there?

5. Are the narrator's motives clearer in retrospect than they were at the time of the trip? Do different things seem important?

Further Reading

Roberts, David. "The Short Fiction of R. V. Cassill," *Critique,* IX (No. 1), 56-70.

Willa Cather   *Paul's Case*   (p. 139)

Though Cather has labeled her story "a study in temperament," thereby appearing to disclaim any moral bias or judgment, the climate of our times usually leads class discussion on a wild chase to fix the blame for

Paul's pathetic finish. Because he is young and misunderstood by parents and teachers, it is all too easy
for young and presumptively misunderstood students (a
preponderant majority, always) to blame them. While no
one can flatly demonstrate such an interpretation to be
wrong, it has the demerit of being facile and of co-
opting into the category of protest literature an author
who has a more enigmatic view of justice to offer.

The chastity of Cather's style and manner may pass
for colorless flatness requiring little attention. But
her full resources are only grasped by noting that the
lucid style continually makes fine discriminations which
should be carefully registered by the reader. The discriminations of style serve a meticulous and equally
discriminating observation. Thus, in the third paragraph we read that his "insult [to his English teacher]
was so involuntary and definitely personal as to be
unforgettable." At first thought the adjective involuntary may seem to mitigate or even contradict the
force of definitely personal. An act which is involuntary may hardly seem to deserve the term insult. But
involuntary also suggests that in an unguarded moment
he has let the cat out of the bag, exposing the full
fury of his "physical revulsion"--something inappropriate to animals of the same species--and shocking in the
extreme. Then, remembering that insult carries the
meaning of trauma or physical injury to a part of the
body, we get a measure of how broad the gulf is that
teachers or parents would have to cross to reach him.

Truly they misunderstand him. By the same token,
this is not from lack of trying or, except under the
provocations of the moment, from lack of charity toward
him. "His teachers . . . [were] humiliated to have felt
so vindictive toward a mere boy . . . and to have set
each other on, as it were, in the gruesome game of in-
temperate reproach." Note, as well, that Paul's temperament (a term not exactly conterminous with character,
inclination, behavior, will, desire or any other approx-
imate synonym) conspires to mislead all his guardians
and keep them off his track. The fault lies not with
them but with the incompatibility of his temperament and
the circumstances of his life. We may always feel the
injustice of such incompatibility, but to lay it at the
door of any human agency, group or individual is another
matter. It seems, finally, to be an instance of cosmic
injustice, a flaw in the nature of things, to be grieved
by the very admission that it is beyond remedy. "Paul's
Case" does not fit the traditional pattern of tragedy,

but it is closer in spirit to tragedy than to protest literature, which would assign the blame and
imply a remedy.

The straw that breaks Paul's back and leads directly to his suicide is the support offered by his
father in the unfolding of the crisis. Even if we
go so far as to find in his father's action elements
of selfishness and insensitivity, it is not easy to
conceive a better alternative. And when we read,
"He had the old feeling . . . , the sinking sensation
that the play was over," we understand that life is
only acceptable to such a temperament as Paul's when
it is a play--i.e., when it is briefly transformed by
special stimulations into something different from
its fundamental reality. The curiously restrained
language of the next to last paragraph implies that
his plight is, and has been, irremediable. As well
he might, he perceives "the folly of his haste,"
but not because he has repented his course or conceived any realistically acceptable alternative to
folly. It has been the very tissue of that folly
to stake his life on the grasp for the unattainable.
The "Adriatic water, the yellow of Algerian sands,"
are objects of the same inordinate desire as was
always hurrying him to this doom. Trying to find
life outside "the design of things" is, alas, a folly
for which no forgiveness is conceivable.

For students too readily inclined to blame his
disaster on poverty or unworthy parents and teachers,
it may be a broadening exercise to imagine different
environing circumstances that would have sustained a
"temperament" like Paul's. If his theft had never
been discovered and the money from it had never run
out, would he have been fulfilled?

Questions

1. If you feel that Paul has been unjustly treated
by parents, teachers, or society at large, explain the
injustice.

2. If, on the other hand, you feel he suffers from
a defect of character, define it.

3. What is the connection between Paul's fascination
with the theater and his crime?

4. Why is his father's repayment of the stolen money
"worse than jail"?

5. Does Paul repent at the moment of his death? If
you think he does not, how do you interpret the end?

See also "Questions for Comparing the Author's Stories," p. 32 of this *Handbook*.

Further Reading

Brown, Edward K. and Leon Edel, *Willa Cather: A Critical Biography*. New York: Alfred A. Knopf, 1953, pp. 121-122.

Daiches, David, *Willa Cather: A Critical Introduction*. Ithaca: Cornell University Press, 1951, pp. 145-147.

Rubin, Larry. "The Homosexual Matrix in Willa Cather's 'Paul's Case,'" *Studies in Short Fiction*, 12 (1975), 127-131.

Stouck, David. *Willa Cather's Imagination*. Lincoln: University of Nebraska Press, 1975, p. 180.

Van Ghent, Dorothy. *Willa Cather*. Minneapolis: University of Minnesota Press, 1964.

Willa Cather   *The Old Beauty*   (p. 156)

The first section establishes the milieu of the present action. Aix-les-Bains is a fashionable watering place, a point of rendezvous for those in the upper strata of European society, particularly the elderly. From the setting we get an impression of the environment in which Gabrielle has spent her life.

In the <u>real</u> chronology of events this first section has a penultimate place. Gabrielle is already dead. Seabury has not yet sent the telegram which he will send before the story is concluded. We are told, through Seabury's musings over the telegram, that "Lord H-- would recognize that this death was more than the death of an individual. To him her name would recall a society whose manners, dress, conventions, loyalties, codes of honour, were different from anything existing in the world today."

Next--with a jump backward in the present time frame--we see Gabrielle through Seabury's eyes. Certainly this is a very restricted glimpse, for he sees her as a stranger. He cannot identify her by name. The woman who passes under his scrutiny--and that of the reader--is disfigured by the ravishing of time.

The next frame through which we look at the still indistinct silhouette of Gabrielle is provided by the Englishwoman, Mrs. Thompson. Mrs. Thompson provides a name for the "gaunt-cheeked old woman" and also improves the identification with an appropriate emotional coloration by saying "It's very sad when those beautiful ones have to grow old, isn't it?"

There is a natural progression to the next section in which Seabury recalls "the whole romantic story" of the woman who was so famous throughout the world as Lady Longstreet. Here, in summary form, we are given the history of her life, as it might be known to anyone who bothered to keep up with the doings of celebrities. This quite impersonal profile is kept consistent with the preceding representation by Seabury's melancholy recognition of her rarity. ". . . where was there such a creature in the world today?"

Then, through the reminiscences of Gabrielle's companion Cherry Beamish, we are given what seems a much more intimate view of the aged beauty's personality, her tastes and preferences, and the difficulties attending her adaptation to the manners, morals, and styles of the postwar world. Part of the definition of Gabrielle is accomplished by sheer contrast to the personality of Cherry, who says, "If only she had a swarm of young nieces and nephews, as I have, she'd see things quite differently and she'd be much happier."

Up to the beginning of Section IX we follow a consistently developing focus on a beautiful woman in her terminal years. But the image, thus developed, provides no _story_, except in the loosest sense. Nothing is happening around which meanings can be crystallized. The author seems to have accepted an intentionally handicapped strategy for coming at what is essential in the plight of this rare and rarely gifted person. And, on the other hand, there has been no preparation for what is now to be revealed when the last of the Chinese boxes is opened and we read of the scene Seabury witnessed long ago.

Suddenly there is a flash of wickedness out of the soft-edged nostalgia and the melancholy of Gabrielle's decline. A flash of terror, the majesty of evil, "_the power of the dog . . ._"

Almost as suddenly, the Chinese boxes are closed again, one after the other, and through the rest of the story we seem to be led farther and farther away from anything that will make that tableau of evil comprehensible. Later episodes of the present action,

including Gabrielle's death as well as the encounter
on the road with the insolent young American women,
seem designed to distract us from contemplation or
speculation on the significance of that moment of
extreme peril boxed in so many layers of varied
circumstance.

Yet there is one tantalizing clue to this well-
concealed significance. It is flicked before our
eyes in the obviously symbolic episode in which
Gabrielle sits by the well of the monastery and, with
a little mirror drawn from her handbag, causes a re-
flection of light to play into its depths. "That yellow ray seemed to waken the black water at the bottom. . . ."

If we match the language of this passage with a
much earlier passage describing Seabury's meditations,
we may understand that this beam of light somehow
equates with Gabrielle's choice to tell him about the
evil that once almost overcame her. ". . . her talk
brought back not only the men, but their period; its
security, the solid exterior, the exotic contradictions
behind the screen, the deep, claret-colored closing
years of Victoria's reign. Nobody ever recognizes a
period until it has gone by, he reflected: until it
lies behind one it is merely everyday life." (See end
of Section IV.) Her beam of light--her tale of sexual
assault--may have exposed the "exotic contradictions"
behind the apparently "solid exterior" or "screen" of
Victorian proprieties.

Questions

1. How important are the changes brought about in
the world by World War I? What represents the postwar
world, what the world that has passed?

2. In what ways is Gabrielle's character representative of the age in which she was a celebrity?

3. Is Seabury's point of view a natural one for
telling Gabrielle's story?

4. Interpret Seabury's feeling that "in this world
people have to pay an extortionate price for any ex-
ceptional gift whatever."

5. Interpret the phrase *"the power of the dog"* (in
Section IX) in terms of its relation to the story as
a whole.

6. What is the importance of the scene in
Gabrielle's house in New York (Section IX)?

7. What symbolism do you find in Gabrielle's playing with the hand mirror (Section XII)? Why does she wear a "contemptuous smile" at this time?

8. How much does the accident on the mountain road contribute to Gabrielle's death?

Willa Cather—
Questions for Comparing the Author's Stories

1. Does the same view of life's ironies color both of Cather's stories?

2. Is Gabrielle's fate as a beautiful woman comparable to Paul's as an estranged youth?

3. What stylistic similarities show the author's temperament and particular concerns in the two stories?

4. Does the author appear to be more emotionally detached in one story than in the other?

John Cheever   *The Enormous Radio* (p. 182)
                (Shorter Edition, p. 65)

In this early story of John Cheever, the scene, the characters and the situation are all realistically and colorfully developed. Only the aberrant performance of the huge radio the Westcotts bring into their apartment breaks the discipline of fidelity to a shrewdly observed segment of contemporary life. The radio is thus the only element of fantasy the author has permitted himself in assembling his design; first, it serves as a means of penetrating the surfaces of the lives of the other tenants of the apartment building, and then, by its accumulation of evidence that all is not as it appears around them, it trips the Westcotts themselves into a painful and perhaps shattering reconsideration of the skeletons hidden in their own closet. The fantasy of the literally impossible radio may be considered as the engine that drives the plot, moving it step-by-step to the point at which the Westcotts are forced to admit they share the ugly shortcomings which have been exposed in the lives around them.

The Westcotts are not presented, in the beginning, as an extaordinary or unusual couple. Their place of

abode, their manners and tastes, their expectations
of the future, and indeed their personalities (which
have been molded to conform to the outward aspects
of their lifestyle) are painstakingly built from details that would typify a norm of urban life in our
time. They "differed from their friends, classmates,
and their neighbors only in an interest they shared
in serious music." If there are sleeping dogs hidden
behind the furniture of their lives, they, like their
neighbors, prefer to let them lie. In a word, they
are far from making a deliberate and conscious choice
to follow the Socratic precept, to examine their lives
or ask whether they have not built on sand.

Perhaps we are meant to understand that their interest in music, the difference that leads them to
acquire the inquisitorial radio, is simultaneously a
flaw in their otherwise invulnerable exterior and a
blessing that leads them out of subhuman complacency,
that saves them from the living death of smugness and
the smothering complacency that accompany the requirements of maintaining their masquerade of success and
happiness.

Clearly the author has intended to pose a paradox
in forcing upon his characters the fabulous radio which
will mechanically shred the veil the Westcotts and
their neighbors have drawn over their secret lives.
But the paradox and the aspect of fable worked into
this superficially realistic story are ancient and
traditional, however modern the appearances and furnishings may be. The paradox is the primal one of the
human pair forced out of (a sort of) Eden by having
eaten from the tree of knowledge. Are they better off
for having lost their paradise of ignorance? Or are
they ruined?

Somewhat shyly Cheever refuses to offer any verdict
or even the hint of an answer to such questions. At
the end we read that the voice coming from the radio
is now "suave and noncommittal." Surely this implies
that the author refuses to commit himself to a verdict,
but just as surely the Westcotts now will have to
shape their own answers to the questions that have been
so flagrantly posed. So will thoughtful readers of
the story, and in shaping their answers they will necessarily record their agreement or disagreement with
the Socratic maxim.

It might be useful to consider this story in conjunction with de Maupassant's "The Necklace," for in
both a bourgeois couple has been shaken from its super-

ficially comfortable perch and exposed to the brutal truth of life.

Questions

1. What, if anything, significantly distinguishes the Westcotts from the other tenants of their building? From the other young couples of their time and social position?

2. Is there anything in the story besides the radio itself that could be labeled an element of fantasy?

3. Is most of the information brought by the radio about the Westcotts' neighbors shocking or sordid? What exceptions can you note? What do all the exposures of private lives add up to?

4. Does possession of the radio give the Westcotts any advantage over their neighbors? Disadvantage? Explain.

5. Socrates said that the "unexamined life is not worth living." Does the outcome of this story support or contradict his view?

See also "Questions for Comparing the Author's Stories, p. 37 of this *Handbook*.

Further Reading

Kendle, Burton. "Cheever's Use of Mythology in 'The Enormous Radio,'" *Studies in Short Fiction,* 4 (1967), 262-264.

Peden, William H., *The American Short Story: Continuity and Change, 1940-1975*. Boston: Houghton Mifflin, 1975, pp. 32-33.

John Cheever   *The Fourth Alarm* (p. 192)
(Shorter Edition, p. 74)

Whatever else we make of this story, we had better find it funny--for all of its oblique, sad, satiric pronouncement on matters of genuine moral concern is dependent on the skillful employment of comic devices and the grotesquerie of the basic situation. The even

tone of the narrator--his apparent unawareness of the
stunning inconsistencies and disproportions in what he
reports--is perhaps chief among the comic devices.
Does he know what he is saying? Is his matter-of-fact
mingling of sobriety, sentiment, and outlandish disorder a symptom of shock? Is he ridiculously unaware
of the ridiculous extremes reached in his attempts to
accommodate himself to his wife's "career"?

The first paragraph exposes the flight of his impulses back and forth across the chaos of his world
from the ridiculous to the sublime. "In order to see
anything--a leaf or a blade of grass--you have, I
think, to know the keenness of love." The cadences as
well as the content of this sentence are grave and
meditative--altogether suitable, we might feel, for
the mood of a late summer Sunday morning in the late
summer of a decent man's life. But immediately the
idea of "love" is modulated into the prospects of
sexual relief to be obtained from any accessible or
acceptable female. Swiftly modulated again into the
notion that passing a football might "do it"--i.e.,
serve as substitute for the marital love he has been
denied.

Recollections of his wife's progress from strict
mother and teacher to participant in a nude show and
orgiastic "love pile" show the same stunning disproportions and absurd rationalizations we saw first in
his impulses. Presumably his present mental disarray
is the result of the chaos into which he tried to
follow his wife. "The fitness of what I did then . . .
still confuses me," he says in a pitifully comic
understatement that amply proves his many-layered
confusion.

Gamely the narrator shows up in the theater to witness one of his wife's performances. But instead of
being able to follow what goes on before his eyes he
flies away into a nostalgic reverie of an innocent
movie he saw as a boy. Returning from his own fugue,
he attempts a ridiculously far-fetched explanation of
what his wife is up to. While she is being "mounted
in public by a naked stranger" her husband tries to
console himself with the notion that this is her way
of recollecting moments of noble tenderness, her artistic remembrance of things past.

Clinging to a sense of duty when all other guides
to conduct fail him, he goes so far as to strip naked
when he is commanded to do so. (Note, of course, the
comic inversion of the meaning of "duty.") We see a

man being lured into a collective insanity--and the
suspense in the story lurks in the question of what
can possibly save him once he has gone this far.

The answer is both comic--ludicrous--and ambiguously profound. "Buck naked," among scornful
strangers, he has no identity of his own to resist
their commands and temptations--except his wallet,
watch, and car keys. Not much. But, as Cheever
tells the story, enough. These few "lendings" can
be, in the pinch, enough to protect and sustain "my
essence, the shadow of myself . . . my name."

Here the theme asserts itself. And in the midst
of hilarious farce it turns out to be grave and
serious. (In fact it is very close to the theme of
Conrad's darkly ponderous *Heart of Darkness*, though
the comparison may seem far-fetched on first readings
of either.) The narrator, lost in a moral and social
chaos without bearings, hits on "some marvelously
practical and obdurate part of myself." The drowning
man has clutched at straws--and learned the smallest
straw can save him if he has the character to use it
rightly.

Questions

1. What is contributed by the "deadpan" tone of the
narration? Is it credible that a sophisticated man
would speak so levelly about his wife's escapades?

2. Is Bertha a believably consistent character?
How do you reconcile her strictness as a parent and
teacher with her behavior on the stage?

3. What is Cheever satirizing? What positive values
does his narrator cling to? Does his nostalgia have
any real worth, or is it an escape from reality?

4. Is the subject matter essentially comic or has
the treatment emphasized the comic aspects of it?

5. In what ways could the story by taken as a
modern version of the story of Adam and Eve?

6. What do wallet, wristwatch, and car keys represent to the narrator?

See also "Questions for Comparing the Author's
Stories," p. 37 of this *Handbook*.

John Cheever—
Questions for Comparing the Author's Stories

1. What elements of social satire do you find in each of the stories? Do they indicate moral preferences on the author's part?

2. How much has the author concerned himself with accurately representing contemporary lifestyles?

3. Discuss the author's use of grotesque turns in commonplace reality.

4. What changes in American standards and expectations are registered between the earlier story, "The Enormous Radio," and "The Fourth Alarm"? (Note that the latter is unmistakably tuned to the Sixties.)

Anton Chekhov   *The Lady with the Pet Dog* (p. 196)
(Shorter Edition, p. 79)

Yalta may be taken to represent any resort, where people come together unencumbered by their normal social restraints and unsupported by the routines of their usual lives. For better or worse they are relatively free to follow the whims of their nature. Gurov, a middle-aged, unhappily married man, is indulging his talents and appetite for seduction when he picks up Anna. His numerous past affairs have never touched him deeply. He does not expect much from his brief affair with Anna except diversion. When they part to go home, he realizes he has not made her happy. Not yet comprehending what has happened to him, he muses "that there had now been another episode or adventure in his life, and it, too, was at an end, and nothing was left of it but a memory."

For her part Anna has come to Yalta for a little relief from a joyless marriage to a man she cannot respect. She cannot believe that Gurov will respect her after she has yielded to him so easily. In her simplicity she believes "the Evil One has led me astray." Her last words to him are "we ought never to have met."

It is part of the developing irony of the story that Gurov only begins to understand the meaning of their encounter when he has gone back to Moscow. (The irony of the whole is that of a dissynchronization in lives

that might have been fulfilled by different timing.
". . . only now when his head was gray he had fallen
in love, really, truly— for the first time. . . .")
Amid the hypocrisies and shallowness of civilized routine in Moscow the memory of Anna's awkward sincerity
glows and grows in Gurov's mind until he has to go find
her. His first glimpse of her in her home town shows a
"little, undistinguished woman, lost in a provincial
crowd, with a vulgar lorgnette in her hand." But at
the same time he understands that there is no one in
the world "so precious and important to him." In this
apparent discrepancy between objective evaluation and
love, Chekhov is saying something radically important
about falling in love. It is echoed and reinforced by
a comment about Gurov himself: "He always seemed to
women different from what he was, and they loved in
him not himself, but the man whom their imagination
created and whom they had been eagerly seeking all
their lives. . . ."

Love must be partly founded on illusion, then, but
in itself it is the most compelling of realities.
There are different "layers" in every life, layers
with contradictory qualities and tendencies. There is
public life and personal life. "The personal life of
every individual is based on secrecy, . . ." and sometimes, tragically, it may remain secret to the individual himself until it is too late to do anything
about it.

The story ends equivocally and ambiguously— in a
way that should be stressed as peculiarly Chekhovian.
The last paragraph is built of a flat antithesis between seeming and what is clear. It seems to Gurov
and Anna that a solution is near; it is clear to them
that the solution is still far off. Again the idea is
sounded of a life tragically divided into layers that
cannot be reconciled.

Questions

1. What has the resort atmosphere of Yalta to do
with the way Gurov and Anna become lovers? Does it
help mislead Gurov about what is really happening to
him?

2. What is the importance of Anna's "awkwardness,"
"angularity," and pathetic simplicity in shaping
Gurov's feelings? Of the "coarse arrogance" and "light
irony" in his treatment of her?

3. Does the story suggest that a person's public life and the attitudes formed by it can never by reconciled with the personal life? Consider the antithesis stated in the last paragraph in shaping your answer.

4. What does the story say about Time (or timing) in its relation to human affairs?

5. What is the point of view and how does it help bring out the essence of the situation described?

6. How are the three different settings of the story related to the developing action?

See also "Questions for Comparing the Author's Stories," p. 43 of this *Handbook*.

Further Reading

Winner, Thomas. *Chekhov and His Prose*. New York: Holt, Rinehart and Winston, 1966, pp. 216-225.

Anton Chekhov   *A Visit to Friends* (p. 210)

The best and most poignant of Chekhov's work may remind us of Eliot's line: "Mankind can not bear very much reality." The pathos of this story comes from the apparently casual realism with which the author reports a brief interlude in lives woven from the commonest contradictions of ordinary human nature —a realism so clear-eyed, for all its apparent calm, that it exposes the fatality which underlies both grief and hope. All the characters are caught in the same inexorable current. Plainly Sergey Sergeich is a flawed character. He is bombastic, hypocritical, and deliberately self-deceiving. He calls himself an idealist to hide—from himself as well as others— the destructive treachery of his behavior to those who admire or tolerate him. But Podgorin, who is in many essential ways his opposite, fares no better—is, in fact, as trapped and tormented and frustrated by his honesty and compassion as Sergey is by his moral sloth. The women characters are all, in their various ways, lovable, talented, still emanating some of their youthful promise. True, Varya is being worn down by her

work as a physician. Tatyana is squandering her
strength and talents in motherhood and an unworthy
marriage. But neither of these women is finished.
And Nadezhda is at the blossoming peak of her charm.
Podgorin feels this and knows it, is urged on by the
sensible Varya to take his happiness "while it offers
itself to you freely." There is no single or major
obstacle to his claiming the blooming girl as his wife.
We feel that if he had even made a sound to let
Nadezhda know he was in the tower when she came through
the moonlight looking for him, the outcome of the episode—and all the future—might have been different.
It is Chekhov's genius to have so balanced the conflicting traits in Podgorin's character and the conflicting motivational impressions he has taken in
during his stay that we can pretty well understand why
he is incapable of revealing his presence. And to be
incapable of revealing his presence is to deserve the
quiet, ineluctable damnation of the girl's "No one
there." Inadequate to master the banal fatality that
keeps him silent while the moment of opportunity
passes, he is indeed, literally, "no one." Now even
the three days he has promised to stay seem "intermi-
nable." That is to say: All time and all its fractions
are the victorious enemy of human wishes.

That this tragic statement should be delivered so
quietly and, as it were, so easily may be the most
terrifying and impressive thing about the story. In
terms of its delicate nuances it is worth comparing—
and contrasting—with *The Darling,* a story in which
rather bold and simple outlines serve the author's
purposes.

Questions

1. Who has changed more, Podgorin or his friends,
during the time they have not seen each other?
2. Can you find a consistent line of motivation for
Podgorin? What are the main ingredients of his present
character and how are these decisive? How important is
his feeling for Sergey Losev in determining the outcome?
3. Why doesn't Podgorin speak to Nadezhda when she
is standing under the balcony of the tower? What is
the full meaning of her declaration "No one there"?

4. Account for the repetitions of the doggerel verse about "Old Bruin." Is it related to theme or action?

See also "Questions for Comparing the Author's Stories, p. 43 of this *Handbook*.

Anton Chekhov   *The Darling* (p. 225)
                 (Shorter Edition, p. 93)

Olenka is a ridiculous, contradictory little woman and Chekhov makes fun of her—tenderly, with a tenderness that turns little by little into reverence. She is ridiculous because she is completely uncritical of those she loves (and she is inconsistent and undiscriminating in bestowing her love). When she is married to the theater manager she declares sincerely that nothing on earth is so important as the stage. Married somewhat later to a businessman, she can say without a vestige of doubt that theaters are "nonsense," a waste of time. In a word, her capacity for loving transcends the claims of consistency or objectivity. Naturally and simply she obeys the Emersonian injunction to "give all to Love, nothing withhold." Even her subconsciousness is committed to the object of her love. When she is married to a timber merchant she dreams of logs, beams, and boards. (A Freudian interpretation might make much of her dream that "a whole regiment of six-inch beams forty feet high, standing on end, was marching upon the timber yard." But a Freudian interpretation might impose on the story a solemnity out of keeping with its tender comedy.)
At the death of her second husband her vocation of love is threatened. No matter. With majestic serenity she takes in the veterinary surgeon who used to come to her for chaste sympathy. "In any one else this would have been censured, but no one could think ill of Olenka; everything she did was so natural." Her uncritical compliance with his opinions is an embarrassment to the veterinary, but even his impatience with her is transformed into a stepping stone to happiness by her natural affection.
The veterinary goes away—as men always do, the author seems to say—as all earthly things vanish

while the impulse to love is more enduring. "And what was the worst of all, she had no opinions of any sort." Men are thus defined, for purposes of the story, as the opinionated sex. Opinions are clearly trivial in comparison with love, but opinions are <u>meaning</u> (of a sort) and love seeks meaning in all things and to give meaning to all things. "One sees a bottle, for instance, or the rain, or a peasant driving in his cart, but what the bottle is for, or the rain, or the peasant, and what is the meaning of it, one can't say, and could not even for a thousand rubles." Probably we hear the voice of the author in this sentence, gently intruding into the story to generalize and reinforce his theme.

The veterinary returns—as men are apt to do—inconveniently encumbered with the wife to whom he has been reconciled, a "thin, plain lady, with short hair and a peevish expression." No matter. The couple has brought her a male (the boy Sasha) in whom she can invest her affections and who will give her opinions—of a sort. "'An island is a piece of land,' she repeated, and this was the first opinion to which she gave utterance with positive conviction after so many years of silence and dearth of ideas." It may not be much of an opinion in the world's eyes. That matters far less than her ability to seize on it and from it germinate new meanings for all the otherwise inert details of life.

It matters little, either, that Sasha is a normally crude and unresponsive little boy who has no capacity for loving her as she loves him. Her vocation for loving has been restored to her. Wryly and obliquely the story has been delivered of its theme; Love will find its ways to conquer, perfectly natural, though not always obvious ways.

Like *The Lady with the Pet Dog,* this is a love story that may revise some conventional opinions about sexual love. It might be placed in comparison with Lawrence's *The Horse Dealer's Daughter*—another love story with a special angle of approach.

Questions

1. What is the theme of the story? Does the presentation of the theme seem more important in this story than the rendition of individual characters or social manners?

2. Why is it so important to Olenka to have "opinions"? Are they of any value in themselves? Do they stand for something else the author chooses not to name?

3. What is the attitude of the community toward Olenka? Does she care?

4. Does Olenka settle for less and less as she moves through a series of relations with men? How does her progress affect the tone and theme of the story?

5. What is the author's attitude toward his main character?

See also "Questions for Comparing the Author's Stories," below.

Further Reading

Poggiola, Renato. *The Phoenix and the Spider.* Cambridge, Mass.: Harvard University Press, 1957. pp. 124-130.

Winner, Thomas. *Chekhov and His Prose.* New York: Holt, Rinehart and Winston, 1966, pp. 209-216.

Anton Chekhov—
Questions for Comparing the Author's Stories

1. Compare tone and author's attitude in *The Lady with the Pet Dog* with those in *The Darling.* How does he indicate where his sympathies lie?

2. To what extent does the passivity of characters contribute to their fate in the three Chekhov stories?

3. Compare the kinds of ironies in these three stories and discuss the means by which the author reveals them.

4. Do the three stories support the sometimes stated criticism that Chekhov's stories are inconclusive?

5. Compare the character of Gurov in *The Lady with the Pet Dog* with that of Podgorin in *A Visit to Friends.*

Kate Chopin   *Désirée's Baby*   (p. 235)
                (Shorter Edition, p. 103)

Nothing is so terrible—or so satisfying to our requirement for equilibrium—as poetic justice. Here,
in a story carefully adjusted to a surprise ending that
will reveal poetic justice in its neatest form, Armand
is punished by a revelation calculated to destroy him
using the very thing that motivated him to destroy his
wife and child. He had adhered arrogantly to the code
of white superiority, only to discover that he is, as
judged by that code, a black.

Aside from the moral implicit in such an outcome,
the chief interest of the story may be in its representation of a way of life and the folkways of a region
at an earlier point in history. Armand Aubigny is the
seigneur of his domain, carrying into a part of the
American South the reckless imperiousness of his feudal
forebears in Europe. Désirée's adoptive family shows
a gentler aspect of the same social formation. Madame
Valmondé in particular is a woman whose disposition to
make a treasure of the foundling Désirée meets no con-
straints. Indeed, it is important to the story that
Désirée should have been spared all the hard knocks of
experience so that her vulnerability to Armand's rejection will be maximized. Socially insulated, she
has no alternative resources to summon in a time of
crisis. She must die when the narrow presumptions of
her existence as wife and mother crumble.

Questions

   1. Is the tragedy caused by social attitudes about
race or by the arrogance and weakness of individuals?
   2. Is Armand being true to his own character when
he sends Désirée away?
   3. Why doesn't Désirée return to her mother's house?
   4. Are Armand's parents to blame for having concealed their secret?
   5. Why has the author concealed the crucial information about Armand's parentage until the last paragraph
of the story?
   6. Are the time, place, and other circumstances essential to the pattern of the action? Could the same
events take place in another environment?

Further Reading

Arner, Robert D. "Pride and Prejudice: Kate Chopin's
    'Désirée's Baby,'" *Mississippi Quarterly,* 25 (1972),
    131-140.
Rankin, Daniel S., *Kate Chopin and Her Creole Stories.*
    Philadelphia: University of Pennsylvania Press,
    1932, pp. 133-134.

Arthur C. Clarke *The Star* (p. 240)

Among its other uses and pleasures, science fiction
sets up hypothetical future circumstances to draw a
clearer schematic diagram of enduring enigmas than
could be done with the materials of our present life.
Here Clarke is posing an everlasting riddle of religious faith: Why, if God is good, does he permit or
even employ means that we can only understand as evil
in carrying forth His designs?

The Jesuit explorer finds proof that God burned a
vast, resourceful, and presumably good "human" civilization—and every last one of its citizens—to provide
the flaring Star of Bethlehem that announced to men on
earth the birth of Jesus among them. It is important
in the arrangement of the story that the narrator
should be a man of faith among agnostic or atheistic
fellows on the spacecraft, for the impact of the discovery on him is necessarily more sharply focused than
for the others. For them the coincidence is essentially meaningless. For him it must be evidence that
the design, in which he believes, is either malevolent
or composed of elements that cannot be reconciled with
the concept of a merciful, just, or loving God. There
is no question of the discovery's making him doubt the
existence of God. The cutting edge of the dilemma
proposed in the story is, rather, that this additional
proof of God's existence drives the man of faith to the
verge of rebellion on moral grounds. The traditional
crisis of faith—doubt of God's existence—would be a
positive comfort compared to the conviction that God
is a cruel joker. Humanistic values are set in stark
opposition to those of the Deity.

The relatively quiet tone of the narration—the
absence of rant and rhetoric—is one of the most

puzzling riddles that might be dealt with in a discussion. Assuming that the shock of the discovery on the Jesuit is the greatest that could be imagined, why does he not howl his grief? Assuming that what he trusted most has betrayed his faith most savagely, has he nowhere at all to turn for either comfort or defiance? Assuming that Clarke set out to write the ultimate horror story, did he deliberately keep it cool to minimize the effect of that horror? Perhaps he meant to show that total despair is the quietest of emotions, a collapse into silence.

Questions

1. How important is the individual character of the narrator as distinct from his formal beliefs? Why is the discovery of the dead civilization more painful for him than for the other scientists on the voyage?

2. Has anything at all been proved about the nature of God by the discovery of the dead planet? What inferences might be drawn about God's motives in choosing an inhabited part of the universe to destroy in announcing to men the birth of Christ?

3. Why did the race that knew itself doomed use its last strength to preserve "loveliness"?

4. Is the central issue of the story the mercy of God? If the narrator has wholly rejected his faith, is this rejection the result of a moral or an intellectual decision?

5. How is this story relevant to your own religious views and values?

Samuel Clemens (Mark Twain)   *The Notorious Jumping Frog of Calaveras County* (p. 246)
(Shorter Edition, p. 108)

The content of this story is unquestionably trivial; the prestidigitation of the author is unquestionably masterful. Here Clemens is showing off his tricks in full confidence that they themselves will become the substance lacking in the material named by the title. He uses not one, but two first-person narrators to filter, distort, and reanimate the events recounted.

By attributing the basic story to a narrator set up to be suspect from the beginning, the first narrator can disclaim responsibility for its elements of incredibility and at the same time milk the profit of its droll absurdity, its frolicking linguistic patterns and the license of its irreverent spirit. And then, behind his impersonations of both narrators, Clemens can seem to share the reader's amused sufferance of the first narrator's prissiness as well as his scornful delight in Simon Wheeler.

Like a savage who really cannot make out the intent of a missionary's question, Simon begins his tale with a cavalier and feckless shift of interest to Jim Smiley, though he was asked about a Rev. Leonidas W. Smiley. And before he can come to what is significant even about Jim, he has to place Jim in relation to an environmental calendar that has no bearing whatever on Jim's great passion for gambling.

Having named this passion—and having effectively reduced Jim Smiley to a two-dimensional cartoon figure of The Gambler—Simon begins to enlarge this figure to a breadth and length (though not a depth) comically in excess of ordinary measures. Clemens is not only incorporating the qualities of the tall tale, characteristic of America's barbarous frontier, but is showing us a hint of its genesis, suggesting it is rooted in the expansionist passion to go beyond the beyond.

The comedy of paradox is the device used in exploiting Smiley's mare and his bull-pup. The story of the decrepit horse is the ancient fable of the tortoise and the hare reoutfitted for this rerun chiefly by the boisterous explosion of language describing how the mare cavorts down the track. The fabulous simpleton who overcomes his more resourceful adversaries by sheer persistence is here reincarnated as Smiley's bull-pup—only to be overcome by the reversal that pits him against an adversary apparently more disadvantaged than he is—a dog with no hind legs for him to get his grip on.

The frog, which must stand at the peak of this series of illustrative creatures, does not at first appear to be as remarkable as the horse or the dog. But very slyly Clemens (through the voice of Simon) lets us know there is something human about this long-limbed beast. "Smiley said all a frog wanted was an education —and I believe him." And then, "You never see a frog so modest and straightfor'ard as he was, for all he was so gifted." Discreetly, with a discretion that is itself part of the fun, Clemens has prepared us to care about Dan'l's victory or defeat, just as if the frog were a human contestant.

Then, in another brilliantly executed shift of focus, Smiley himself replaces the frog as the center of interest. It is Smiley who will go to the mat with the stranger, Smiley who must win or lose in the long-prepared showdown. The whole remarkable narrative contrivance works to show us Smiley outsmarting himself, falling into the trap he has set for himself. He is the familiar American figure of the Hustler, the pool shark acting clumsy until he has lured the stranger into betting with him, the gambler with an ace up his sleeve, the con man of frontier legend. Our pleasure in the climax of the action is not merely in seeing the con man conned—it is the pleasure of noting him as his own victim. And if we end suspecting that all the way through Clemens has been conning us, and that we have conned ourselves into the maze of the entertainment, then the whole transaction of storytelling has been successfully concluded.

Questions

1. What are the differences in character and cultural background between the first narrator and Simon Wheeler?
2. Discuss the relationship between the episode of the frog-jumping contest and Simon Wheeler's prologue to it. Which is more important—prologue or episode?
3. Select and list some examples of the peculiarities in Wheeler's language. List some of his figurative expressions.
4. What is accomplished by giving a touch of human personality to the frog Dan'l Webster?
5. What does the story say about the extent of human gullibility?
6. How do various elements of the story contribute to its tone? Do they all work harmoniously, or is there contradiction between one element and another?

Further Reading

Baender, Paul. "The 'Jumping Frog' as a Comedian's First Virtue," *Modern Philology*, 60 (1963), 192–200.
Mellard, James M. *Four Modes: A Rhetoric of Modern Fiction*. New York: Macmillan, 1973.

Joseph Conrad   *Heart of Darkness*   (p. 251)
                  (Shorter Edition, p. 113)

It is noteworthy that we do not enter this story
directly. The first several paragraphs are spoken by
a first-person narrator who is never named and who
will have no more relation to the story Marlow tells
of his African adventure than the others who listen to
it passively on the deck of their becalmed yacht. The
language which sets this scene—at the borderline between civilization and the enveloping darkness all
around—is solemn, stately, almost grandiloquent and
ceremonial, like that of a sermon preached as a memor-
ial elegy: "The tidal current runs to and fro in its
unceasing service, crowded with memories of men and
ships it has borne to the rest of home or to the bat-
tles of the sea." After such organ tones have established a mood suitable for meditation, when Marlow
first begins to talk, we hear the irregular rhythms and
fragmentary constructions typical of oral recollections.
A fumbling for words. Sudden flights of association.
A colloquial listing of picturesque details. Occasional
shifts to indicate he is aware of the other men present
on the deck. But as his story moves, the language persistently resumes the literary eloquence of the opening,
and this elegiac voice dominates the account of the
quest in search of Kurtz. Before Marlow really
launches into his recollections we are warned not to
look for significance within whatever pattern of action
may develop. ". . . Marlow was not typical . . . and to
him the meaning of an episode was not inside like a
kernel but outside, enveloping the tale which brought
it out only as a glow brings out a haze. . . ." So we
must be extraordinarily responsive to the voice in
which Marlow frames his pronouncements and slants the
light of meditation on all that he saw on his journey.
Since this is presented in straightforward chronological fashion, the first things Marlow has to tell are
how he went to Brussels and got the job as captain of a
Congo steamboat. People encountered there are ticked
off with a wry, faintly sarcastic enumeration of salient impressions they left with him, so they do not
emerge as flesh and blood humans but rather as disem-
bodied gestures, phrases, and humors. The visit to his
aunt before departure provides Marlow with an occasion
for making the first of his important distinctions between the "world of their own" which women inhabit and
the world of fact which will show him a kaleidoscope of
horrors as he travels.

The account of his trip down the African coast is
as factual as that of his meetings with company offi-
cials in Brussels—but here again the facts seem dis-
connected as in some beginning nightmare. "Watching
a coast as it slips by the ship is like thinking about
an enigma," he says. And the French warship firing
her guns "into a continent" from offshore—and making
nothing happen by the bombardment because "Nothing
could happen" prompts him to think "There was a touch
of insanity in the proceeding, a sense of lugubrious
drollery. . . ." Such summary interpretations provide essential guidelines for the reader caught in
the flicker of absurdly incoherent details noted on
that thirty-day trip down the coast.

Once arrived, Marlow soon comes to see the whole
colonial enterprise in Africa as a "merry dance of
death and trade" presided over by "a flabby, pretending
weak-eyed devil of a rapacious and pitiless folly."
Glimpses of a chain gang and of sick black laborers
turned out to die in the airless shade of a grove bring
his disgust to a peak and prepare for his realization
that the best he can expect out here is a "choice of
nightmares."

Just as important as Marlow's voice to the shape and
effect of the whole is the author's tactic of keeping
the major figure of Kurtz offstage. Kurtz takes shape
bit by bit as a moral preoccupation of Marlow's before
he is physically in view and in fact before any reliable specifications of his character have been made.
When Marlow first begins to hear of Kurtz he seems to
be, at least potentially, a heroic alternative to the
disgusting incarnations of the "flabby devil"—the
hypocritical white functionaries who have created all
this devastation in the name of progress. At the
Central Station Marlow gets some vague hint that the
sinking of his steamboat was part of a plot to leave
Kurtz without aid until disease had finished him off.
It is also suggested that Kurtz is a "universal genius"
whose ideas and policies might lift the control of
colonialism out of the hands of the "sordid buccaneers"
who have made such a brutal mess out of it. Above all,
Marlow is lured into the deep reaches of the continent
by the prospect of talking to Kurtz—"The man presented
himself as a voice." This must be construed to mean
that even if hopes of reform are vain, still Kurtz's
"gifts" might throw some light, make some sense of the
hideous enigma into which Marlow has wandered. Thus,
when the steamboat is repaired and the last stretch of
the journey begins, Marlow can still suppose that a

rescue of Kurtz will represent a victory, of sorts, for decency and enlightenment.

But once the corruption of the white men's stations has been left behind, the spirit of the wilderness asserts itself with unforseen authority. "Coming up that river was like travelling back to the earliest beginnings of the world, when vegetation rioted on the earth and the big trees were kings." Here we must not minimize the sinister ambiguity of the verb <u>rioted</u> and the dream-distorted perception of the trees <u>as kings.</u> This poetic disorientation of language stresses Marlow's discovery of zones of reality that civilized consciousness refuses to take into account. The wilderness is not a benevolent or neutral backdrop for the human drama. ". . . this stillness of life did not in the least resemble a peace. It was the stillness of an implacable force brooding over an inscrutable intention." It is as if the landscape uttered a warning of the "moral shock" to come when Kurtz is found, though that warning cannot yet be deciphered.

Among other things *Heart of Darkness* is obviously an adventure story, and in the section describing the approach to the Inner Station we find an abundance of suspense, armed conflict, and perilous brushes with the hazards of river navigation. A written warning is found near a deserted hut. A blinding fog traps the steamer as the shrieking natives threaten to attack. A midstream island forces the boat to pass so close to the shore as to be in easy range of spears and arrows. Cannibalism is in prospect. The helmsman is killed and his blood fills Marlow's shoes. The white passengers fire a fusillade into the jungle and the attackers are at last driven off by blasts of the steamer's whistle.

In spite of so much melee, students often have a hard time visualizing this crescendo of action or even keeping straight in their minds what is going on. It is not hard to see why. Marlow's voice has asserted itself dominantly heretofore, intruding its luminous haze between events and the reader's gaze, and even in this sequence of action Marlow keeps up his speculative digressions. The headman's eagerness to eat the flesh of the attackers becomes the occasion for Marlow to reflect on the weaknesses and restraints of which morality is composed. When arrows come flying out of the jungle foliage, Marlow—through whose eyes we have to see everything we are going to see—notices "sticks, little sticks, were flying about." The gunfire which would be so loud a part of the general melee in actuality is pretty well subdued by references to it as "squirts." In a word, Marlow's voice is poorly suited to rendering such action with the kind of impact it would surely have on a wide screen with full sound effects. Yet it would seem important to visualize the action if only as a means of measuring how far Marlow has gone in transposing it to fit into the flow of his major concerns. So, in discussing these passages it will be worth your time to isolate and paraphrase the continuity of events that bring the tin-pot steamer through the last stretch of the voyage.

And then note how Marlow breaks into the most suspenseful part of his narrative to anticipate not only Kurtz's death but the final encounter, back in Brussels, with Kurtz's fiancée. "Girl! What? Did I mention a girl? Oh, she is out of it . . . Oh, she had to be out of it. . . ." Since references to her are so skimpy at this point, we must assume that Conrad is here including them as a device for promoting the curiosity that builds suspense. But they also serve as an index of how far he has gone beyond reliance on the overt action to maintain the suspense. How, when Marlow and Kurtz are about to meet, all the issues of the story are changed.

The central question is no longer whether Kurtz can be rescued, or whether there can be some sort of alliance between him and Marlow against the "flabby devil" of a corrupt colonialism. Henceforward the issue is whether there exists a way for Marlow to save himself from the discovery that this anticipated ally is more deeply corrupted and committed to evil than his enemies are. The naive young Russian may be satisfied to think that Kurtz's "gifts" of creative intelligence excuse his crimes. Marlow knows better. He knows that the worst manifestation of which mankind is capable is a corruption of the best. All Europe has contributed to making Kurtz a representative, a standard bearer of its best. In the wilderness, no longer limited by the restraints of civilization, he has used all his talents to magnify the scope of the evil, of the "abominations" Marlow must charge him with.

No critical examination of *Heart of Darkness* should skip an examination of the way Conrad has worked to convey the meaning of that somewhat lackluster and obsolescent term "abomination." Certain physical evidence is offered—the rotting heads on the poles around his house, the fact that he has required some chiefs of

the tribes that serve him to crawl when they approach
him. Marlow's rhetorical devices strain obsessively—
sometimes with mocking understatement, sometimes with
passionate solemnity—to express the enormity of
Kurtz's fall. (Understatement: "there was something
wanting in him—some small matter . . ." Solemnity:
"What made this emotion so overpowering was . . . the
moral shock I received, as if something altogether
monstrous, intolerable to thought and odious to the
soul, had been thrust on me unexpectedly.") Kurtz is
called "hollow at the core." The footnote he has added
to his high-minded pamphlet is a summons to genocide:
"Exterminate all the brutes." The horrors taking place
are said to exceed "the usual commonplace deadly danger
. . . which . . . was positively welcome and composing."
But perhaps what is finally most persuasive of all is
the sense of Marlow's despair of conveying the real di-
mension of depravity to his listeners—to people like
us. "You can't understand. How could you? . . . too
dull even to know you are being assaulted by the powers
of darkness." By recognizing the limits that secular
civilization has put on our understanding, we concede
the immensity of the evil that passes understanding.

It is noteworthy that Conrad does not invoke predictable sexual allusions or imagery in his struggle to
define the abomination. The majestic black woman who
appears to have been Kurtz's consort is clearly labeled
as a personification of the wilderness that permitted
him his hellish liberty. Yet all the devices that
qualify her image contribute to making her seem more
pathetic than depraved or evil. So the flaw in Kurtz
cannot be understood as a fleshly perversion. It must
be seen as a perversion of the soul—and seen as beyond
the forgiveness that may be relevant to major crimes of
violence or lust.

As the story nears its end we are told that in his
damnation Kurtz yet achieved a victory. "That is why I
have remained loyal to Kurtz to the last and even
beyond," Marlow says. The victory consists—for whatever we are to make of it—simply and precisely in
Kurtz pronouncing his own career to be "The horror."
This expression "had candor, it had conviction, it had
a vibrating note of revolt in its whisper, it had the
appalling face of a glimpsed truth." This ability to
recognize one's own perdition would seem to be the only
positive value on a major scale to be left in the
resolution of the story.

Against the devastation of such major values as
honor, justice, truthfulness, charity, wisdom, and

fortitude the secondary value—the English virtue—of duty, of absorption in the task at hand, is proposed as the most reliable alternative or compensation. "Rivets!" Marlow holds himself steady against disgust and disillusion by devotion to the task of refloating and then navigating his poor old steamer. At the very end of the action, when he visits Kurtz's bereaved lover, Marlow forfeits the major value of truthfulness for the minor value of consoling her in her grief. Yet somehow this forfeit seems to be transfigured and transformed so that lowly duty to human conventions and to the protection of the weak becomes fidelity—a fidelity that incorporates his loyalty to Kurtz and his concern for the deceived woman and becomes the one major value that makes up for the loss of all others.

Or perhaps it does not. No discussion of this story should end on a note too positive or reassuring. Conrad did not give it its title for nothing.

Questions

1. Interpret the first narrator's statement that "to Marlow the meaning of an episode was not inside like a kernel but outside, enveloping the tale which brought it out only as a glow brings out a haze." How does this apply to Marlow's report of the episodes that make up the novella?

2. What is the relation of the present setting (the deck of the yacht anchored in the Thames) to what Marlow has to say about Africa?

3. What is Marlow's attitude toward the people in Brussels who hire him and send him to Africa? Toward the things he witnesses on his sea voyage?

4. Why is Marlow appalled by what he sees on his arrival in Africa? What does he mean when he speaks of seeing "devils"? Of "seeing" Kurtz—when in fact he has not yet laid eyes on him? What special sense is given to the term "seeing" throughout the novella?

5. Marlow says he does not "at first" grasp the significance of the wreck of the steamboat. What significance does he later find in this circumstance?

6. What is the relation of the young Russian to Kurtz? What ironies lie in the young man's opinion of Kurtz? Is Marlow aware of these ironies or does he merely report what the young man says?

7. Of what significance is the "barbarous and superb" black woman, Kurtz's consort? By what con-

trasts and similarities is she related to Kurtz's "Intended"?

8. What does Marlow mean when he calls Kurtz "hollow"?

9. Why does Kurtz try to escape from the ship that has rescued him?

10. How is Kurtz's report on "The Suppression of Savage Customs" related to the meaning of the whole novella and to the tone that emerges from Marlow's sarcasm?

11. What is said about colonialism? Are these comments essential to the theme?

12. What elements of optimism and pessimism mingle in the conclusion? To what does Kurtz's pronouncement "The horror! The horror!" apply?

13. What is Marlow's ultimate judgment of Kurtz? What factors in his knowledge of Kurtz are most important in the formation of this judgment?

Further Reading

Boyle, Ted E. "Marlow's Lie in 'Heart of Darkness,'" *Studies in Short Fiction*, 1 (Winter 1964), 150-163.

Guetti, James. "'Heart of Darkness' and the Failure of the Imagination," *Sewanee Review*, LXXIII (Summer 1965), 488-504

Johnson, Bruce. "Names, Naming, and the 'Inscrutable' in Conrad's 'Heart of Darkness,'" *Texas Studies in Literature and Language*, 12 (Winter 1971), 675-688.

Levin, Gerald. "The Skepticism of Marlow," *Twentieth Century Fiction*, III (January 1958), 177-184.

Martin, David M. "The Function of the Intended in Conrad's 'Heart of Darkness,'" *Studies in Short Fiction*, II (1974), 27-33.

McCall, Dan. "The Meaning in Darkness," *College English*, XXXIX (May 1968), 620-627.

Pierce, William P. "An Artistic Flaw in 'Heart of Darkness,'" *Conradiana*, 1 (Summer 1969), 72-80.

Robert Coover   *The Babysitter* (p. 322)
                 (Shorter Edition, p. 184)

With a story as complex in organization—and dis-organization—as this one, you may choose to stop short of a full explication of the details and devices used

by the author to keep the multiple points of view distinct and the chronology relatively intelligible. Even
if a number of clues are missed, the main characters
and the main lines of comic development should be clear
enough to the average attentive reader to permit a
level of comprehension from which reasonable discussion
can proceed. And especially since some of the clues to
what is going on at any particular time are deliberately planted false leads, it is probably well to begin
with some general specifications that can be stated
with confidence.

First, the situation. Harry Tucker and his wife
Dolly go out for the evening to a party at the house of
friends. Their three children are left at home with a
babysitter. Her boyfriend Jack and his pal Mark are
playing a pinball machine and discussing the possibility of calling on—and perhaps raping—the babysitter
while the adult Tuckers are gone. In the course of the
evening all these characters have fantasies about how
the evening might go and also about how it is going.
In the early part of the story it appears possible to
distinguish these fantasies from reality. By the time
it is finished such a distinction is literally impossible. The author does not resolve the tangle of false
clues and overlapping fantasies he has created.

Mr. Tucker's fantasies consist in imagining various
returns to his own house, where he sees himself sexually involved with the babysitter. These fantasies
spin out from the fact that on a previous occasion the
babysitter bathed in the Tucker bathroom and left pubic
hair in the tub. Mrs. Tucker's fantasies are set off
by the tightness of her girdle and her anxieties about
her increasing weight. Jack and Mark evidently find
the pinball machine a surrogate for the body of the
babysitter. They handle it and talk to it as if they
were in the midst of the sexual ravishment they intend
to visit on the girl. Her fantasies (oddly enough) are
for the most part coordinated with the fantasies of the
four males (including young Jimmy) who have sexual designs on her, though near the end of the story when we
read that the baby is drowned in the bathtub this detail has blended not only with Mrs. Tucker's anxieties
about her children but with the general chaos that
seems to have descended on the community and all its
inhabitants.

Second, the shifting point of view. Each paragraph
is presented from the point of view of a different
character. Usually, and particularly in the first half
of the story, we can tell whose point of view the

author is taking by the data included in the paragraph. Masculine or feminine pronouns in combination with such details as proper names, girdles, towels, coin slots, television set, cake of soap, and a multitude of other props usually establish not only the character and his location but the place of the scenic fragment in the general chronology of the evening. Thus, even the cryptic fifth paragraph can be pinned down with exactitude by matching it with later information about young Jimmy's lecherous thoughts of the babysitter.

But in at least one paragraph describing what is appearing on the TV it is impossible to ascertain either the point of view or the point in time. And, when the fantasies of the various characters are most entangled, our initial hypotheses about the whereabouts of characters and the time sequence become impossible to sustain. Perhaps some paragraphs describe actual bathroom experiences of the babysitter on a previous occasion. Perhaps Mark and Jack have never left the drugstore where they were playing the pinball machine. There are simply so many uncertainties one had best conclude that the author has made use of certain realistic devices and illusions only to abandon them in favor of playing comic variations on the possibilities in the situation he has imagined, content to have contrived a ribald pastiche.

Questions

1. What comment does the story make about the way we live now? About such features of American life as babysitting, cocktail parties, and pinball machines?

2. Cite some instances in which fact blurs into fantasy. How do these blurrings comment on the social patterns in which the characters exist and act?

3. Why is the story separated into multiple points of view? Do these shifts from paragraph to paragraph help to keep the characters and the strands of action relatively distinct?

4. How are the images of the television screen related to the actions of the real characters?

5. The characters can be categorized in three distinct age levels: adults, adolescents, and children. Is there more consistency and rationality at one level than at the others?

6. Is it easier to keep the characters and situation straight at the beginning or at the end? How does the relative confusion or clarity relate to the meaning of the story as a whole?

Mark Costello   *Murphy's Xmas*   (p. 344)

It is an ambition of many writers of short stories
to pack as much observation and experience as possible
into a brief space. Formal variations (or eccentricities) in stories we call experimental emphasize this
concern, and it might be well to consider *Murphy's Xmas*
as a type of miniaturized novel, for an immense number
of relationships, actions, perceptions, and chronolo-
gies have here been telescoped into a few thousand
words. Many of the unconventional transitions, the un-
orthodox punctuation and paragraphing that will strike
(and perhaps baffle) the reader have been invented to
accommodate the extraordinary profusion of characters
and events. The main plot line itself has been trimmed,
bent, and broken up to fit the economy of the overall
design.

A necessary part of reading is to take hold of that
plot and, so to speak, unfold it so we can comprehend
the way its ramifications lace through the form the
author has finally achieved for his text. The plot action begins (chronologically speaking) when Murphy's
wife tricks him into making her pregnant though he has
separated from her and is living with the younger woman
named Annie. The plot is complicated when Murphy, compelled by family obligations, must leave Annie within
reach of his lecherous friend Glover to drive his pregnant wife and their young son to visit parents in
Illinois. There, motivated as much by his anxiety
about Annie as by the torment of having to explain to
his parents why he is divorcing, he seeks release by
again having intercourse with his wife. The price of
this relief is his increased vulnerability to the
pleadings of his son and his parents that he resume his
role as husband and father. To help himself resist
these pleas, Murphy indulges in jealous fantasies about
what Annie and Glover are doing in his absence.

In the course of developing the plot line and showing its psychological and moral subtleties, the author
has to deal with Murphy's relationships to three male
and three female characters, all of them except Glover
part of the unstable structure of Murphy's love. The
concept of fatherhood, its duties and anguishes, must
be dovetailed with the equally elaborate variations on
the theme of love between the sexes, his bonds to
mother, wife, and lover. Nimble transitions help to
keep all these relationships simultaneously before our
eyes—as if a juggler were keeping control of six balls
in the air.

The first few lines show the speed of transition as well as the suppression of detail we would ordinarily expect. The drunken Murphy is no sooner "out in the headlights" to fight (with person or persons unknown) than he is "waking up the next afternoon with Annie kissing his crucified right fist." The word blue which ends the fifth paragraph is made to do double duty, terminating one thought, one sentence, and beginning another, as it could not in conventional syntax. The extraordinary image of Annie's "shy skeleton waltzing away with his in a fit of ribbons" (in the sixth paragraph) is a dense compound of coital sensations and their accompanying fantasies with anticipations of the Christmas season beginning. All the complex considerations that must have gone into Murphy's decision to make the long holiday trek with his estranged wife and son are also reduced to an image—Murphy's shocking vision of his son "strewn across the wet December roadside, his toys and intestines glistening under the wheels of semi trucks." (The shocking juxtaposition of toys and intestines is typical of the author's reliance on word play and imagery to load the narrative to its maximum potential.) A little farther along the image of Lincoln's coffin—called into Murphy's mind by their passage through Springfield, Illinois—and the morbid associations of the coffin slip over without transitional explanation into the morbid associations related to Mrs. Murphy's womb, which is so ominously preparing to produce an unwanted child. The recollection of how she tricked him into making her pregnant swiftly prepares for his refusal to face her parents.

When he desperately phones Annie in Missouri, the slurring elisions of the prose transform her innocent report of Glover's visit into the gibbering voice of Murphy's jealousy. Thus one experience after another is phantasmagorically transformed until finally all the challenges Murphy must face in his various relationships are welded into a constricting circle of undifferentiated pressure that squeezes him, figuratively speaking, to death.

Questions

1. What are the relations between Murphy's intentions and the circumstances in which he must operate? Between his psychological state and his real interests?

2. In what ways does imagery function in explaining the action and its psychological accompaniment?

3. Discuss the concept and the actuality of father-hood as it appears here.

4. In what ways are form and language appropriate to the subject matter? Do they give us any clues as to how the author feels about his main character?

5. In what ways is the technique comparable to that of contemporary films?

6. What does it mean to say that Murphy "knows" he is dead? Is this merely figurative language?

Stephen Crane   *The Open Boat*   (p. 357)
                 (Shorter Edition, p. 206)

Literary craftsmen have long admired the audacity and precision of the first sentence: "None of them knew the color of the sky." Not only do these few words plunge the reader immediately into the experience being rendered, they also summarize with great economy the anxiety of men watching for the next antic of the waves so fixedly they cannot register any other aspects of their environment. The rest of the opening paragraph exploits the breakthrough of the beginning words and establishes the transfixed consciousness through which the reader perceives the adventure.

Certainly this is the consciousness of the corre-spondent, but it also presumes, successfully, to be the common consciousness of all four of the men in the boat. We are never particularly aware of his distinction from the other three. He is presented as objectively as everything else. Some of the metaphors and allusions must be his alone—consider the ironic pathos of his speculations on "A soldier of the Legion"—but the mus-cular discomforts of rowing, the chilly precariousness as they huddle to sleep, and even the resentment at the indifference of the natural universe can be accepted so naturally as shared experience that we easily believe such an ordeal dissolves the barriers that in easier times separate one man's consciousness from that of his fellows.

It is this overall sense of immersion in and recog-nition of a common fate that gives point to the corre-spondent's knowledge that this "was the best experience of his life." The following specification that "no one said that it was so" defines a relation preserved throughout between the reportage of objective fact and the no less objective recording of accompanying states of awareness.

The dialogue is very low-key, understated, the probable speech patterns of exhausted men. But it is set in counterpoint to some very elaborate figurative language, much of it devoted to a sort of personification of the sea and a rhetorical expression of its moods. The remark at the end, that the man felt they could be interpreters of the voice of the sea, is an extension of a long series of interpretive images that speak for the sea. The conflict in the story—superficially nothing more than a prolonged struggle for survival—might be altogether too simple to make good fiction if we did not have the sense that the subtle complexity of the human soul was matched against an at least equally subtle complexity in the power the men must confront.

Suspense and irony are raised to a crescendo by the unforeseen problems that emerge when the little boat comes in sight of land and is actually observed by people on shore. The test on the men becomes a test of their ability to compose themselves in face of the mocking riddles of their condition. "Was I brought here merely to have my nose dragged away as I was about to nibble the sacred cheese of life?" "A distinction between right and wrong seems absurdly clear to a man" at those moments when clarity is absurdly irrelevant. He "wishes to throw bricks at the temple, and he hates deeply the fact that there are no bricks and no temple." These hideous and unjust contradictions—of the sort that must be faced by everybody in extremis— are articulated almost lightheartedly, perhaps because it would be unbearable not to joke about them.

A shark—or perhaps more than one—trails the little boat for a while until it grows "bored at the delay." Significantly in the paragraph that reports its disappearance the shark is called the "thing." This is a slight shift in names which leaves open the possibility that the referent is not an actual shark but the "design of darkness"—as Robert Frost once called it— that has moved so inscrutably to lure the men into their plight. Perhaps there is a suggestion that beyond the horror of an ineffable designing power there is a worse horror—nothingness, meaningless, the total void.

Though three of the four men are saved—saved as capriciously as they have been cast in danger—the survivors have glimpsed the promised end of their

lives. After such knowledge, what can one do but in-
dulge the flippant irony that is the prevalent tone of
Crane's telling?

Questions

1. What is the major conflict of this story? What
minor conflicts accompany it?

2. Why does the indifference of nature to the fate
of the men seem worse than hostility?

3. How do the men in the boat feel about each
other? How is this revealed?

4. What is the meaning of the correspondent's remembrance of a sentimental verse about "a soldier of the
Legion"?

5. Interpret the tone and meaning of the expression
"nibble the sacred cheese of life."

6. Pick out examples and discuss the use of figurative language. Are statements made in such language
consistent with the meaning of the events described?

See also "Questions for Comparing the Author's
Stories," p. 65 of this *Handbook*.

Further Reading

Buitenhuis, Peter. "The Essentials of Life: 'The Open
    Boat' as Existentialist Fiction," *Modern Fiction
    Studies*, V (Autumn 1959), 243-250.

Burns, Landon C., Jr. "On 'The Open Boat,'" *Studies in
    Short Fiction*, III (Summer 1966), 455-457.

Frederick, John T. "The Fifth Man in 'The Open Boat,'"
    CEA Critic, XXX (May 1968), 1-14, *passim*.

Going, William T. "William Higgins and Crane's 'The
    Open Boat': A Note about Fact and Fiction," *Papers
    on Language and Literature*, I (Winter 1965), 79-82.

Gullason, Thomas A. "The New Criticism and the Older
    Ones: Another Ride in 'The Open Boat,'" *CEA Critic*,
    XXXII (June 1969), 8.

Kissane, Leedice. "Interpretation Through Language: A
    Study of Metaphors in Stephen Crane's 'The Open
    Boat,'" *Rendezvous*, 1 (1966), 18-22.

LaFrance, Marston. *A Reading of Stephen Crane*. New
    York: Oxford, 1971, pp. 195-205.

Stallman, R.W. "The Land-Sea Irony in 'The Open
    Boat,'" *CEA Critic*, XXX (May 1968), 15.

Stephen Crane   *The Blue Hotel* (p. 376)

It may be said that Crane's ironic conception rises
from his recognition of a disparity between the obligations of conscience and the obligations of our legal
system. Acting with all propriety, as far as we can
determine, the agencies of the law determined that responsibility for the Swede's death lay exclusively with
the man who knifed him. That the sentence imposed for
the killing was "light" can be justified by our realization that the gambler was not only provoked but assaulted before he responded with the fatal stroke of
his knife. The court honorably performed its assigned
task.

But the all important question of whether justice
was done remains open to the conscience after the case
is legally closed, for Crane has designed this moral
fable to show how many different ways <u>might</u> have been
followed—to how many dead ends or misty uncertainties
—in the search for ultimate responsibility. "A thousand things might have happened," the Easterner remarks
after the event, and it follows logically from this
that there were a thousand sins of omission contributing to the fatal outcome. The number of positive con-
tributions would be equally great.

Certainly the Swede himself <u>can</u> be considered responsible for what happens to h<u>i</u>m. Or if he is sick—
"daffy," "crazy," "frightened out of his boots"—his
illness or simply his unlucky encounter with a milieu
he can not interpret sanely <u>might</u> be singled out as the
true cause of the disaster. (The author is playing a
strange game when he refers in his own language to the
Swede's body as a "citadel of virtue, wisdom and
power." This is hard to square with the picture we are
given of the beserk stranger, alternating between mad
cowardice and mad belligerence.) Or we could equally
say that Scully's attempts to keep the peace were, in
the circumstances, fatal. Or say that Scully's attempts to keep the peace were hypocritical, based on
greed, not warm concern. Yet, in fact, there is hardly
anything we can say about the contributory causes except that it is impossible to single out any one of
them and prove that the guilt lodges exclusively here
and not elsewhere.

This is the success of Crane's design. He has shown
what a labyrinthine path the conscience must take in
such matters, without much hope of a conclusive answer.
However, it must be noted that the last section of the

story contains some limping attempts to minimize the scale of the problems thus far opened up. The Easterner's disclosure of Johnnie's cheating can be seized on, all too easily, as the one clue that explains everything. In fact, it answers none of the riddles of responsibility, and the Easterner's prejudice that "usually there are from a dozen to forty women really involved in every murder" ought to show that there are drastic handicaps to his moral vision of human affairs.

Questions

1. What ironies lie in the fact that the action takes place in Nebraska? Consider that everyone associates violence and danger with "The West." Is Nebraska somehow transformed into "The West"?

2. Is Scully acting from good motives in trying to keep peace in his hotel? Does the purity or impurity of his motives have anything to do with the outcome of the action?

3. Is Johnnie a victim or an aggressor? What does the story as a whole say about innocence and guilt?

4. How much faith can we have in the interpretation of the case given by the Easterner in the last section of the story? Is this just one man's opinion or is it a wise summary of all that has happened?

5. At one point the author tells us that the Swede's body is a "citadel of virtue, wisdom, power." Does this appear to be true when you take into account the man's behavior? If you see a discrepancy, account for it.

See also "Questions for Comparing the Author's Stories," p. 65 of this *Handbook*.

Further Reading

Gibson, Donald. "'The Blue Hotel' and the Ideal of Human Courage." *Texas Studies in Literature and Language*, VI (Autumn 1964), 388-397.

LaFrance, Marston. *A Reading of Stephen Crane*. New York: Oxford, 1971, pp. 221-332.

Maclean, Hugh N. "The Two Worlds of 'The Blue Hotel,'" *Modern Fiction Studies*, V (Autumn 1959), 260-270.

Narveson, Robert. "Conceit in 'The Blue Hotel,'" *Prairie Schooner*, XLIII (Summer 1969), 187-191.

Wenig, Sister Mary Anthony. "Heroic Convention in 'The Blue Hotel,'" *Stephen Crane Newsletter,* VI (1968), 6-7.

Westbrook, Max. "Stephen Crane's Social Ethic," *American Quarterly,* XIV (Winter 1962), 593-595.

Stephen Crane—
Questions for Comparing the Author's Stories

1. Compare tone and imagery of *The Open Boat* and *The Blue Hotel.* In which is the meaning of the story most dependent on these elements?

2. Since the human conflict is obviously more important in *The Blue Hotel* than in *The Open Boat,* one might expect the ironies of fate to be essentially different in the two stories. Are they? In which is plot most important?

3. Are there differences in realism in the two stories? (Remember that *The Open Boat* was based on an actual experience of the author.)

Isak Dinesen   *Sorrow-Acre* (p. 399)

Obviously the setting plays an extraordinarily important part in this story. Not only is it exotic and picturesque and peopled with figures who might seem to belong in a fairy tale; the landscape has a potency to shape its inhabitants, and it is more than faintly suggested that the old lord is, essentially, the voice of the land on which he and his like have lived "a thousand years." His values are rooted in the soil of Denmark, as the traditions he upholds are those of men and women whose lives are shaped by their attachment to the land.

The essential conflict, from which the theme of the story rises, is between the conservative tradition of the Danish landholder and the appeals of the New World and England, where Adam has been exposed to "the great new ideas of the age"—the Utopian ideals of freedom and democracy that urge him to reject what he feels to be his uncle's tyranny and emigrate to America.

Adam is not directly involved in the action of the story. He has no decision to make except to which of

the conflicting political and philosophic views of
life he will commit himself—will he stay or go? He is
only a witness, yet in a real sense he is the central
character of the story. The author uses him to examine
and sort out the evidence and finally to point up the
meaning of what takes place in the rye field by decid-
ing to stay. His submission to the dreadful justice of
the landholding tradition testifies to the persuasiveness of all his uncle believes in.

In the beginning Adam leans toward departure. If he
were to speak to the land "as to the mother of his
race," he would ask "Is it only my body that you want
. . . while you reject my imagination, energy and emotions?" The "great, new ideas" invite him to go where
imagination, energy, and emotion will have freer play.

Intellectually and emotionally Adam is troubled by
the bargain that his uncle has made with Anne-Marie—
that she could save her son only by the enormous task
of mowing the big rye field by herself between sunrise
and sunset. He has looked up to his uncle all his
life. "What was he to do . . . if . . . his second
father's figure [should] take on to him a horrible aspect, as a symbol of the tyranny and oppression of the
world?" As the day of trial progresses, Adam comes to
the point of pleading with the old man to call it off.

But the old man refuses, saying patiently that he
has given his word to Anne-Marie. "Anne-Marie might
well feel that I am making light of her exploit, if
now, at the eleventh hour, I did nullify it by a second
word." The exchange between the two men culminates
with Adam's declaration that he will go away. "England
. . . was not far enough away; deeper water than the
North Sea must now be laid between him and Denmark. . . .
'I shall go to America, to the new world.'"

His uncle does not try to dissuade him—in fact says
without any apparent intention of mocking Adam's innocence, "Take service there . . . with the power which
will give you an easier bragain than this: That with
your own life you may buy the life of your son."

Though he does not at once grasp the deep irony of
the comment, it catches Adam's ear—repeating the idea
voiced in the little French tune his "aunt" has sung to
him. And it seems to him presently that in the spectacle and example his uncle has provided he has seen,
here in Denmark, the vision of "the oneness of the
world." As he declares at last that he will stay,
"a long, loud roll of thunder broke the stillness of
the afternoon. . . . The landscape had spoken. He

remembered that twelve hours ago he had put a question to it. . . . Here it gave him its answer."

Even if he does not stay in the field to see the end of Anne-Marie's trial, it is the spectacle through which his uncle and the land have reached him, spoken to him. It has spoken, as well, to all its workers who have come to watch the woman finish her task. And when she finishes her mowing a "great stir, and a sound like a manifold deep sigh, ran through the crowd." The spectacle of the dying woman in the arms of the son she has saved seems to complete some necessary ritual, profoundly understood by all who have witnessed it. Rather than lament for her, some "wandered on, up and down the stubble, imitating and measuring her course from one end of the rye field to the other. . . ."

The poetic justice of such a conclusion (like that in Tolstoy's *God Sees the Truth, but Waits*—which might be read for comparison) is likely to jar heavily against the preconceptions of a majority of American students. How many of them, in Adam's place, would finally accept the tragic tradition personified and articulated by his uncle? Once they understand the story to be a challenge to libertarian American prejudices, the stage is set for an open discussion of the alternative value systems.

Questions

1. What is the importance of the physical setting? Of the traditions of the landowners? Of the descriptions of the young wife and her role?

2. Give a full summary of the old lord's ideas of law, power, and justice. In what ways are Adam's ideas opposed to these? Does Anne-Marie oppose or accept them?

3. What does the old lord mean when he says that Anne-Marie is not an ordinary person? Why is her accomplishment believable?

4. How does the story comment on democracy and aristocracy? Does the author seem to take sides?

5. Why does Adam give up his plan of going to America?

6. Discuss the story as a representation of conflicting ideas of justice. As an allegory based on Christian theology.

7. How do the values set forth by the story fit with your own sense of right and justice?

Arthur Conan Doyle   *A Scandal in Bohemia*   (p. 425)

Whatever else it may be for most students, this story will give them a brush with the legendary Sherlock Holmes and—from the first page onward—a chance to measure Doyle's extraordinarily popular conception of the way the intellect works. For Holmes is conceived as, above all, an intellectual machine. "He never spoke of the softer passions, save with a gibe and a sneer. . . . Grit in a sensitive instrument . . . would not be more disturbing than a strong emotion in a nature such as his." This cold-blooded thinking machine alternates "between cocaine and ambition." And the sort of mysteries to which such an intellect is attracted are not those of the human soul or motivation (except in a crude mechanical sense) but the mysteries of matters of fact. Holmes says (in a trademark phrase) that he "deduces" things. Actually what we observe is an ingenious display of inductive reasoning, not deductive. To put it as strongly as it deserves, his reasoning processes are pseudoscientific. Bright students will quickly see that he makes no distinction between hypotheses and conclusions. He seizes on possibilities as certainties with a recklessness that should appall anyone with scientific training. Nevertheless, like Superman or Tarzan, Sherlock Holmes is one of the prominent icons of popular mythology and no doubt deserves study for that reason alone.

It must be noted that the trick he uses to get Irene Adler to disclose the location of the photograph depends on his knowledge of what "a woman"—every woman, every time—will do when she thinks her house is on fire. "It is a perfectly overpowering impulse . . . ," he says. As stated, this is perfectly overpowering nonsense, but it fits with the mechanistic and simplistic conception of character and motivation that prevails throughout.

Only confusion can result from measuring this story with the standards appropriate for serious fiction. Much of the activity that supplies color and suspense is merely stage business—the rush to the church when Irene marries, for example. The King's ultimate confidence that he is safe after Irene's departure is based on nothing material—he has not gained possession of the photo that worried him so much. Misusing the word <u>inviolate</u> for <u>inviolable</u>, he merely decides to accept her promise that she will trouble him no more. So the resolution of the story is as paper-thin as all of the characters are.

On the other hand, examining the piece as an example of the popular culture of a period in which character stereotypes and public values were somewhat different than they are now should make for lively discussion. Bohemian kings and clever adventuresses are not exactly the staple of contemporary pop literature, but the exposure and threats of exposure of public figures continue in new forms. Asking students to imagine contemporary equivalents for the characters and predicaments here should turn up illuminating opinions of the evolution of manners.

Questions

1. What does Holmes have in common with other "super-heroes" of popular literature, film, and television?

2. Are Holmes's methods truly scientific? To what extent is he a lucky gambler?

3. For what qualities does Holmes admire Irene Adler more than all other women? What other values are expressed by the story?

4. Trace lines of motivation for the various actions performed by the main characters. For instance: Why is Irene Adler in such a hurry to get married? Why does she suppose that leaving England will get Holmes off her trail?

5. How does Watson function in the design of the story? Does his admiration for Holmes's cleverness make the reader take it for granted?

Ralph Ellison   *King of the Bingo Game*   (p. 443)
               (Shorter Edition, p. 225)

Here is a highly successful fusion of technique and meaning; the important and moving statement of the story is intensified and extended by narrative devices which, without calling attention to themselves, permit the author to pass beyond realism without taxing the reader's credulity. First we note that the name of the central character is never given. The significance of this device is revealed when we learn that "somehow he had forgotten his own name." In the mysteriously symbolic trial with the bingo wheel he has become simply "me"—a man with responsibilities he cannot meet and hungers he cannot satisfy, who nevertheless believes that as long as he can keep the wheel running he is impregnable, perhaps even omnipotent, since he has taken God's place in control of chance.

Not only is the chief character's name omitted, the author has locked himself into a point of view so closely identified with his character's awareness that all objective measures of what is really happening are drastically minimized. Except for one sentence in the last paragraph, no data comes into the story except what is filtered and transformed by the mental state and processes of the player. Such extraordinary strictness in limiting the point of view has the effect of giving authority to ideas and impressions that might be dismissed more readily as mental aberration if we saw the episode as, say, another member of the audience in the theater would see it. It is almost as if this were a first-person narration—though the author retains the privilege of using his own language to clarify and articulate the experience of his character. Because the world is thus reduced to a world perceived by passion and need, the author gains at least a rhetorical advantage in persuading us that reality is what it seems to the man with his finger on the button of power and control. Such rhetorical advantage enhances the force of the theme—which is close to the Existentialist idea that a man may, in the extremity of his need, when he has forgotten his name (that is, his social identity) seize the power to control his destiny, though he may not be able to sustain his power against physical opposition. The "king" of the story has achieved a transcendental kingship, which need not be considered illusory merely because it has little temporal effect or duration. The "king" has known who he is while he holds the button, and Existentialists affirm that this is victory. He has "a sense of himself that he had never known before." It is a triumph of self-possession.

The setting in the shabby theater, amid a mocking and essentially uncomprehending crowd is important in the design of the story, as is the illness of the player's wife. The latter circumstance provides the dynamic motivation for the extreme psychological concentration required to carry the main character to the visionary point at which he knows who he truly is. A comparison with D. H. Lawrence's *Rocking-Horse Winner* could be valuable, for it also is a story in which social and psychological patterns are pushed into the realm of metaphysics. Sir James Frazer's *The Golden Bough* will provide ideas about kingship that illuminate Ellison's conception and explain the ambiguity of his title.

Questions

1. How does the actual physical setting provide the symbols used in constructing the theme? How do the actual needs of the main character prepare him for what he feels when he is holding down the button and making the wheel run?

2. Is his sense of power hallucination or insight?

3. What is the significance of his forgetting his own name?

4. Interpret, by paraphrasing, the symbolic significance of the wheel.

5. What is the significance of the end of the story? Of the fact that the wheel comes to rest on the double-zero?

William Faulkner   *A Rose for Emily*   (p. 451)
            (Shorter Edition, p. 233)

The narrator seems to have no character of his own distinct from that of the town for which he speaks, using the pronoun "we" to stress that sentiments toward Emily Grierson and the information on which they are based are collective, not individual. At the same time it must be noted that if he speaks for the town, he speaks for its better side, for its tolerant, reflective, and patient acceptance of events shocking enough in themselves. There is ripeness and passivity in the narrative tone; the sad, calm sobriety that passes no judgment on Miss Emily or on those of her townspeople who are baffled and sometimes outraged by her perversity.

Just as the contending passions of Miss Emily, Homer Barron, and the townspeople are dissolved by the even charity of the narrator's tone, so the chronology is softly blurred as memory moves back and forth to retrieve one or another part of the pattern of the tale. We are told that the old men of the town have grown confused about whether Emily was their contemporary, "confusing time with its mathematical progression, as the old do, to whom all the past is not a diminishing road, but, instead, a huge meadow . . . divided from them now by the narrow bottleneck of the most recent decade of years." This nonlinear image of past time seems to have been effectively adopted by the narrator.

What he sees in this "meadow" of the past is a series of abbreviated and fragmentary actions. "We had long thought of [Emily and her father] as a tableau; Miss Emily a slender figure in white in the background, her father a spraddled silhouette in the foreground, his back to her and clutching a horsewhip. . . ." The other glimpses of Emily in her later years are hardly more than tableaux. She appears a motionless figure in her window when the townsmen come into her yard to sprinkle lime to suppress the stench. She appears at her door after her father's death to deny that he is dead. We see her—almost as in a still picture— driving with Homer Barron in his yellow-wheeled buggy. When she goes to the drug store to buy poison she speaks, but so elliptically that the effect of tableau hardly gives way to that of dramatic involvement and complication. We might say that the story is presented less like a movie than like a series of slides pro- jecting still pictures on the screen—or like pages from a family album showing the title character at various decisive moments of her life. It is important to note that the images do not come in a strictly pro- gressive chronological sequence, but in a pattern that will preserve the suspense of her secret while it moves toward the revelation of the last clause of the last sentence.

Emily, we discover, has refused not only to accept the possibility that her lover could desert her but, after she has poisoned him, refused to accept the fact that death has changed her relationship with him. All these years she has slept with the corpse of her dead lover as if his death and decay were beneath her notice.

The grotesque ugliness of this circumstance is muted by the oblique manner in which the story has been told. There is humor in the gruesome resolution, and the dis- tance preserved by Faulkner's ingenious narrative strategies has prepared us to see Miss Emily as an allegorical figure even while we believe her to be a most eccentric individual. Allegorically she seems to represent a certain stubbornness in the South that re- fused ever to recognize that the old times were gone beyond recall. She clung "to that which has robbed her, as people will." By her clinging she goes mad. But even in her mad refusal to admit change she remains something of a monument to the old values and virtues. She is, in the eyes of the narrator, "dear, inescapable, impervious, tranquil and perverse." Just as we must not slight the force of the last adjective, we would miss the theme of the story if we ignored the first one. As in much of his other fiction, Faulkner does not here look cheerfully at progress nor admit easily the merits of change.

Questions

1. Account for the use of the pronoun "we" by the narrator.
2. How is Faulkner's handling of chronology expressive of the nature of memory?
3. What does Emily represent to her town and her region? What attitudes toward social classes figure in the action and how do these change?
4. What is the relation between comic elements and the melancholy or shocking ingredients of the story?
5. What does Homer Barron represent? How important is it that he is a Yankee?
6. What motives can you attribute to Emily for her killing of Homer Barron? How are these motives related to the theme?

See also "Questions for Comparing the Author's Stories," p. 80 of this *Handbook*.

Further Reading

Brooks, Cleanth, and Robert Penn Warren. *The Scope of Fiction*. New York: Appleton-Century-Crofts, Inc., 1960.

Kobler, J.F. "Faulkner's 'A Rose for Emily,'" *The Explicator*, 32 (1974), Item 65.

McGlynn, Paul D. "The Chronology of 'A Rose for Emily,'" *Studies in Short Fiction*, VI (Summer 1969), 461-462.

Stone, Edward. "Usher, Poquelin, and Miss Emily: The Progress of Southern Gothicism," *Georgia Review*, XIV (Winter 1960), 433-443.

William Faulkner   *That Evening Sun*   (p. 459)

Readers of Faulkner's complete works will be
prompted to identify the narrator of "That Evening
Sun" as Quentin Compson, who, with his siblings
Candace and Jason, also figures prominently in *The
Sound and the Fury* and who reappears in *Absalom,
Absalom!*, telling his Harvard roommate stories of
the South. Nancy can be seen as the black woman
Nancy Mannigoe of a much later novel, *Requiem for a
Nun*. If one accepts this identification it leads
automatically to the conclusion that her fear of
being murdered by Jesus never materialized.

However, one is well-advised to tread lightly in
making such identifications, paying due respect to
Faulkner's occasional inconsistencies and reconsiderations. When, as he often did, he resumed the account of a character whose tale was incomplete in an
earlier work, sometimes only the superficial data
about that character remain consistent, and sometimes
not even that is reliable. Sometimes information subsequently supplied radically changes the significance
of things we believed to be definitive. Thus identifying the narrator of "That Evening Sun" will pose a
discouraging problem if we dwell on Faulkner's fictive
afterthought that Nancy survived to become the saintly
murderess of *Requiem for a Nun*. With that in mind we
might properly wonder why the short story was not
rounded out by having Quentin supply that information
in the present instance. Since the story is being
told from a perspective of some fifteen years, the
Quentin we hear at the beginning would certainly have
known Nancy was not killed by Jesus on the night the
story ends.

To say that this specific information would be
anticlimactic and would have vitiated the effect of
the story as it stands is perhaps merely to note that
it is better to take Faulkner's works as discrete en-
tities rather than as fragments of a continuing saga
—and to highlight the extent to which this story depends on effect achieved at the expense of withholding
information.

After a sweepeing beginning that promises a sum-
mational view of Nancy in her relation to Jesus and
the other characters who figure in the story, the broad
perspective of fifteen years is thereafter deliberately
suppressed, choked down so far that we are not even
given Quentin's childish interpretations of what is
going on. From something like omniscience, the narra-

tion funnels down to a tight-lipped, objective understatement. The concluding scenes cannot, in the form
Faulkner chose for them, inform the reader as to whether
or not there is any substance to Nancy's fear of Jesus.

Of course, there is a reason for this radical narrowing of focus. It is a device to build suspense. It
might be compared to the tactic of a filmmaker playing
on the nerves of the audience of a thriller by holding
the camera to the shot of a hand turning a doorknob instead of revealing figure and face. Is it the hand of
a killer who will attack when he has opened the door?
There is no way to know from the limited information
given, but the buildup has suggested this as probable,
so the audience is breathless with anxiety.

Here Faulkner has laid on many suggestions that
Nancy will be killed. The story ends with the strong
suggestion she will not live through the night.
Quentin's question, "Who will do our laundry now?" suggests he knows this to be the case. Perhaps he has
sensed it from his father—the father's natural reticence in the presence of the children being understood
as a signal that the knowledgeable adult has, in fact,
given up hope of saving the terrified woman. At the
very least, the unrelieved crescendo of tension has
overshadowed the anticipation of any other outcome.

If this were all, we might conclude Faulkner has
tricked us into a false belief, limiting our admiration
to a respect for the grim and gaudy coloration he has
supplied for his entertainment. It may be enough to
admire the virtuosity of his showmanship.

But there is another, and perhaps more impressive,
explanation for his drastically confining the narrative
means to Quentin's muted perceptions. Concentrating on
these at the moment of their impact dramatizes the magnitude of the shock when a child realizes that horrors
can happen to terrified flesh and blood. It is a recognition which does not belong in the world of children,
we feel, and it may be argued that the shock of recognition is as frightful as the hypothetical murder might be
in itself. Whether or not Nancy will be killed, something awful has happened to the children, to Quentin
particularly. So the effect Faulkner achieves by a radical amputation of the informational ingredient in his
story redirects our apprehensions, making us suspect it
is Quentin's story more than Nancy's. Unmistakably he
has suffered a major violation, whatever may become of
her.

Questions

1. In what different ways does each of the three children respond to Nancy's fears?

2. Since we are never told whether Nancy's fears are objectively justified, what is the point of the story?

3. What function in the story is served by the father of the children? What seems to be his state of mind at the end?

4. Taking into account the opening paragraphs, comment on the differences between past and present times. Is there something about Nancy's character or predicament that requires the setting of the past?

5. How does limiting the story to a child's point of view exaggerate the effect of the story?

See also "Questions for Comparing the Author's Stories," p. 80 of this *Handbook*.

Further Reading

Lee, Jim.   "The Problem of Nancy in Faulkner's 'That Evening Sun,'" *Smith-Central Bulletin*, Winter 1961, 49-50.

Sanders, Barry.   "Faulkner's Fire Imagery in 'That Evening Sun,'" *Studies in Short Fiction*, Fall 1967, 69-71.

Slabery, Robert M.   "Quentin Compson's Lost Childhood," *Studies in Short Fiction*, Spring 1964, 173-183.

William Faulkner   *Barn Burning*   (p. 473)
(Shorter Edition, p. 241)

This scene opens in a country store being used on this day as a courtroom. Mr. Snopes is on trial for burning the barn of a man named Harris.

But the scene is so strongly colored and oddly re-organized by the point of view through which it is presented that it may not be recognized immediately and the information necessary to follow the significance of the action appears only bit by bit. As is often the case with Faulkner's fiction, readers must be constantly alert to catch information as it drifts past.

They must make a constant effort to reconstruct the common world from the partly deranged perceptions of the characters through which it is reported.

The point of view here is that of the boy, Colonel Sartoris Snopes. But a further specification must be made. Rather frequently the boy's perceptions are reported in a rhetorical language which could only be the author's attempt to extend or translate the special flavor of the boy's perceptual experience. Thus, in the second sentence of the first paragraph we find that we are seeing the interior of the store through the eyes of a boy who is not only breathless with anxiety about the outcome of his father's trial but also hungry. The rendition of this necessarily complex state of mind is accomplished by complex syntax and language ("the solid, squat, dynamic shapes of tin cans whose labels his stomach read . . .") supplied by the far more sophisticated consciousness of the author. The intrusion of rhetoric supplied like an echo of the boy's awareness by the broader consciousness may be remarked farther on in this passage as in many others: "Older the boy might have remarked this and wondered why not a big [fire]: why should not a man who had not only seen the waste and voracious prodigality of war, but who had in his blood an inherent voracious prodigality with material not his own, have burned everything in sight?" We must concede that Faulkner adheres to a single point of view —while marveling at how enormously he stretches it.

In any case the difficulties are going to be such for many student readers that it will be necessary to help them hold onto the story line. It must be followed if they are to understand the meaning of the test on the boy and his resolution of the tangled loyalties that bind him.

The trial that opens the story concludes without a finding of guilt, but with the Judge ordering the barn-burning elder Snopes to get his family out of town before dark. On the move, when they are camped in a grove, the father accuses the boy of having been on the point of giving evidence against him and says, "You got to learn to stick to your own blood or you ain't going to have any blood to stick to you."

From their new home the boy walks with his father to the house of Major de Spain, the plantation owner for whom Snopes will work as a sharecropper. The boy's first sight of this big house *"big as a courthouse"* awakens another loyalty which will compete with the loyalty of blood (that is of kinship). *"People whose lives are a*

*part of this peace and dignity are beyond his touch. .
. ."* The boy has, in a word, beheld the vision of a
lawful civilization with claims superior to the outlaw
code by which his father has always lived and by which
he will die.

At the door of the de Spain house, Snopes deliberately scrapes horse manure from his boot on an expensive rug. The gesture is his declaration of independence.

De Spain responds by riding to the Snopes shack with
the rug and ordering Snopes to clean it. The womenfolk
of the Snopes household would have, presumably, done a
proper job of cleaning the rug. But the father, to
show that he will not be belittled by his boss, cleans
the rug with lye and a sharp stone—deliberately ruin-
ing it in his compliance with the letter of the in-
structions de Spain gave him. The ruined rug is returned by night and flung down (as a gauntlet might be
flung) on the de Spain porch.

De Spain demands twenty bushels of corn as compensation for destruction of the rug. The boy spontane-
ously rebels against what he considers the injustice
of de Spain's demand, "He won't git no twenty bushels!
He won't git none! We'll gether hit and hide hit!"

His father has other plans. First he takes de Spain
to court to get the claim for damages set aside.
Failing in this, he prepares to burn down de Spain's
barn. Now the boy is confronted with the flat necessity of making a choice. He must side with his father
in the crime, try to warn de Spain, or run away from
both obligations. *"I could run on and on and never
look back, never need to see his face again."*

In the event, he escapes from his family, runs to
de Spain's house. His warning comes too late for de
Spain to prevent the burning of the barn, but in time
to bring de Spain on the scene, where he (presumably)
kills Snopes.

The story ends with a peculiar and delicately
phrased reconciliation of the opposite claims of the
boy's loyalty. In a practical sense he has, of course,
betrayed his father. But in another sense by delivering the old outlaw he has reclaimed him for those ideal
principles of justice that were, in any event, going to
triumph. "He was brave!" the boy cries out in his
grief and despair. This may be all that can be said
for his father. It is enough. The Luciferian pride
which drove him is justly measured by such an epitaph.
The "slow constellations" wheeling on as the story ends

may be taken as a literary allusion to "the army of unalterable law" in George Meredith's famous poem *Lucifer
in Starlight*.

Questions

1. By what values does the boy's father live? Does
the boy renounce all of them in the end? Is there a
sense in which the boy is being true to his father by
betraying him?

2. How is the principal conflict related to the
"peace and joy" the boy feels at the sight of Major de
Spain's house?

3. How is the language related to the point of view?
Is it always appropriate to the experience being related or undergone by the point of view character?

4. Discuss concepts of justice that emerge from the
story. What does the story say about the evolution of
justice from its primitive to its more civilized forms?

5. How do the shifts of scene and setting serve to
express the meaning of the unfolding action?

6. Is the tone essentially optimistic or pessimistic?

See also "Questions for Comparing the Author's
Stories, p. 80 of this *Handbook*.

Further Reading

Johnston, Kenneth G. "Time of Decline: Pickett's
    Charge and the Broken Clock in Faulkner's 'Barn
    Burning,'" *Studies in Short Fiction*, 11 (1974),
    434-436.

Mitchell, Charles. "The Wounded Will of Faulkner's
    'Barn Burning,'" *Modern Fiction Studies*, XI (Summer
    1965), 185-189.

Wilson, Gayle Edward. "'Being Pulled Two Ways': The
    Nature of Sarty's Choice in 'Barn Burning,'"
    Mississippi Quarterly, 24 (Summer 1971), 279-288.

William Faulkner—
Questions for Comparing the Author's Stories

1. Discuss the similarity of the opening commentary in "A Rose for Emily" and "That Evening Sun." Why does the detached, remote comment of the narrator persist through the former and not the latter?

2. Does "That Evening Sun" seem more like a fragment of a longer story than the two other Faulkner stories in this text?

3. Students who have read *The Sound and the Fury* should discuss the relationship between the novel and "That Evening Sun." Is the narrator of the short story consistent with the character of Quentin in the novel? (The question of age may be touched on here. How old was Quentin when he died?)

F. Scott Fitzgerald   *Babylon Revisited* (p. 489)
                       (Shorter Edition, p. 256)

Most of Fitzgerald's stories, including *Babylon Revisited*, were written for popular magazines of his day. Therefore, along with the merits of his fiction, we might profitably study some of the stereotyped formulas that were prevalent in the commercial folklore of the early part of this century. (It is counterproductive snobbery to pretend that no great writer uses such formulas. As with any conventions, the question is always to what end he uses them. Since a great many people model themselves on and see themselves most distinctly in the stereotypes of the commercial media, these should never be dismissed out of hand as untrue to life.)

Consider the specifications given Charlie Wales to make him a glamorous and "sympathetic" character. He is handsome—"good to look at." He is rich. His wealth has come from that combination of luck and hard work that Americans of his period were taught to admire. He was even richer before he lost a lot of money in the stock market crash of 1929. We are never told any particulars about his investments or his judgment in making and managing them. His financial misfortune comes across as an undifferentiated part of a much publicized national disaster. His misdemeanors during the period of his dissipation have nothing vicious or

ugly about them. He has mastered his alcoholism by
personal will-power.

His daughter Honoria is so beautiful that she cap-
tures the stares of diners in the restaurant where he
takes her to lunch. His wish to reclaim her is, as far
as we are told, prompted by nonambivalent paternal love
and the anticipation of spending quiet Sundays at home
with her while he watches her grow up and prepare for
marriage. She, in turn, has a clearcut, fully conscious preference for living with him rather than continuing in the home provided by Lincoln and the prud-
ishly neurotic (nonsympathetic) Marion.

In a word the outlines of the principal characters
and their life situation are (designedly) suitable for
soap opera. But how the story really works dawns on us
as we reflect that there might have been a living,
breathing, suffering Charlie Wales who could not conceive or shape his life except by the patterns of the
soap opera. That—and not the hackneyed lamentations
for his lost youth or his "nice thoughts and dreams"—
may be the true pathos with which we are confronted, as
it may have been the true genius of Fitzgerald to show
that Americans locked into a commercially romanticized
misinterpretation of themselves never really possess
their youth any more than they possess their middle
years or old age. To be Charlie Wales is the real
anguish. His disappointing failure to carry Honoria
home with him pales by comparison. The somewhat contrived intervention of Duncan Schaeffer and Lorraine
Quarrles does not impressively manifest the fate that
has doomed Charlie—but doesn't hide it either. They
come like ghosts out of the past he is hoping will not
be resurrected against him. We note in their appearance the machinery of conscious contrivance. But since
the past was more ghastly in its emptiness than Charlie
knows how to admit, it does not matter much whether
they intrude on his designs. (The sense of real ghosts
lurking behind the contrivances of the story is what
distinguishes Fitzgerald's novels *The Great Gatsby* and
Tender Is the Night and accounts for their enduring
power.)

As he has trimmed his characters to fit the requirements of mass-circulation magazines, Fitzgerald has
patterned his narrative to keep the conflicts perfectly
clear and the issues easy to grasp. His expertise in
managing the unfolding story line offers an eminently
teachable example of exposition, complication, and resolution. Exposition in the first section provides not

misinterpreted himself then,
and misinterprets himself now in not
recognizing that the past, too, was
hackneyed, and not merely dissipated

only the essential information we will need to understand what comes later, it prompts us with firm guidelines to concentrate on the specific issues to be resolved and hints at the positions to be taken by major characters. The dialogue is carefully shaped to give information and show dramatic progress at the same time as it reveals character. Early on, Charlie pronounces a judgment—"I spoiled this city for myself"— that is not only consistent with his present mood and character but definitive of all we will learn about his past here. The present conflict will be with his sister-in-law—and when he encounters her we are told that she wears an expression of "unalterable distrust." In the expository phases of the narration we learn of Charlie's recovered financial position and his method of balancing himself against the temptations of alcohol. But the full disclosure of his present mission in Paris is withheld until Section III—i.e., it comes as a sort of summary explanation of what he means to reap from his rehabilitation.

The chance meeting with Schaeffer and Lorraine Quarrles in Section II, followed by her beseeching letter, prepare us to expect that these ghosts from the past will decisively intervene at the climax of the action—tipping the scales against Charlie. Just how badly things have turned out is signaled by Lincoln's declaration that arrangements for Honoria's return must be allowed to "slide for six months." This is a clear-cut indication that Charlie's mission has failed. A few lifelike ambiguities may remain, but the conflict of the story has been neatly, pathetically, resolved.

Such skillful management of the economies of his material permits Fitzgerald the double advantage of convincing the uncritical reader that everything necessary has been said, while the more sophisticated reader can continue to mull a number of pungent riddles about the relation between character and fate, between the commitments of the past and the encumbrances of the present.

Questions

1. Considered thematically, what does the story have to say about the relation between the Past, Present, and Future? Can Charlie Wales ever achieve the happiness he looks forward to? Did he ever have a chance of reaching it?

2. Near the beginning of Section IV Charlie agrees not to press for legal guardianship of his daughter— "wanting only the tangible, visible child." What does this language indicate about his conception of fatherhood?

3. An old axiom tells us that "character is fate." What are the fatal flaws in Charlie's character?

4. Define the roles of Duncan Schaeffer and Lorraine Quarrles in the past and present action. How do you interpret the statement that "they wanted to draw a certain sustenance from Charlie's strength." What sort of sustenance can he give them?

5. Discuss Charlie's self-criticism. Is it adequate? Is Marion's mistrust of him ill-founded? Is she clinging to narrow resentments or sizing him up well?

Further Reading

Edenbaum, Robert I.   "'Babylon Revisited': A Psychological Note on F. Scott Fitzgerald," *Literature and Psychology*, XVIII (1968), 27-29.
Gross, Seymour L.   "Fitzgerald's 'Babylon Revisited,'" *College English*, XXV (November 1963), 128-135.
Male, Roy R.   "'Babylon Revisited': A Story of the Exile's Return," *Studies in Short Fiction*, 11 (Spring 1965), 270-277.
Piper, Henry Dan. *F. Scott Fitzgerald: A Critical Biography*, pp. 165-166.

Gustave Flaubert   *The Legend of Saint Julian the Hospitaller* (p. 506)

The last paragraph declares this to be "the story . . . as it is given on the stained-glass window of a church in my birthplace." The hidden clue in this declaration is the fact that stained-glass windows are pictorial rather than verbal narratives. And Flaubert has indeed revamped the form in which legends were traditionally told by pictorializing—intensifying color and detail—every phase of his narrative. This modernization and elaboration of narrative method is as fascinating to the student of fiction as is the progress of the plot.

Flaubert begins by creating a world of pictorial

detail. Eight paragraphs set the scene before Julian's
father appears on it, wandering through the castle in
his fox-skin cape or riding his mule among the wheat-
fields of the countryside. We are told not merely that
Julian's mother is, as a young bride, haughty (that
would be specification enough for a pure legend) but
also that she is "pale and serious." Flaubert devotes
a paragraph to rendering the feast that celebrates
Julian's birth before he tells us that the young mother
was absent from it, resting in her room when she receives the prophecy of her son's destiny. Such vivid
and scrupulous attention to the visible can be noted in
literally every phase of the story, especially in those
that deal with supernatural occurrences. Note, for
instance, the precise rendering of the passage in which
the stag Julian has shot pronounces the curse. Finally
the transformation of the leper into Christ shows a
serial development as even in its continuity as it
might be in cinematic form.

(But even the term _pictorial_ does not suffice to explain the scope of art lavished to keep us constantly
aware of the physical world inhabited by the characters. Sounds and smell, heat and cold, hardness and
softness are as distinctly represented as visible form
and color.)

It must be stressed that the extraordinary craft
committed to recreating a semblance of the sensuous
world is neither art for art's sake nor mere ornamenta-
tion of a tale that would mean the same in a sparser
telling. At least the craft reminds us forcibly that
the lives of saints are lived moment by moment and
through sensation, just as we live ours.

The larger lines of Julian's evolution are as painstakingly developed as the momentary scenes or the lists
of dogs and falcons. Julian's lust for hunting begins
in his excessive annoyance with the mouse in the
chapel. It expands to monstrous proportions as he
kills more and larger animals, discovering a "voluptuousness of killing" that he has been trained to appreciate by the voluptuousness of his life in general,
his position as the spoiled son of a lord. It climaxes
in the hallucinatory scene of animals crowding on him
to be killed and in the slaughter of stags in the
enclosed valley. This surfeit of blood prepares him
to renounce hunting, one would think, even without the
prophetic curse he hears from the stag killed by his
last arrow.

After he has fled from home to evade fulfillment of

the prophecy, his occupation as a warrior continues the
course he has begun as a hunter and killer of animals.
He renounces hunting while his military exploits bring
him to the pinnacle of worldly success. But the passion
for blood has not been completely exterminated by the
voluptuousness of his life in peacetime. "Sometimes, in
his dreams, he fancied himself like Adam in the midst
of Paradise, surrounded by all the beasts; by merely
extending his arm, he was able to kill them. . . ." On
the night when his parents have finally caught up with
him, Julian goes out into the darkness expecting relief
from, once again, killing animals. His impotence and
frustration in this magical sequence prepares him to do
what he has feared most. "The thirst for carnage stirred
afresh within him, he desired to slaughter men." Compelled by this desire, he slaughters his mother and
father. It is true that he has mistaken the identity of
the couple in his bed—just as obvious that the mistake
would not have occurred if he were not ready to make it.

In his last phase as penitent, Julian longs for the
society of men but is kept from it both by their repul-
sion at his ultimate crime and by his unbearable envy
of their relative innocence. Descending the scale, he
wants communion with animals. They flee from him. Even
the wind brings sounds of horror to his ears, the sun
appears to stain the sky with blood. He would kill himself except that a vision of his father prevents it.

The miracle—toward which the whole narrative has
been tending—does not come without preparation any
more than anything else in the story has. Julian's ab-
jection is at least as extreme as his passion for
killing once was. He is utterly purged of concern for
himself, therefore capable of excesses of danger, morti-
fication, and charity. The appearance to him of Christ
in the guise of the leper merely climaxes the progress
toward saintliness elaborated in the last section of
the story—but when it happens we are made to see that
everything, every excess and every horror of his past,
has also been a preparation for his being carried to
Heaven. Certainly the legend declares that God works in
mysterious ways, but if the road to Julian's sainthood
has been crooked, he has followed continuously the path
of excess—suggesting that to be a great sinner may be
true preparation for being a great saint. The enigma
and paradox of God's ways as presented by Flaubert are
in some ways kin to that recounted by Tolstoy in *God
Sees the Truth, but Waits*. The circumstances of

Tolstoy's story are altogether more humble. The theme
may be the same.

Questions

1. How many times does Julian's life change direction? Are all the courses he follows necessary to
bring him to sainthood?

2. If you leave the supernatural out of account,
does the remainder of the story seem psychologically
true? Explain Julian's psychological motivations at
the main stages of his life.

3. Can the three major prophecies about Julian be
explained as wishes? How might the wishes influence
the development of his character?

4. What major paradoxes do you find in the action
and its outcome?

5. In the last paragraph the author tells us his
story was "given" by a stained glass window. What
special qualities of description and narration seem
to reflect this pictorial source?

6. How has the author shaped the tone of the story
to fit his legendary subject matter?

E. M. Forster   *The Road from Colonus* (p. 526)

Most of the stories that we label fantasy seem to
have been constructed to answer an original question
that begins: "What if . . .?" What if this or that
human capacity were to progress beyond the limits of
present possibility or probability? What if we could
travel through time as we travel through space? What
if we voyaged to a country where all the human inhabitants were only six inches tall? In *The Road from
Colonus* Forster has not postulated any surprising
transformations in the outward, visible world. He has,
rather, structured both language and event to make us
ponder the conceivable discrepancies between the outer
and visible event, on the one hand, and its inner
reality.

Outwardly, Mr. Lucas is and remains Mr. Lucas, a
rather irascible old Englishman who is fulfilling his
lifetime dream of visiting Greece, while, predictably,
he finds it disappointing in its bleak modernization.

Since he is old—as Oedipus was—and is accompanied on
his travels by his daughter—as Oedipus was by his
daughter Antigone—he is, to an extent, playing the
"role of Oedipus." Just as Oedipus and Antigone came
to a sacred grove in Colonus at the end of their wanderings (see Sophocles' *Oedipus at Colonus*) the Lucases
come upon a grove of plane trees, so unexpected in the
desolation of the landscape as to appear miraculous. At
least to the eye, this grove suggests the <u>sacred</u>. And
within the grove there is a shrine with emblems of
divinity around a mysterious and improbable spring
flowing out of the dark.

Thus there are, in Forster's presentation, some
powerful correspondences between old Mr. Lucas's situation and that of Oedipus. But these correspondences can
be dismissed as merely fortuitous, in the nature of
shallow coincidence or a joke. That it should be Mrs.
Forman who alludes to Lucas's Oedipal role tends to
make us believe the correspondence is merely formal,
for Mrs. Forman is a flat representation of a type of
a shallowly erudite tourist, an English person of
broad but shallow learning.

Even readers who have not pondered the Oedipus
legend will note that the author has not assigned to
Mr. Lucas the salient characteristic of the legendary
model—his blindness.

Or has he? We certainly find no statement to the
effect that the Englishman suffers any physical impair-
ment of his vision. But a careful examination of the
opening passages will reveal that Forster has played
very subtly and carefully with nuances of expression
involving "sight" and "see" and "eyes." For instance,
we are not told that Lucas saw the grove—only that he
"came in sight" of it. On arrival he is "glad even
that he should not see" his daughter for a while. These
extremely delicate hints (there are more than I have
noted) become more meaningful when they are recognized
as preparation for the forceful statements about seeing
made after Lucas has submitted to the spell of the
grove and the spring. ". . . when he opened his eyes,
something unimagined, indefinable, had passed over all
things, and made them intelligible and good." When he
imagines staying at the Khan, he foresees that he will
"watch the bats flit about within the globe of shade,
and see the moon turn the golden patterns into silver
—one such night would place him beyond relapse. . . ."

In effect, Forster <u>has</u> said that Mr. Lucas was
blind as Oedipus until he wandered here. (Readers

familiar with Forster's novels, particularly *A Room
with a View*, will remember how many complex figurative
meanings he attaches to the verb see.)

This brings us to the fanciful question he has meant
to pose by the story as a whole. What if a full-sighted
modern man should be blind to the inner reality of the
role he is playing—blind until he comes to a certain
spot on earth where his eyes open on mystic natural
signals which identify the place as his true destination? Mr. Lucas "was aroused at last by a shock—the
shock of an arrival perhaps . . . in a brief space of
time, [he] had discovered not only Greece but England
and all the world and life. . . ." Therefore "there
seemed nothing ludicrous in the desire to hang within
the tree another votive offering—a little model of an
entire man." (Note that "an entire man" is not a blind
man—another oblique comment tending to imply that
vision has been restored to Oedipus-Lucas while he remains here.) While the scales are gone from his eyes
he sees the truth of inward reality—that he has come
home as an entire man to a harmonious and meaningful
world.

But the irony of conflict between inner and outward
reality cannot be resolved so easily—as we see from
the remainder of the story. Lucas's contemporaries,
who have not undergone the restoration of true vision
that he has experienced, kidnap him. They put him on a
mule and carry him back to the "blindness" of daily
life.

Once back in London—which here serves as a synonym
for the kingdom of those blind to inner reality—Mr.
Lucas cannot stand the sound of running water. (We remember that within the grove of plane trees in Greece
it was just this sound that served to catalyze the
other influences, that made him "see.") The irony of
the end is the revelation that he would have been dead
if he had been allowed to remain at the Khan—and that
he is, in another, and probably less attractive sense,
dead in England. This last paradoxical twist on the
ideas of death and life is compatible with the paradoxes of appearance and reality that make up the con-
ceptual structure of the whole.

Questions

1. What is the importance of the setting? Of the
references to mythology and antiquity?

2. The myth of Oedipus tells us that he blinded him-
self. What does this circumstance have to do with Mr.
Lucas. Why does he try to "settle down" to the role of
Oedipus?

3. What contrasts does Forster make between modern
life and the life or spirit of antiquity?

4. Is Mr. Lucas lucky or unlucky to have escaped the
fall of the tree?

5. Briefly state the theme of the story and relate
it to the tone.

Further Reading

Stone, Wilfred. *The Cane and the Mountain*. Stanford:
   Stanford University Press, 1966.

Mary E. Wilkins Freeman   *The Revolt of "Mother"*
                  (p. 536)

In a story so straightforward in design and so
simple in its characterization, there might seem to be
few mysteries requiring discussion. Sarah looks meek
and is meek in her behavior, and she "looked as if the
meekness had been the result of her own will, never of
the will of another." She is, in fact, a woman of
steadfast and unequivocal determination when circumstances require, at last, that she should question and
thwart her husband's intention. The action, including
Adoniram's complete submission, follows from her determination as from a law of nature.

Yet there may be some lively controversy about the
significance of her act in terms of its probable consequences. It is made sufficiently plain that Sarah
has always meekly accepted her role as servant to the
master of the house until she takes the step of converting the fine new barn to a family dwelling. Has
she, by this step, merely redefined and set limits on
her role as servant? Or has she begun a process that
can only end with a reversal of the lines of family
authority? Though she declares to Adoniram, "I've
done my duty by you forty year, an' I'm goin' to do
it now . . .," at the same time we may guess from his
tears and the authorial comment that he "was like a
fortress . . . [which] went down the instant the right

besieging tools were used" that his reign is finished.

It is an old observation that, once revolt against any established order is set in motion, the extent of its consequences are unpredictable. Even though Sarah herself may intend to restabilize the situation after her modest gain has been consolidated, the impact of her example on her children and on the community at large must still be reckoned. The uncertainty about what will follow is probably, in some form, in the mind of the minister who comes to question— if not exactly to protest—the move to the barn, and it surely animates the concerned curiosity of the "knot of men" who gather to watch for fireworks at Adoniram's return.

Theirs is a "conservative" impulse in the purest sense of the word. The author does not really hint that they would condemn Sarah's modest reform, but rather clearly implies they are troubled by the portent of change. From our present point of view, it might be easy to mock these men as being merely fearful that her example might cost them the perquisites and the privileges of male authority they have unrightfully assumed. Our sympathies must almost automatically go with Sarah —unless we feel she means to settle for too little after all. But, writing for another age, the author has taken some pains to draw a historic parallel between Sarah and the heroic forefathers who made a limited revolution that did not roll on to anarchy. ("The barn threshold might have been Plymouth Rock from her bearing.") Perhaps when all the men come to understand this parallel their disquiet will be allayed. Nevertheless, in principle, the story may be an occasion for arguments pro and con on the effects of revolt.

Questions

1. Discuss the importance of the setting and the period in relation to the story.
2. What is the role of the children in the action?
3. Has the success of Sarah's revolt established her as head of the house?
4. Why does Adoniram weep at the end of the story?
5. Of what concern to the minister and the other villagers is Sarah's revolt?

Further Reading

Gallagher, Edward T.   "Freeman's 'The Revolt of
    Mother,'" *Explicator*, 27 (1969), Item 48.
Westbrook, Perry D. *Acres of Flint: Writers of Rural
    New England, 1870-1900*. Washington: Scarecrow, 1951,
    p. 114.
-----. *Mary Wilkins Freeman*. New York: Twayne, 1967.

Mavis Gallant   *Acceptance of Their Ways* (p. 549)

This picture of decayed gentility—of "infirm
nicety"—is notable chiefly for the sharpness of its
observation, for the way the author has selected and
measured the distortions of manners and the perversion
of reasonable values among aging women with a particular background. The note of the narration is gingery
and might be called satiric, except that the characters
are so far gone in the degenerations of old age that
they are hardly worth satirizing. They are, in themselves, satires of the attitudes and manners that once
sustained them as members of a social structure con-
sisting largely of artifice, reductions to absurdity of
its pretenses and sterile disciplines.

The management of tone by language and selection of
detail is particularly important to the success of this
story. Mrs. Freeport and Mrs. Garnett merit neither admiration nor respect, but a more solemn tone that
seemed to condemn the ugliness and pettiness of their
ways might drag the story down to their level and omit
the saving tolerance of laughter, which retrieves, perhaps, some sense that there is a sort of beauty even in
the grotesquerie to which life has brought them. The
inclusion of Lily—who is altogether more roguish and
vital than the other two ladies—also functions to suggest that sport, meaning, and merriment can be extracted even from the shoddiest of circumstances. In
fact, Lily emerges as an embodiment of the creative
principle. Her judgments of her companions are about
as grotesque as they are, and we might well wonder if
she is not crazy to hang around in such company. But
the author delicately and humorously suggests there is
a touch of the artist in Lily, that her companions feed
her incessant imaginative play with life.

The story should be particularly rewarding if the language is closely studied, for it displays both a remarkable precision in rendering the scene and characters and a very considerable range of tones expressive of comic nuances. For example, these characteristic sentences: "Illiberal by circumstance, grudging only because she imitated the behavior of other women, she became, drunk, an old forgotten Lily-girl, tender and warm, able to shed a happy tear and open a closed fist." "An excellent cook, she had dreamed of being a poisoner, but decided to leave that to the loonies; it was no real way to get on."

Questions

1. Why does Lily admire and try to emulate the women with whom she lives?
2. What does the story say about the price of gentility and the manners it engenders?
3. What is the tone and what elements of the story establish it?
4. To what extent are Lily's feelings mixed, her values confused?
5. Is Mrs. Freeport sincere in her remorse after Mrs. Garnett leaves?
6. Discuss the handling of the point of view and its contribution to the story.

Gabriel García Márquez   *The Handsomest Drowned Man in the World* (p. 556)
(Shorter Edition, p. 274)

The strangely compelling situation and development of this story are structured on an interaction between the village and the stranger who comes from the sea. Being already dead before any of the villagers encounter him, the stranger, of course, cannot bring them any tidings in his own voice, cannot tell them anything he might have known about what life is or what it might be. But because of certain qualities in the corpse (size and handsomeness) and the impenetrable mystery of his origin, he draws like a sponge on the imagination of the villagers who must somehow dispose of him.

It is hardly too much to say they had no imagination
—or at least did not recognize it or exercise it—
until they were enticed to fill in the blanks of the
mystery the drowned man presents them with. It is probably significant that children and women begin the
process of reconstructing Esteban from their imagination—the children by their play, the women by comparing
their menfolk unfavorably with what the drowned man
might have been in his life. The wishful thinking of the
women leads them into "a maze of fantasy," in the midst
of which the oldest woman declares, "He has the face of
someone called Esteban," and then we are told, "It was
true."

This authorial statement should not be taken as the
intrusion of an omniscient author telling us what the
drowned man's name was in his lifetime. Rather, it
should be understood as a somewhat oblique and cryptic
declaration that this is the way "truth" is established
in matters that lie beyond the reach of observation or
rational verification. Since the woman who uttered this
truth was marked "with more compassion than passion,"
the proportions of that necessary mixture would seem to
be the formula from which springs the particular truth
that generates myths.

Out of compassion the women begin to elaborate and
complicate their knowledge of what Esteban's existence
must have been. His gifts of size and beauty must have
been accompanied by certain frustrations and humilia-
tions, since he was not like the ordinary men they are
familiar with. It is by their compassion for his em-
barrassments that the women can come to declare "he's
ours."

The men of the village are harder to persuade, but
at length their skepticism and jealousy are overcome
by the aspect of death in the stranger's appearance.
The shamefulness of the dead body convinces them of his
"sincerity," and they are moved by this conviction to
honor him with funeral ceremonies. The structure of the
ceremony, which requires that he be provided with hon-
orary parents, continues the process of myth-building,
transforming Esteban from stranger to "kinsman."

Before Esteban came to the village, it was composed
of "odd wooden houses that had stone courtyards with no
flowers," but the villagers have transformed themselves
by the acts of imagination that led to their adoption
of the strange kinsman. ". . . Things would be different from then on . . . their houses would have wider
doors, higher ceilings, stronger floors . . . they were

going to break their backs digging for springs among the stones and planting flowers on the cliffs . . . ."

And just as their own parochial imaginations have generated the myth of a godlike visitor who came from the sea and became one of them, their efforts and their arts will stabilize and extend the myth so that all those who pass the island on ships will recognize the blessing that came to the village from the recognition that they belong to Esteban.

Thus the story may be taken as a fanciful but persuasive exposition of the way myths are born and how they become entwined with the lives of a culture.

Questions

1. What changes are made in the appearance of the village and in the lives of the villagers by Esteban's presence among them?

2. How do the villagers "know" the drowned man's name is Esteban?

3. Why are the women quicker than the men to respond to Esteban's presence?

4. What is indicated by the interest that passing ships take in the "promontory of roses on the horizon"?

5. What does the story say about the way myths originate?

6. How are we supposed to understand the subtitle?

Maxim Gorky   *The Hermit*   (p. 561)

The relation of the narrator to the chief character is like that of a reporter writing a "profile" of an interesting person for *The New Yorker*. Nothing links the two men in any significant action. The narrator is purely the observer and listener. The form of his account is natural and apparently artless. After the setting is established and a physical description of Savel given, the old man launches into a summary history of his past life. "Savel spoke with remarkable ease. . . . [he] spun his yarn with such convincing simplicity . . . that I feared to interrupt him with questions," the narrator tells us. Yet at the same time, almost from the beginning of Savel's remarkable account of his early years, marriage, and wanderings,

"I realized that the old man was the possessor of living gems [of speech or expression] able to conceal all filthy and criminal lies with their bewitching power. . . ." Here we are let in on the puzzle that will provide the intellectual suspense of the whole and that will be somewhat ambiguously answered by the statement of the theme: Are the events Savel touches on truly "filthy and criminal"? His behavior with his wife and with other women would appear so by conventional standards. He very strongly hints that he has committed incest with his lovely daughter when she was hardly more than a child. Is Savel "concealing" the wickedness of these and other acts? Or is he revealing them to be part of a life which is altogether redeemed by love?

When the narrator returns to the hermit's cave on subsequent occasions, he not only hears more of Savel's recollections but sees the old man in the role of counselor and confidant of people in trouble. Bit by bit skepticism is overcome and the full magnificence of Savel's wisdom overpowers the narrator's doubts. He never gives a flat statement of approval, of course, but the powerful drift of the story is toward a revelation that Savel has risen beyond the measures of conventional morality to a vision of life as altogether glorious and good. While the narrator is at pains to note the old man's repulsive physical features, he constantly remarks the beautiful harmonies in his movements. ". . . he seemed almost handsome, with the beauty of a life whose confusion was multicolored and intricate. And his outward disfigurement gave a particular emphasis to that beauty." Savel's delight in his daughter's beauty qualifies and transforms whatever judgment we might be tempted to make of the facts of that case.

Savel has a special power over women and a special power from women. These powers are as much sexual as they are spiritual—or, rather, an extraordinary identification is made here between the sexual and the spiritual. The aberrations of sexual impulse are shown to be undiminished by his advanced age. "The soul knows no laws, it takes no account of years." He understands from personal experience Olesha's impulse to beat up a woman irrespective of love or adoration for her, and such sympathy makes him the marvelous healer he finally appears to be.

For Father Savel—as for the poet Yeats—life is a dance, and dancing "means the soul is at play, friend."

The narrator rather straightforwardly announces his

theme in concluding that the source of Savel's morality
and power is "a love which knows nothing but itself and
marvels at itself." The ideas and values expressed in
this story might well be compared with those of Walt
Whitman. For reference see Whitman's *Faces, I Sing the
Body Electric, A Woman Waits for Me,* or *Song of Myself.*

Questions

1. What relationship exists between the narrator and
Father Savel? Is the character of the narrator changed
by what he sees and hears?

2. Is the hermit physically ugly or beautiful? Has
his life been sinful and ugly? By what standards? What
standards are applicable to him?

3. Does the story attempt to justify Savel's anar-
chistic views? Does it succeed?

4. What are Savel's views about women? How has he
gained the power over them that he claims? Or do you
believe his claims? Do his spiritual powers derive from
his special relationship to women?

5. Are Savel's views about the appropriate punishment for murder consistent with his other principles?

6. Why does he say he stole the doll he gives to the
little girl instead of admitting he bought it?

James B. Hall *A View of the Beach* (p. 583)

Amusingly, the narrator emerges as a type less
familiar in American literature than in life—the
Decadent Yokel. Although he has a temperamental and
spiritual kinship with them, he has never heard of the
European Decadents of the nineteenth century. His
world-weariness came on him not from a surfeit of
sophistication but from an adolescent disappointment
in which the promise of glamor was snatched away by
the fortuitous intervention of the drunken cook whom
he and Ceely rouse when Ceely leaps down from the retaining wall. Although there is a degree of ambiguity
about the fateful jump (the narrator says he pushed
her, and that already seems a gesture of rejection or
severance from her), it seems clear that she had been
leading him on to some kind of sexual fulfillment of
the romantic promises implicit in the trip to Florida.

However vague he may have been about what was supposed
to happen there, it was unquestionably to be an experience of a magnitude to shatter and change him forever.

Instead of the liberating convulsion, the initiation
into glamorous mysteries, he gets only a shock of fear
and incongruity as the drunken cook waddles toward the
ocean and Ceely flees. The importance of the episode is
underlined by the fact that, subsequently, he "made a
break" with the banalities of life back in Ohio with
his mother and returned to Miami—like someone in a
permanent daze, forever unable to grasp the reality of
his loss though he is forever unable to recover from
it. At the end we see that he has made his frustration
into a life style, frozen at the one moment of time
when, he feels, everything might have gone differently.

There is a pathetic irony in the fact that the episode crucial to him appears to have left no mark at all
on Ceely. She marries offhandedly. The comment that she
"did not inherit her mother's brains" distinguishes her
from the narrator who is a victim of what might be
called thinking too much, or brooding fruitlessly on
the ways of chance. Mrs. Herdston, too, is another such
victim, for in her grotesque way she also has sought a
significance in the picturesque details of life which
workaday people pass over. Like him, she cares too
much, and is replaced by the right-thinking members of
the school board as soon as they dare. With the boy's
seafaring father she has stirred romantic expectations
in him that leave him eviscerated when they collapse.

The most notable technical feature of the story—
the displacement of the account of what happened when
Ceely leaped down into the dark—is difficult to account for with certainty. Perhaps the author used the
device merely for an effect of suspense, sleight-of-
hand to tease and entertain the reader. But perhaps it
also helps illustrate the profound confusion into which
the narrator was plunged by the brutal swiftness of his
disappointment.

Questions

1. How do the narrator's expectations of the trip
differ from Mrs. Herdston's? From Ceely's?

2. Why has the author displaced the account of what
happened when Ceely jumped from the sea wall, post-
poning it so it comes as a memory rather than as part

of the continuous sequence of action on the evening it
happened?

   3. Does the narrator learn anything about himself or
about life from his second visit to the beach?

   4. What have Ceely's marriage and Mrs. Herdston's
death to do with the theme of the story?

   5. What does the story say about coincidence? About
glamor and disappointment and their effect on the
narrator's life?

Nathaniel Hawthorne   *Young Goodman Brown*   (p. 589)
              (Shorter Edition, p. 279)

   This may appear to be a story without a resolution
since, near the end, the question is boldly stated:
"Had Goodman Brown fallen asleep in the forest and only
dreamed a wild dream of a witch-meeting?" If he merely
dreamed and if all the evidence of his waking life con-
tradicts the message of the dream, then the dream cannot, strictly, be said to have taught him anything he
need believe. Nothing happened. And yet the last paragraph of the story declares that something has happened.
Though his wife Faith may not have met him at the
witch's revel deep in the forest, still he has lost his
faith in her—and that loss, in itself, may be precisely
the evil he bargained for when he committed himself to
going into the forest with the intent of meeting the
devil. Finding himself (though only in a dream) drawn
step by step to the evil he does not want and tries
vainly to hold back from, he is perhaps necessarily
condemned to believe that the power of evil has equal
attraction for all other mortals. That indeed is a sad
"if not a desperate" conclusion to live with. An evil
sufficient to spoil any life, something in the nature
of a self-fulfilling prophecy.

   One reads only a few paragraphs into the story before grasping that its method is allegorical rather
than realistic. The old man first encountered in the
forest has attributes that rather quickly identify him
as the devil. (The wary reader will note something
disturbing in the old man's first speech. How could he
have come so quickly "through" Boston to his rendezvous
near Salem?) The people encountered on their way to the
diabolic communion are all those to whom Brown has
looked for examples of righteousness. The cloud that

darkens the gleam of heaven above the dark woods emits, among other voices, the voice of Faith Brown "entreating for some favor, which, perhaps, it would grieve her to obtain. . . ." A pink ribbon tumbles from the cloud, a token that Faith has passed beyond her wavering husband on her way to join the wicked revel. The master of the gathering promises the young couple that "By the sympathy of your human hearts for sin, ye shall scent out all the places . . . where crime has been committed, and shall exult to behold the whole earth one stain of guilt, one mighty blood spot." Perhaps the allegory means to tell us that this is precisely the formula by which mortals lose their faith, by the discovery of their own sympathy for sin.

Yet the allegory would not be so persuasive as it seems to be if it were built merely from doctrinal or dogmatic ideas of sin. The symbols of detail, the symbolic names and characters are psychological as well as theological and they seem to have, in the story, the ambiguity of figures in a real dream, susceptible to a shimmering variety of interpretations. For example, the twig that has been aflame before Brown's last minute revolt sprinkles his cheek with "the coldest dew" when he finds himself alone in the forest solitude. Doesn't this ghastly cold suggest that he has somehow broken faith with Faith when they were on the verge of communion?

Some vestiges of the trials of Adam and Eve show their traces here, along with some of the paradoxes of sin and punishment that poets have found in that Biblical story.

Questions

1. How are elements of the supernatural related to the psychology of Brown and other characters? Does it matter whether or not Brown merely dreamed the witch-meeting?

2. What was Brown's initial motive for going into the forest? Is this motive consistent with his reluctance to go along with the devil after they have met?

3. How do you interpret Brown's refusal to accept his wife's joyful welcome on his return?

4. How does the last paragraph relate to the action and theme of the story? What comment does it make on the workings of the devil?

See also "Questions for Comparing the Author's Stories," p. 103 of this *Handbook*.

Further Reading

Cochran, Robert W. "Hawthorne's Choice: The Veil or the Jaundiced Eye," *College English*, XXIII (February 1962), 342-344.

Crews, Frederick S. *The Sins of the Fathers: Hawthorne's Psychological Themes.* New York: Oxford University Press, 1966.

Hurley, Paul J. "Young Goodman Brown's 'Heart of Darkness,'" *American Literature*, XXXVII (January 1966), 410-419.

Paulits, Walter J. "Ambivalence in 'Young Goodman Brown,'" *American Literature*, XLI (January 1970), 577-584.

Walsh, Thomas F., Jr. "The Bedeviling of Young Goodman Brown," *Modern Language Quarterly*, XIX (June 1958), 331-336.

Nathaniel Hawthorne   *The Birthmark* (p. 600)

The Faust legend has been called the central myth of modern man because it embodies the archetypal pattern of the scientific attempt to gain mastery over nature. *The Birthmark* is Hawthorne's version of this legend.

The mark on Georgiana's cheek is explicitly said to express "the ineludible gripe in which mortality clutches the highest and purest of earthly mould, degrading them into kindred with the lowest." Her husband Aylmer, in his role as Faustian scientist, strives to eradicate the blemish. That is, he stakes everything on transcending the condition of nature in which we are all bound. He rebels against the limitations of mortality and by his rebellion brings on tragedy. His confidence in the power of science to change the human condition has blinded him to the wisdom of patient submission. The moral is very plain.

Yet Hawthorne's rendition of the mythic tale has some special emphases that we must note. For one thing, we see that from the first Aylmer's concern, well-meant as it may be, makes the blemish worse. "It needed but a glance with the peculiar expression that his face often wore to change the roses of her cheek into a deathlike paleness, amid which the crimson hand was brought strongly out. . . ." Her sensitivity to his concern is so great it gives her the power to share his dream and recall it to him though he had forgotten it on waking. The dream is, of course, prophetic of the fatal outcome of his experimental treatments of her. "Truth often finds its way to the mind close muffled in robes of sleep, and then speaks with uncompromising directness of matters in regard to which we practice an unconscious self-deception during our waking moments."

Hawthorne's psychological theory may here be stated in archaic or even quaintly primitive terms. We can't believe, literally, in Georgiana's ability to know what Aylmer dreamed. But however primitive or allegorical the psychology may be, it is sound. Locating "unconscious self-deception" in those waking hours that are supposed to be the province of consciousness is quite equal to the boldness of twentieth-century psychology. And, as far as the allegorical plot is concerned, the shared dream has the ironic function of making Georgiana an accomplice in her husband's Faustian crime —if not the prime mover. It is she who declares "let the attempt be made at whatever risk" to rid her of the birthmark.

Hawthorne's cast of characters is shaped to indicate that the inescapable divisions and contradictions in human nature are more pronounced in men than in women. Aylmer is "a type of the spiritual element." His assistant Aminadab represents "man's physical nature." At least Georgiana contains both elements and might, Hawthorne hints, harmonize them happily enough if only men were not so absolutistic in one direction or the other. Aminadab cherishes the birthmark that Aylmer is committed to eradicate.

The main bulk of the story, lying between the decision to get rid of the birthmark and the trial of the potion Aylmer has concocted, is devoted to placing Aylmer in the tradition he represents. In his scientific library Georgiana reads of ancient and medieval naturalists who sought from "Nature a power above Nature, and from physics a sway over the spiritual world." She comes to see that her husband is at the van of this glorious (if mistaken, doomed) quest. And if there are no actual plot complications in these pages, still a significant change is made in the way we view the action. What began as a merely passionate choice on Georgiana's part acquires the additional nobility of intellectual volition. Even when she finds that her husband's "most splendid successes were almost invariably failures" and sees his scientific logs to be "as melancholy a record as ever mortal hand had penned," she wishes to commit her fate to its continuation.

This "moral advancement" as Hawthorne calls it intensifies the moral ambiguity of the story as a whole (in keeping with the moral ambiguity that Goethe, among others, found in the Faust legend). For though the story seems to end with a pat warning against tampering with the natural, this conventional admonition comes after a demonstration that men and women achieve the zenith of their humanity by defiance of that warning, by their quest for transcendence.

Questions

1. What is the significance of the mark on Georgiana's cheek? What does each of the three main characters represent?

2. What does the story say about the secrets of nature? About our attempts to learn them? Is Hawthorne's attitude toward science valid in light of modern scientific knowledge and practice?

3. What is the reletion between Aylmer's love for science and his love for Georgiana?

4. Why do Aylmer's experiments with a plant and with photography turn into mortifying failures when he tries to demonstrate them to his wife?

5. The moral attached to the end of the story is plainly stated. Is it contradicted to any degree by the story itself?

See also "Questions for Comparing the Author's Stories," p. 103 of this *Handbook*.

Further Reading

Crews, Frederick C. *The Sins of the Fathers: Hawthorne's Psychological Themes*, pp. 111 ff.; 125 ff.; 158 ff.
Franklin, H. Bruce. *Future Perfect: American Science Fiction of the Nineteenth Century*. New York: Oxford University Press, 1966.

Walsh, Thomas F. "Character Complexity in Hawthorne's 'The Birthmark,'" *Emerson Studies Quarterly*, No. 23 (2nd Quater 1961), 12-15.

Nathaniel Hawthorne—
Questions for Comparing the Author's Stories

1. Compare the use of supernatural elements in *Young Goodman Brown* and *The Birthmark*.
2. Do the two stories display consistent attitudes about the role and qualities of women?
3. Which of the central characters bears the greatest personal responsibility for his own fate?

Ernest Hemingway   *Hills Like White Elephants* (p. 613)
                    (Shorter Edition, p. 290)

One way of coming at the heart of this story is to note, first, what has been left out. Stripped bare of the ordinary signs by which character is revealed, the story depends on setting and dialogue alone. But the setting has little to tell us about the two strangers except that they are in a place foreign to them. The dialogue is far from eloquent. It consists of the speech between two people who know each other so well that they need not explain anything. Surely it is the very absence of explanation that eloquently stresses their intimacy, as elsewhere in the story it is the absence of explanation that causes the reader to make the most of the few clues given. The hotel labels on their bags suggest homelessness, and this adds poignancy to the girl's implied wish to keep the child she is bearing rather than abort it as the man wants, for babies suggest stable homes and an end to wandering. The girl's fanciful notion that the hills across the river look like white elephants suggests a poetic nature, and the man's irritably literal response to her observation tells us that though they are deeply involved in intimacy, they are just as deeply incompatible. The horror lies in this ironic incongruity.

And the horror is perhaps even more impressive to us because it has come through without the usual embroidery of preparatory explanation and without the expected fanfare of emotion. Hemingway's tactic is to understate everything. When the girl says, "It isn't ours anymore," the language seems as flat as a table top. But the despair encapsulated in it reverberates as we take in the strangeness and the ambiguity of her declaration.

The world never belonged to the two of them in any legal or literal sense, of course. The "they" who took it away are not mortal judges or powers. What is implied is that true ownership of "the world" has to do with a worthiness to possess that they have squandered. Or that has been bled out of them by the operation of laws that can be inferred by their results but not named. She is saying more than she—or anyone—knows how to explain. She is, in her desperate certainty, like Eve looking back on Eden and seeing only the glitter of light on the sword of the angel who has driven them out.

When she says, "And we could have all this. . . . And we could have everything and every day we make it more impossible," her voice is given a sort of oracular weight by the use of the three <u>ands</u> (technically <u>polysyndeton</u>, a device found often in the prose of the King James Bible and the poetry of Walt Whitman as well as in Hemingway). Childlike and seeming to come from a trance of vision, the desperation of her pronouncement is all the more shocking because it is so quietly delivered. No wonder her companion asks "What did you say?" He does not want to believe what she has discovered.

Just as much as he depends on the shock effect of his understatements, Hemingway relies on a carefully controlled and modulated sequence as he presents his single scene with dramatic objectivity. By starting the quarrel so quietly that we hardly realize his characters <u>are</u> quarreling, the author maximizes the impact of those moments when the lover-antagonists expose the full measure of their hostility. The girl's final, quiet threat to scream comes at the end of an interchange that has exhausted the possibilities of real reconciliation between them. The apparent lightheartedness of the last few sentences is an intentionally bad disguise for the fact that everything is over.

Questions

1. Why has Hemingway provided so little information about the past lives and circumstances of the charac-

ters? What qualities of the dialogue make up for the
lack of descriptions of gestures, appearance, and other
identifying signs?

2. The girl seems to make a slip of the tongue when
she says, "They don't really look like white elephants.
I just meant the coloring of their skin through the
trees." As stated this means that hills have skins.
What is expressed by this confusion in her speech?

3. Does the man seriously try to understand the
girl's feeling about an abortion? Does she misunderstand his concern?

4. What is the significance of the setting?

5. Has the quarrel been resolved when the story ends?

Further Reading

Kraus, W. Keith. "Ernest Hemingway's 'Hills Like White
    Elephants': A Note on a 'Reasonable' Source," *English
    Record*, 21 (December 1970), 23-27.
Lid, Richard W. "Hemingway and the Need for Speech,"
    Modern Fiction Studies, VIII (Winter 1962-1963),
    403-407.

Shirley Jackson *The Lottery* (p. 617)
            (Shorter Edition, p. 294)

It seems clear that this story would not work without a carefully controlled objectivity in the narration. The effect depends on a gradually dawning sense
that something extraordinary and sinister is taking
place—followed by a swift crescendo of revelation at
the end. Even the revelation of what the townspeople
are up to is made dramatically. For the author to have
used the point of view of an informed character would
have been to give away the surprise prematurely.
Further, the eeriness of the proceedings would be seriously diminished if the participants were not seen to
be taking it all as a matter of course.

Yet, even without the effective unleashing of a grim
surprise, the story would contain a good deal to interest us. The picture of villagers gathering for a
ceremonial holiday is detailed and skillfully composed.
Even if the black box were not part of a fatal ritual,
its part in the legend of community life would be a

fascinating index to the folkways of the villagers. Conflict between tradition and progress focuses in argument about the appearance of the box and the proper ways to use it. Finally, even if we had known from the beginning that Mrs. Hutchinson was to be the victim, there would be suspense until we learned how she and her assailants behaved as the drawing went on.

That is to say the story offers more than the shudder of excitement provided by its special effects. It is a study of the blind spots in a society dominated by unexamined tradition. As allegory it warns that those who live by conformity may die from it. As a study of mass psychology it shows how a multitude of trivial individual sentiments can coalesce into a monolith of evil.

Questions

1. What are the first signs that something odd is taking place? The first signs of something sinister? The conclusive signs that the outcome will be dreadful?

2. What does the author accomplish by showing how familiar the proceedings are to the villagers? What does she show about mass psychology?

3. What is the theme of the story? Is it consistent with the tone?

4. Why do you suppose the author chose not to use the point of view of any of the characters?

5. What ironies are involved in the villagers' ideas of fairness?

6. What social rituals similar to the lottery do you participate in?

W. W. Jacobs *The Monkey's Paw* (p. 625)

The success of a horror story like this one depends on the author's maintaining a careful balance between revelation and concealment. If he presumes too far in the direction of insisting on the intervention of the supernatural or tries to bring its workings into full light, he risks losing his capital of credibility. His effects are in danger of evaporating by exposure to the full light of day. Belief in spectral presences flourishes in the dark.

Here the balance between credibility and impossibility is very skillfully maintained by a graded reduction in the amount and pertinence of the evidence that the three wishes made by Mr. White are granted. There is brutally strong (but still inconclusive) evidence that the first wish was granted. The son's death and the compensation of two hundred pounds might have been a coincidence. That is, the causal connection between wish and fulfillment is not established by anything even mentioned in the story. Only superstition supports the relation between the wish and the son's death, though of course the Whites in their grief are extremely vulnerable to such superstition.

There is nothing to support the belief that the second wish is granted except the noise at the door, which <u>might</u> have been misinterpreted by the old people whose minds have been turned in a certain direction by grief and guilt at the thought of having profited by their son's death. Only silence, following the noise at the door, supports a belief that the third wish has been granted. In a word, a psychological explanation is ready at hand and is easier to sustain than a supernatural one. The author has very neatly refrained from making a single declaration that might overtax the credulity of the reader. Yet, by his arrangement of the pattern of the wishes and an increasing momentum of suggestion, the reader has been induced to follow the psychological path of the parents and to be sure that the last wish was that the son might be dead again and at peace—though this is never stated. The effect of the story, then, is accomplished by careful craftsmanship in the telling. Like most effects unsupported by specific substructures of evidence, this one begins to melt when we reflect that <u>if</u> the second wish had been truly granted, the old man may have been very foolish to wish his son dead again without at least having a look to see what shape the young man was in—or asking his preference in the matter.

Questions

1. How do the comments about chess in the first two paragraphs foreshadow the main developments of the action?

2. How much of the story can be explained by the psychology of the parents?

3. Is there any real evidence that the second and third wishes were granted?

4. What is the moral of the story? How much does your answer depend on the way you answered Question 3?

Further Reading

Harkey, J. H.   "Foreshadowing in 'The Monkey's Paw,'" *Studies in Short Fiction*, 6, 653-654.

Henry James *The Tree of Knowledge* (p. 634)
(Shorter Edition, p. 301)

For better or for worse no reader of any level of sophistication can enter into James's fiction without taking on the puzzle of his style. Its circumlocutions almost unavoidably create an initial uncertainty as to what on earth he is talking about. It is a style so adroit in making distinctions that it often doesn't make those clear declarations that point the line of thought in most good prose. Substance fades behind pronouns of unclear reference. Eccentric imagery dims the reality it is presumably intended to illumine. We must begin *The Tree of Knowledge* by wading through a maze of interdependent allusions before we are eventually told, flat out, that Brench "despised Mallow's statues and adored Mallow's wife, yet was distinctly fond of Mallow. . . ." We may well wonder why James did not begin with this sentence and suspend his ramifying qualifications from it instead of building them up like a house of cards to be capped by it. We may wonder even more whether James supposes he is really giving us a picture of the landscape when he says Brench and the Mallows live where "the soft declivity of Hampstead began at that time to confess in broken accents to Saint John's Wood."

But student readers can be eased over the difficulties of the style with a little prompting—and even be persuaded that the mannerisms of expression are particularly appropriate to the characters and the rarified conflicts of this particular story. The Mallows and Brench are anything but effective, pragmatic people with concrete problems to solve, so a more earthy style might fail altogether to render their feelings and cal-

culations. Thus, Brench's chief task in life is to
<u>refrain</u> from saying what he knows, out of delicacy and
a firmly suppressed affection for his friend's wife.
His relation to the Mallows has been long sustained by
just such qualifications and reservations as figure in
James's style. To blurt the truth would be to wreck the
whole house of cards.

The threat to family happiness rises when the son
Lance grows up and has to be sent to Paris to prepare
him to follow in the Master's footsteps—or even go
beyond! Peter Brench opposes Lance's going. His fear is
simply that Lance will learn enough to see through the
fraud of his father's horrible and wrongheaded work. If
Lance detects the fraud, Mrs. Mallow may also learn the
truth. If she learns the truth, Peter's care in keeping
it from her will have been in vain. The pretty structure of illusions will come tumbling down, and after
investing so much of their lives in the lie the adult
characters have nothing to substitute for it.

Lance <u>must</u> go to Paris. The structure of lies they
have lived by requires it. Since his father has worked
so bravely in the face of public neglect, how could his
son lack the daring required to make his own commitment?
And the logical consequence of his mislabeled quest in
Paris is that he does, in fact, learn exactly what
Peter feared he would.

But there is another turn to the screw—typically
Jamesian and considerably more somber in its implications than anything that has led up to it. Brench—who
has a very large stake in not being a fool; who has
dedicated his life and given up many of its opportunities for the sake of keeping his beloved Mrs. Mallow
comfortably wrapped in the cocoon of her illusions—
Brench learns that she has never really had any illusions about her husband's supposed gift.

At last, like other Jamesian characters with noble
intentions and generous commitments, he must face the
fact that his efforts have been wasted. Beyond that,
he must descend to the uncomfortable assumption that
the object of his courtly love has been guided all
along by motives that must be distasteful to him.
Either the pure woman has a taste for fraud and deception or she is fond enough of the connubial state to
ignore the fraud that is part of it. She has lost her
spiritual luster in Brench's eyes. She has become a
creature of the sensual world that he, alas, has re-
nounced for her sake.

Questions

1. What meanings do you find in the title and how are these related to the story?

2. Why doesn't Peter Brench want Lance to go to Paris? Is Brench justifiably proud of preserving the Mallows' illusions? Has he made unwarranted assumptions?

3. Is Brench finally the victim of his own illusions? Is he more severely damaged by the coming of knowledge than Lance is?

4. How seriously should we take Brench's love for Mrs. Mallow? How does he demonstrate it?

5. How many of the four main characters are truly concerned with sparing the feelings of others?

6. Discuss the author's use of figurative language. In what ways is it appropriate to the subject matter?

7. How would you characterize the kind of language used throughout the story? How do its qualities relate to the chosen point of view?

See also "Questions for Comparing the Author's Stories," p. 113 of this *Handbook*.

Further Reading

Bellman, Samuel I. "Henry James's 'The Tree of Knowledge': A Biblical Parallel," *Studies in Short Fiction*, I (Spring 1964), 226-228.

Henry James *The Jolly Corner* (p. 646)

When we have abandoned one possible major alternative for the sake of another which will definitively shape our personality, it not infrequently happens that we are haunted by questions about (if not the specter of) the person we might have been if we had chosen otherwise. Perhaps the easiest illustration of this proposition for the majority of students will come from asking them to imagine the persons they might now be if they had chosen not to come to college. Most will come up readily with a partial portrait—including fragmentary details of appearance, lifestyle, feelings, level of prosperity, etc.—and by doing so will find

themselves in a situation analagous to Brydon's when he
returns to New York and is haunted by an image of the
self he might have been if he had not gone to live for
more than thirty years in Europe.

To be sure, this power to imagine an alternative
self is a psychological phenomenon which normally stops
short of a conviction that the abandoned "self" has any
actual existence. We keep to the rational distinction
between the hypothetical self and the historical one.
But James has taken the storyteller's option of proceeding as if the hypothetical and historical personalities had equal claims to be the real self, and he has
constructed his ghost story on that assumption.

There may be some guilt as well as curiosity in
Brydon's quest for his ghostly alter ego, for, in
fanciful terms appropriate to the fictive projection
James is making, it may be said that Brydon aborted the
potential of the other self by forsaking New York. Miss
Staverton's cryptic suggestion that Brydon's shadow
self might be a better man is also an implication of
guilt.

Brydon has a fundamental inclination to dislike the
"other." He goes beyond Staverton's epithet of "monstrous" to characterize the ghost as "quite hideous and
offensive." This anticipatory revulsion is consistent
with his dislike of the changes he has noted on his return to his native city. The novelties, "the famous
things . . . [are] his sources of dismay." Since we see
in his knack for managing business affairs that he
would have accomplished just these "famous things" if
he had chosen to live the other life in New York, we
can understand the grounds for hostility between the
ghostly self and the actual man. The ways of life are
antipathetic; so would be the men who lived them,
though both would be Spencer Brydon.

So far we are on fairly safe ground in postulating
that the conflict in this ghost story is a transposi-
tion into fictive objectivity of matters that are at
least psychologically explicable. (Could there be an
encounter between actual and hypothetical self, these
would be the feelings engendered.) Such parallelism
between psychic reality and fictive parody becomes
more tenuous in the long passages pertaining to the
search through the old house when Brydon gradually becomes aware that his ghostly other self is feeling
harder pressed, is growing wrathful and preparing for
confrontation. Perhaps a psychological grounding is

possible here, too. If the "ghost" is a mirror image of Brydon's psyche, then it is Brydon's anxiety for a showdown which is being indirectly represented.

Even such tenuous explanations are unavailable for the details of the other Brydon's appearance at the moment of confrontation. Why should it be the hands of the apparition which are rendered most visually for the reader's contemplation though we are told Brydon sees the whole figure vividly, as if he were painted by "a great modern master"? Two fingers are missing, "as if accidentally shot away," from these "splendid" hands. Splendid hands pertain to the career of an activist, a practical builder of cities—that is, to the career spurned by Brydon during his long expatriation—but why the fingers should appear to be shot away rather than lost in some accident of building defies conjecture. About the face we know only its effect on Brydon, his shock at being confronted by the face of a total stranger.

Subsequently there is some play with the idea that he has actually died in this confrontation, and this may (or may not—perhaps it is inappropriate to grope for certainties in a ghost story) be a thematic sugges-tion that he has no greater claim to be the real Brydon than the one who was denied the fulfillment of actual life. This teasing insinuation is reinforced by the play on pronouns when Miss Staverton says she dreamed she saw "you" and only under pressure corrects this to "him." Finally she says, "You came to yourself," as if she has mystic assurance of the equivalence of the lived and the unlived life. By expressing her affectionate sympathy for both the man and his ghost, she seems to expunge the antipathies between them.

Questions

1. What is Brydon's response to the changes he finds when he returns to New York?

2. How does Miss Staverton whet his curiosity about what he would have been if he had not gone to live abroad?

3. Does the identity of the ghost set this apart from most ghost stories?

4. What is the best explanation you can give for the fact that Brydon's ghost finally turns at bay to con-front him?

5. What is the final relationship between Brydon and

his "other self"—the man he might have been? How does Miss Staverton help resolve the conflict?

See also "Questions for Comparing the Author's Stories," below.

Further Reading

Freedman, William. "Universality in 'The Jolly Corner,'" *Texas Studies in Literature and Language*, Spring 1962, 12-15.

Rosenblatt, Jason P. "Bridegroom and Bride in 'The Jolly Corner,'" *Studies in Short Fiction*, Winter 1977, 282-287.

Henry James—
Questions for Comparing the Author's Stories

1. Comment on stylistic similarities in the two stories. Is James's style as well suited to the suspense of a ghost story as to the comic revelations of "A Tree of Knowledge"?
2. To what extent do both stories depend on the manners and circumstances of a particular social class?
3. What do the two stories say about the difficulties and importance of knowing oneself?
4. What do the stories reveal about James's values and his view of what counts in human experience?

Sarah Orne Jewett *The Flight of Betsey Lane* (p. 673)

As a local colorist, Jewett seems more intent on assembling details to present a favorable and pleasant picture than on analytic examination of either her central character or the setting. That is, the story seems to have sprung from a favorable prejudice toward the simple rural life of the period and the sort of virtues it bred. Betsey is more an emblem in whom those virtues are embodied than a particular individual. There is nothing here to strain one's credulity. The requirements of realism are duly observed and help to give the story its air of wholesome honesty. But, by the same token, one feels it is something less than the whole

story of the old folks in Byfleet Poorhouse. Has old age
ever been so free of miseries as Jewett would have us
believe? We are dealing with a selective realism, the
principle of selection being to choose those circumstances and virtues which highlight the resolution, self-
reliance, and good cheer bred into Americans and reinforced by rural life. The shadows are not so much denied
as ignored.

The common virtues of the type are concentrated in
the figure of Betsey. Old age has made her somewhat
childish, but this childishness is not at all to be con-
fushed with senility. Rather it is the reemergence of
childish zest and benevolence out of the drying husk of
age and bodily decrepitude. The simple beauty of Betsey's
nature seems to have earned the money given her by Mrs.
Strafford. It is not a small sum, but Betsey multiplies
its value by spending it on an adventure, in the best of
American traditions. As Whitman would put it, she takes
to the open road. She is a pioneer to the end, and if her
trip to the Centennial is fairly small potatoes by common
measure, still it is glorious for a woman of Betsey's
limitations.

Everyone Betsey encounters on her trip, from the railroad men who give her her first ride to the wise and
kindly doctor at the fair, is swayed by the verve and
spunk she displays. In the design of the story they serve
the function of character witnesses, testifying to the
aura she emanates in her finest hour. This testimony is
reinforced and underpinned by the general tone of approval with which the author presents her to our imagination. The tone breathes a quiet and uncomplicated faith
in Betsey's capacity to glide over impediments, and it is
the correspondence of this tone with the significance of
events which gives us our best insight into the heroic
dimensions of a simple heart.

Questions

1. What does the story say about the resourcefulness
of country people?

2. What sets Betsey Lane apart from the other inhabitants of the poor farm?

3. How does the tone of the story contribute to our
understanding of Betsey and her adventure?

4. What is there in Betsey's character that makes all
the others sympathetic to her?

5. What qualities in Betsey make her particularly appealing to the American taste?

Further Reading

Carey, Richard. *Sarah Orne Jewett*. New York: Twayne, 1962, 100-108.

James Joyce   *Araby* (p. 690)
              (Shorter Edition, p. 313)

   Fundamentally, this is a story of someone scrutinizing his former, childish self from the vantage of greater maturity. To that scrutiny he brings not merely the wisdom of more experience but also the maturing vision and the concerns of an artist. The events of the story may seem to have little significance except as they are focused, reassessed, and compelled to yield meanings they could not have revealed to the boy at the time of the action. (In a very real sense it is the story of a meeting between two persons, the young boy and the young man he has become.) This distinction between the older and younger selves of the narrator may be most readily demonstrated by considering the language of the story. Its versatility, precision, and resonances weave secondary images around the image of the small boy who dreams of finding romance at a Dublin fair. Scrutinized through the lenses of such language, there is hardly a detail in the story that does not glow with secondary signification.
   Thus the few books found in the house formerly tenanted by a priest become tokens of romantic lore inherited by modern times from the age of chivalry dominated by priestly authority, and the boy's infatuation with Mangan's sister may call to mind the rituals of courtly love. "Her image accompanied me even in places the most hostile to romance." Such language should evoke the figure of a medieval knight errant cherishing the image of his beloved as he explores the drab hazards of the earth. "I imagined that I bore my chalice safely through a throng of foes," he says, and we are reminded that in the artist's eye the figure of the boy conforms to the traditional profile of the "devout communicant" bearing his votive offering. The name of the

fair to which the boy eventually goes—*Araby*—represents both the commercialized romanticism of modern Dublin and its origin in the fascination that the East always held for the romantic imagination of Europe. In a sense the boy repeats the adventure of the Crusaders by going to Araby, and in this sense he incarnates a mythic figure on an endlessly repeated mythic quest.

Yet surely it would be a mistake to emphasize, in a discussion of the story, the mythic shadow that accompanies the boy without giving equal emphasis to the reality of his present circumstances; for the triumph of Joyce's art here is to show that persisting myths are visible in banal present circumstances. Shadows of Crusader and Devout Communicant become desiccated rhetorical debris unless we understand how they are cast by the living boy. His longing for something he cannot quite name will get through to most readers in terms of their own memories of childhood yearnings and frustration. And when they see it as a story of what might have happened to them, then they are in a good position to infer how they, like Joyce the artist, may see the large dimensions of their own past, the secondary significances in things they have been taught to regard as trivial.

Questions

1. What are the chief qualities of the narrator's character? How are these emphasized by the feelings and behavior directed toward Mangan's sister?
2. What is the tone of the story and how is it affected by the narrator's language?
3. Discuss the importance of the setting.
4. Interpret the clause: "I imagined that I bore my chalice safely through a throng of foes."
5. What is the character of the uncle, and how does he affect the boy's wishes and feelings?
6. Is anything gained by the narrator through his frustration and humiliation?

See also "Questions for Comparing the Author's Stories," p. 125 of this *Handbook*.

Further Reading

Friedman, Stanley. "Joyce's 'Araby.'" *The Explicator*, XXIV (January 1966), Item 43.

Garrison, Joseph M. "The Adult Consciousness of the
    Narrator in Joyce's 'Araby,'" *Studies in Short Fic-
    tion*, 10 (1973), 416-419.
Ohmann, Richard. "Reply" [to John Russell's "From
    Style to Meaning in 'Araby'"] *College English*,
    XXVIII (November 1966), 171-173.
Russell, John. "From Style to Meaning in 'Araby,'"
    College English, XXVIII (November 1966), 170-171.
Stone, Harry. "'Araby' and the Writings of James
    Joyce," *Antioch Review*, XXV (Fall 1965), 375-410.

James Joyce   *A Little Cloud* (p. 695)
              (Shorter Edition, p. 318)

Thoreau's remark that "the mass of men lead lives of
quiet desperation" could hardly be better illustrated
than it is by this not quite static portrait. Little
Chandler is fulfilled neither by his marriage nor by his
work. His wife has a pretty face, but he finds "something mean in it," something at the same time "unconscious and ladylike." The way she received the blouse he
bought her as a present is no doubt typical of the un-
satisfying way she accepts anything he may have to give
her, mangling his timid attempts at generosity. His
clerical job provides no outlet for the best of his
mental activity. He is growing older without prospects
of changing his life for the better. And Dublin—which
suffuses and conditions everything in the story with the
potency of a tyrannical character—is a dreary substitute for the exotic places toward which his spirit
yearns.

And his old friend Gallaher has escaped to those
places. That in itself would be enough to excite
Chandler's envy and threaten the "equipoise of his
sensitive nature." Worse, he feels—there is every indication that he is right—that Gallaher is his inferior,
too crude and callow to appreciate properly the liber-
ties he has achieved in England and in Europe. What
Gallaher dotes on as the "immorality" of the world's
capitals would be for Chandler passion, voluptuousness,
and romance. So an awareness of injustice adds fuel to
the fire of his dissatisfaction.

This is _almost_ all that happens in Joyce's story.
Nearly everything he has to say has been said by the
time the two separate after sharing drinks and cigars.

"A dull resentment against his life" has been wakened in Chandler by the encounter, but we do not expect dull resentments to precipitate bold new beginnings in lives so committed to routine as his. Yet the climax of the story is still to come, and what Chandler makes of his resentment reveals Joyce's meaning and his pity.

A better man than Chandler would have grappled for a new direction. A worse man would have taken what satisfaction he could from his envy and forgotten it. Chandler contrives to make his relation to his irremediable life worse—his wakened feelings only motivate him to frighten his infant son and anger his wife. He is, alas, intelligent enough to see in this incident how shamefully inadequate are his impulses to rebellion. His small virtues, then, are worse than none at all, and this irony is what Joyce leaves us to contemplate.

Questions

1. What makes Little Chandler unable to use the fine potentials he feels within himself? Is he truly a better man than his friend Gallaher? How are Chandler's "poetic" sentiments related to his character and his predicament?

2. Do Chandler and Gallaher have the same attitude toward the "immorality" of English and European capitals? Why does Chandler raise the question of their immorality?

3. What does the story say about the provincialism of Dublin?

4. How does the episode with the baby shape the meaning of the story as a whole?

5. In the last paragraph Chandler feels "shame." For what? Has he fallen from his general state of melancholy into something worse?

See also "Questions for Comparing the Author's Stories," p. 125 of this *Handbook*.

James Joyce   *The Dead* (p. 706)

In the time of his artistic apprenticeship Joyce was an enthusiastic admirer of the great poet and dramatist Henrik Ibsen. How much he learned from the Norwegian master and how much of Ibsen's craft Joyce brought over and placed in the mainstream of fiction in English may be seen and demonstrated in this, the longest of the stories from Joyce's *Dubliners.*

Symbolic naturalism is probably the best and most comprehensive term for the strategy that Ibsen and Joyce went so far toward perfecting. Naturalism as such aimed broadly at undistorted reportage of human nature and society. In literature it often produced "a slice of life"—an undoctored sampling of the ebb and flow of life as it is experienced by most of us. The discovery of Ibsen and Joyce was that the more sharply the eye and ear of the naturalist penetrated into the minutiae of daily reality the better they could discern the track of universal magnitudes, magnitudes revealing themselves in the shape of trivial actions, chance words with multiple signification, and banal encounters that set off whole minefields of memory for their characters and for the audience or reader. It is as if the symbolic naturalist, using a microscope, might discover and plot the movement of vast constellations.

It is a good point of departure to observe that nothing happens in this story that would deserve more than a passing note on the society page of a local newspaper. The world should little note nor long remember that the Misses Morkan have held their annual dance. The world, being defined as it is by social norms and legal grids, will go on afterwards as before. There is every reason to guess that the marriage of Gabriel and Gretta Conroy will continue as before. The revelation that Gretta loved a boy named Michael Furey before she knew her husband is not on the scale of revelations that lead to divorce, separation, or any sort of alienation that either the law or society would take cognizance of. It seems reasonable to assume that the pattern of sexual relations between the Conroys—as such things are measured by Masters and Johnson techniques—will show no marked alteration of its normal rhythms just because, for one night, Gabriel's desire has been balked by his wife's melancholy reminiscences.

And yet the reader who follows the pattern of trivial signals as they speak to Gabriel in the course of the evening will have to conclude that all is changed, changed utterly. Gabriel has been led to what Joyce called an epiphany—a moment of transcendent illumination when reality is no longer hidden by the veil of illusions that make up the structure we daily accept as "the world."

If there was no such epiphany at the climax of the
story, we might still appreciate it as a richly tex-
tured slice of Dublin life in another era. A very large
fraction of the material is presented dramatically. The
shade of Ibsen, the dramatist, flirts in the background
when we reflect that *The Dead* is very much like a play
with two important scenes—the more protracted scene of
the party, the more concentrated epilogue scene with
Gabriel and his wife alone in the hotel room.

We would miss much if we did not give due attention
to the variety of characters, the hit and run conflict
of temperaments and ideologies, the social habits and
restraints, the nostalgic reminders of mutability with
which Joyce fills his stage. And the leisurely attention he devotes to furnishings and the food on the
supper table. All this spectacle is the provision of
the naturalist *per se*.

However, it is the sensibility of Gabriel Conroy
that transforms *The Dead* into something beyond the
range of a sociological, naturalistic report on a vanished age. By exploiting Gabriel's point of view, Joyce
is able to demonstrate a pattern in the signals ex-
changed by the interaction of his characters with their
setting, to develop that pattern into a track that
leads on to the land of the dead. For Gabriel is above
all a reader of signals. He does not read them all consciously; he does not interpret all of them in rational
language. His is the Central Intelligence of the story
(to borrow James's specification), but his indefinable
shifts of sympathy, his hurt feelings, his very baffle-
ment in the face of the mystery of love with which
Gretta at last confronts him are as important in following the pattern of revelation as that part of his
nature that we ordinarily label intelligence.

Gabriel's point of view is not used to open the
story. He is not even on the scene in the opening paragraphs, but it may be worth marking out the steps of
modulation in the impersonal narration that prepare for
the reader's acceptance of things as Gabriel sees and
feels them. First the setting is established by sensory
detail—the clang of the "wheezy" doorbell. The generalized definition of the occasion is then given in
terms available to any acquaintance of the Morkan
sisters—"Everybody who knew them came to it." This
is followed presently by a more specific and interpretive qualification of what is going on, as if by an
acquaintance who sympathized effectively with the
sisters' feelings—"They had good reason to be fussy"

and "they were dreadfully afraid. . . ." The progression is from a purely objective presentation to one tinted lightly with sentiment and subjective evaluation.

Yet it is only after the milieu is colored in that Gabriel makes his appearance, and we see him first as he would appear to a stranger looking on and overhearing his dialogue with the maid. Gabriel "smiled at the three syllables she had given his surname"—but his response does not represent the completed transition to his point of view. If we saw the scene on a stage, the skill of the actors could make us aware of the reason for his smile. When he blushes at Lily's bitter comment about men, we are told it is "as if" he had let their small talk veer onto an inappropriate subject. The "as if" signals that this is an interpretation of his embarrassment that might be made by an onlooker acquainted with his character.

We enter fully into his point of view only when we are told that "He was still discomposed by the girl's bitter and sudden retort." The graduated steps by which the reader has been led into the point of view probably make the later transitions out of it less disturbing, even less noticeable than they might have been without such preparation. Greasing the way in greases the way out. There are several passages in the story that apparently take place beyond Gabriel's notice, but the reader is hardly aware of this because Joyce has so deftly evolved the point of view out of the sights and sounds of the milieu.

He assigns to minor, flat characters—particularly Miss Ivors—much of the foreground action that develops the "riot of emotion" in Gabriel which is caught up. Gabriel and Miss Ivors have deeply ingrained allegiances that make them differ on questions of nationalism and the worth of tradition versus change. But their sparring on these issues begins and remains strictly within the social frame imposed by the particular occasion and the frame of manners prevailing in the Dublin of their time. When Miss Ivors calls him a bad name, it is nothing worse than "West Briton." She upsets him by staring at him "with her rabbit's eyes," but she certainly stops short of what we might, in our time and place, consider real verbal abuse. When Gabriel reflects angrily that she had no right to "call him a West Briton before people . . . to make him ridiculous before people" we realize he is exaggerating her offense. Evidently no one except himself heard the epithet.

It is precisely this oversensitized capacity to ex-

aggerate, to make much out of little, that enables him
to guide us into the labyrinth of the spiritual world
behind the social masquerade of his aunts' party. For
if there is a heroic conflict going on, he and Miss
Ivors are not the real antagonists. It is his wife
Gabriel must confront at the bottom of the labyrinth,
and, through her, the ambiguous threat and promise of
a love that his generosity is too small to cope with.

At the beginning of the story we saw no reliable sign
that any conflict existed within the Conroy marriage.
True enough, Gretta made a faintly disparaging reference
to her husband's caution when they arrived. "'Goloshes,'
said Mrs. Conroy. 'That's the latest. . . . Tonight
even, he wanted me to put them on, but I wouldn't. The
next thing he'll buy me will be a diving suit.'" Such a
complaint hardly goes beyond formalized banter. It is
just as important to note the miniature scale of this
discord between them as to point out that it foreshadows
the magnitude of estrangement between them that is finally disclosed. At last we will see that his irritating
caution is indissolubly linked with his generosity,
keeping it inadequate to bridge the gulf between the
ultimate needs of their hearts.

The track between her small-scale, low-keyed complaint and her revelation in the hotel room is the
winding pattern of the whole story. It is a pattern that
seldom shows husband and wife in direct contact with
each other. Their acceleration toward the moment of
confrontation is accomplished through the intermediary
minor characters—like Bartell D'Arcy, who sings an old
song that reminds Gretta of the dead boy whose love for
her is beyond Gabriel's power to match. The wounds
Gabriel takes from Miss Ivors goad him on to ask for the
wound his wife finally inflicts when he has made himself
supremely vulnerable by the tenderness of his desire for
her.

We must give full weight to the slowness and indirec-
tion by which Joyce has opened up this track for us.

In Gabriel's toast to his aunts he alludes to the
"sadder thought that will recur to our minds" in the
very midst of such festivities. Later he will be struck
by the spell of his wife's "grace and mystery" as he
sees her listening to a melancholy song sung by a "voice
made plaintive by distance."

Neither he nor the reader yet guesses how far these
prophetic guidesigns will lead him down from his precarious assurance of stability. The emotions wakened by
"distant music" seem to be leading him to a closer sympathy with Gretta.

In the final scene Gretta's unsolicited praise for his generosity brings them closer—brings him close enough to be defenseless against the revelation of her involvement, once upon a time, with the dead boy. When what she has said first dawns on him, "a shameful consciousness of his own person assailed him. He saw himself as a ludicrous figure . . . a nervous well-meaning sentimentalist . . . idealising his own clownish lusts."

But there is one more turn of the screw of abasement still to come. Still presuming on his adequacy to cope with shame and disappointment, he tricks himself into asking more questions.

"And what did he die of so young, Gretta? Consumption, was it?" Someone who died young of a physical ailment is indeed pitiable—and therefore a formidable rival for Gretta's affections.

But when she answers, quietly, "I think he died for me," the comprehensible pathos of death by disease is replaced by the immeasurable and heroic pathos of a death for love's sake. Then Gabriel knows himself not merely shamed and humiliated but vanquished. Perhaps it is no wonder that "A vague terror seized Gabriel at this answer, as if . . . some impalpable and vindictive being was coming against him, gathering forces against him in its vague world."

Well-intentioned, Gabriel has blundered across the boundary of the mortal world, in which virtues like generosity and humility might yet retrieve him. His rival, his adversary, is dead, therefore deathless, immortal.

In the terms into which the story of a ceremonial, social evening has now been transformed, it is the blunder itself that provides salvation for Gabriel. When his personal and social identity begins to fade into a "grey impalpable world," into the "region where dwell the vast hosts of the dead," his inadequate personal generosity is transfigured.

The play with the concept embodied in the term "generous" is the play of a very great poet, maneuvering the ambiguities of language to provide a climax for his story that no display of action could here achieve. "Generosity" is scaled upward from a term descriptive of a set of actions and a set of attitudes to designate a spiritual state in which desire and will have been surrendered. By accepting the annihilation of his personal desires, Gabriel has achieved a communion beyond the menace of mortality or the alienation of mortal love. No terms except those borrowed from religion will serve for an interpretation of the conclusion to which this masterpiece comes.

Questions

1. What is the central conflict of the story? Among the numerous minor characters, which contribute most to the development of the conflict?

2. What is the significance of the song sung by Bartell D'Arcy? Is it significant that he has a bad cold and sings it hoarsely?

3. What ideological conflicts enter the story? How are they related to personal conflicts?

4. What is the prevailing tone of the party? Is it in conformity with the tone of the whole story?

5. Why do you suppose Joyce gave so complete an itemization of the food on the supper table? Why give Gabriel's speech in full?

6. How does the party prepare the "riot of emotions" in Gabriel's psyche?

7. What suggestions of discord and incompatibility between Gabriel and his wife appear before they go to their hotel room?

8. Gretta tells Gabriel that he is a "very generous person." To what extent is this praise supported by what we learn of him? Has his generosity been modified or lessened by what Gretta tells him of Michael Furey?

9. Since most of the story is told from Gabriel's point of view, what is gained by opening the story before he comes on the scene?

10. The structure may suggest that of a play in two scenes. What would be omitted if the material were presented as a play rather than as fiction? Would the omissions radically alter the meaning?

See also "Questions for Comparing the Author's Stories," p. 125 of this *Handbook*.

Further Reading

Deane, Paul. "Motion Picture Techniques in James Joyce's 'The Dead,'" *James Joyce Quarterly*, VI (Spring 1969), 231-236.

Ellman, Richard. "The Backgrounds of 'The Dead,'" in Robert Scholes and A. Walton Litz, eds., *Dubliners: Text, Criticism, and Notes* (New York, 1969), pp. 388-403.

Kelleher, John V. "Irish History and Mythology in
    James Joyce's 'The Dead,'" *Review of Politics*,
    XXVII (July 1965), 414-433.
Lytle, Andrew. "A Reading of Joyce's 'The Dead,'"
    Sewanee Review, LXXVII (Spring 1969), 193-216.
McKenna, John P. "Joyce's 'The Dead,'" *The Explicator*,
    30 (September 1971), Item 1.
O'Hehir, Brendan P. "Structural Symbol in Joyce's 'The
    Dead,'" *Twentieth Century Fiction*, III (April 1957),
    8-13.
Tate, Allen. "'The Dead,'" in Scholes and Litz, eds.,
    Dubliners: Text, Criticism, and Notes (New York,
    1969), pp. 404-410.

James Joyce—
Questions for Comparing the Author's Stories

1. Compare the use of setting in the three stories by
Joyce. Does the first person narration in *Araby* inhibit
or enhance the author's exploitation of the symbolism
inherent in homely details?

2. Compare the narrator's frustration in *Araby* with
that of Little Chandler in *A Little Cloud*, with Gabriel
Conroy's in *The Dead*.

3. Are the author's sympathies more clearly with the
narrator in *Araby* than with the major characters in the
other two Joyce stories? How does the tone act to build
or deny sympathy with the characters?

Franz Kafka   *The Metamorphosis* (p. 740)

One of the first things that will occur to us as we
grapple with this story is that it is <u>like</u> an account
of terminal illness that afflicts one member of a family
directly while indirectly it reconstructs the whole
fabric of family attitudes and relationships. That is,
Gregor's transformation into a giant insect seems to
equate rather easily with a sick man's feeling that his
whole physical being has been transformed into something
loathsome to himself and others by the onset of his
disease. The varying degrees of compassion, aversion,
panic, hope, and resentment felt by the members of
Gregor's family are, at least, credible tracings of the
feelings that might be generated around the sickbed of a

young man withering from tuberculosis, cancer, or
another of the diseases for which we have a name. The
evolution of these feelings—particularly the change in
the attitude of the sister—might well be considered a
realistic rendition of a family's attempts to cope with
the intrusion of the abnormal into the normal routines
and relationships on which they must found their lives.
Every disease, and particularly those with a fatal outcome, will impinge on the routines of health like something alien and uncanny which must ultimately be rejected if life is to continue. And in the psychological
patterns that Kafka has rather laboriously developed
here we may recognize a high degree of verisimilitude—
a shocking but accurate picture of the way sickness
seems to a dying man and the way the survivors prepare
to cast out the sick person along with his sickness as
the price of resumed health. So, if we were merely to
translate Gregor's transformation as a hyperbolic synonym for, say, tuberculosis or cancer we could rest in an
interpretation of the whole story as a kind of psychological case study. It has, indeed, a strong matrix of
psychological realism.

But, plainly, Kafka is up to something more than
studying the psychology of a diseased young man and the
repercussions of the disease within the family circle.
Even if we suppose that to begin with the transformation into insect form is a stretched metaphor for waking
into sickness, we soon notice that the author is more
interested in his metaphor than in the human condition
it might be taken to represent. As soon as Gregor tries
to use his voice and to get out of bed there begins a
detailed examination of physical changes that goes beyond any requirement of a metaphor that might explain
the distortions of self-awareness that accompany physical disease. It is partly the objective tone of the
prose that persuades us against interpreting Gregor's
perceptions of his new body as hallucination or fever
dream. A variety of subtle signals convinces us that
the story has crossed the boundary between psychological realism and metaphysical fantasy.

By the time Gregor has opened the bedroom door and
his physical change is verified by other eyes, the
fictional presumptions of the fantasy are so firmly
established that the author is able to reverse his
previous tactic. Now, in his address to the chief clerk,
it is Gregor who seems to believe he is unchanged—it
may be the sight of a photograph of himself on the opposite wall that re-establishes his self-image as a

human—while the onlooking family and clerk register
the monstrous change. "I'll put my clothes on at once,
pack up my samples and start off," Gregor offers. But
the chief clerk is struck dumb by what he has seen
emerge from Gregor's bedroom and goes into the hallway
"as if some supernatural power were waiting there to
deliver him"—which suggests that only a supernatural
power could now unscramble the supernatural changes that
have occurred.

When we speak of the supernatural in connection with
this work, it is important to specify that Kafka is not
invoking it to obtain conventional effects of awe and
terror. (Gregor, as monster insect, has almost nothing
in common with the monsters of television or film fantasy that crawl out of the shadows to menace shrieking
heroines.) Primarily, at least, Kafka exploits the
supernatural for its comic possibilities. It is, after
all, ludicrous for a giant bug to harangue a chief
clerk about the petty injustices to which a commercial
traveler is subject. Awe and terror of a very special
and persistent sort may indeed linger in the recesses
of our intuitive imagination when all the implications
of uncertainty seep into our minds. But the primary
effects of Kafka's distortions are not designed to
shock.

When Gregor's sister is inspired to feed him with
garbage instead of the milk that he has previously
enjoyed, no particular comment is made on family relationships as we normally experience them. It is rather
as if the author were playfully examining the logical
consistencies of the alternative world that can be constructed in fiction. In this aspect of the tale, at
least, it is kin to those passages in *Gulliver's
Travels* where Swift seems merely to be indulging in a
boyish delight in testing the possibilities of his toy
armies of little people or the mechanical capacities of
his giants. At the same time, any comparison with
Gulliver's Travels must be hedged with an awareness
that Swift's was a very different sensibility from
Kafka's and that Swift was writing in an age of moral
and philosophical certainty, very unlike Kafka's.

The examinations of the family financial situation
that follow Gregor's disability—particularly references to his hopeless dream of sending his sister to
study the music she loves so much—serve to orchestrate
a homely pathos with the strains of comedy just noted.
But the pathos as well is dissolved in the evolving
re-orientation required by the insuperable change in

Gregor. With quiet patience the author keeps insisting
that what we must deal with is not a domestic tragedy
disguised in fictional metaphor, but an alienation of
such proportions that the family's (or the reader's)
attempts to rationalize it by comparing it to natural
disease must all shatter against an altered reality.
His mother may talk of his "getting better"—and this
reference may tend to equate his alteration with disease. But the words have become utterly meaningless in
the situation as represented. What is "better" for a
giant insect? Language itself is being cast loose from
its anchorages in experience.

Gregor's relationship with his father makes one of
the major parts of the pattern. Here, as with the whole
story, we can pick out many elements of realism and of
the sort of caricature which merely heightens realism.
The father is a pompous, opinionated, ineffective
tyrant, bloated with self-indulgence and parasitically
attached to his wage-earning son; a type who might appear in many a realistic novel of bourgeois life. But
his bombardment of his transformed son with little red
apples—and the imbedding of an apple in Gregor's flesh
—is purely enigmatic. It becomes a symbol that cannot
be exhausted by any rational explanation, however ingenious. It has to be taken as part of the given data
of the tale, consistent with the enigma that the whole
presents. There is certainly no easy or reliable explanation, either, for the fact that in his insect form
Gregor is more susceptible to the influence of music
than ever before. Hearing his sister's violin, he "felt
as if the way were opening before him to the unknown
nourishment he craved." It may be that his approach to
death (represented first by his physical transfiguration) has sensitized him to the meaning of music, re-
moving the obstacles that health and normality put in
the way of his appreciation. In any case, the reference
to the "unknown nourishment" could well be examined in
comparison with the statement of the central character
in the story *The Hunger Artist* who says, "If I had found
[the food I like] . . . I should have made no fuss and
stuffed myself like you or anyone else."

As in *The Hunger Artist*, we may note that the story
ends when the central character has wasted away to
death, while those around him seem to have obtained a
new lease on crude health from his demise. A vigorous
animal replaces the dead Hunger Artist—and here
Gregor's sister flowers into a kind of brutal vitality
after he is out of the way.

Consideration of such developments in the action of both stories may be more helpful in understanding them than the devotion of too much attention to symbols, which cannot be fully rationalized in any case. Like all good fiction, this novella works through a combination of effects, meanings, and patterns. The attempt to find a single "key" to the meaning of the whole may actually obstruct the apprehension of the unity achieved by Kafka's orchestration of various fictional resources.

Questions

1. Is there any real surprise in this novella after the first sentence? What does the author accomplish by accounting at such length for the consequences of Gregor's transformation?
2. Is Gregor increasingly aware of the significance of intrafamily relationships after his transformation?
3. What is the general tone of the story? How is this affected by telling it mostly from Gregor's point of view?
4. In what ways does the character of Gregor's sister change? How do the changes in her attitude toward Gregor contribute to the progress and meaning of the story?
5. In what ways could Gregor's misfortune be compared to a severe or crippling illness in a family situation? Is the focus of the whole story more on the family than on Gregor as an individual? Explain.
6. If you take Gregor's transformation as a metaphorical symbol of guilt, from what does the guilt arise?
7. What roles do the lodgers, the charwoman, and the chief clerk play in the action?
8. What is the meaning of the picture of the woman in furs?

See also "Questions for Comparing the Author's Stories," p. 132 of this *Handbook*.

Further Reading

Greenberg, Martin. "Kafka's 'Metamorphosis' and Modern Spirituality," *Tri-Quarterly*, Number 6, pp. 5-20.
Moss, Leonard. "A Key to the Door Image in 'The Metamorphosis,'" *Modern Fiction Studies*, 17 (Spring 1971), 37-42.

Taylor, Alexander. "The Waking: The Theme of Kafka's
    'Metamorphosis,'" *Studies in Short Fiction*, II
    (Summer 1965), 337-342.
Wolkenfeld, Suzanne. "Christian Symbolism in Kafka's
    'The Metamorphosis,'" *Studies in Short Fiction*, 10
    (1973), 205-207.

Franz Kafka   *A Hunger Artist* (p. 779)
               (Shorter Edition, p. 329)

Kafka delights in tripping up common sense by its
inherent contradictions and reducing the logic of
language to absurdity to show its merely provisional
nature. It is logical to call anyone who excels at
anything an artist in the area of his excellence—
though probably our colloquial word champion fits better
with what is really meant here. Part of Kafka's comic
proposition is that there is no field of human action
that does not have its champion, from pulling the leaves
off daisies to balloon racing to composing poetry.

And there is always a peculiar relationship between
the person who excels and the public at large. What is
easy for him (if it were not in some sense "easy" he
could not do it) is impossible for them, so there is a
difficulty in communication should he try to explain why
he likes to persist in something they would not like at
all. Taking advantage of this is the middleman—the
"impresario" of the story. He makes the unintelligible
impulse to excel intelligible to the public by misin-
terpreting it to them and profits both from his entertaining falsehoods and from their natural curiosity
about activities foreign to their capacities or
preferences.

The curiosity of the public is not insatiable. Without the link of genuine understanding or of reliable
communication with the alienated champion, the ordinary
folk lose interest in spite of the impresario's tricks.
On the other hand, the champion wants to continue in
his specialty—to infinity—simply because it is the
one among his human functions that he does best. There
is, as Kafka's hunger artist testifies, a compulsion at
work that can't be helped, that should not be admired
as self-sacrifice for a goal beyond personal interests.

The story is barren of any details that tend to
personalize or individualize the central character.

Bizarre as his calling may be, nothing suggests there are any determining factors in his history, his early thought, or his sensuous response to life that have pushed him into his career. He exists as a bewildering figure within the bent, distorted world that Kafka has imagined.

Perhaps Kafka is saying that men, caught in the trap of their thought patterns, are inclined to make freaks of themselves while animals—consider the panther that replaces the hunger artist—embody freedom and joy by virtue of their lack of the contradictions suffered by mankind.

Questions

1. What are the usual motives for fasting? Do any of these apply in the case of the protagonist? What allegorical or symbolical meanings can be attached to his fasting?

2. What does he mean when we are told that fasting for him "was the easiest thing in the world"? What does "easy" mean in this context?

3. Does the protagonist fit your usual ideas of (1) an artist, (2) a naturally gifted athlete, or (3) a sideshow freak? How does the story change or develop your identification of him as any of the above?

4. Is it significant that the protagonist's impresario misrepresents him to the public? Why does the hunger artist submit to the dictates of the impresario?

5. Does the fasting man deserve admiration? Does his act represent a human perversity from which animals— like the panther that replaces him—are free?

6. What is the tone of the narration? What is accomplished by the omission of allusions to particular real places, historical events, and persons? Where and when do you imagine the events of the story to have taken place?

See also "Questions for Comparing the Author's Stories," p. 132 of this *Handbook*.

Further Reading

Holtz, William. "'The Hunger Artist': A Way In," *CEA Critic*, XXIX (December 1966), 3.

Moyer, Patricia. "Time and the Artist in Kafka and
    Hawthorne," *Modern Fiction Studies*, IV (Winter
    1958-9), 295-306.
Steinhauer, Harry. "Hungering Artist or Artist in
    Hungering: Kafka's 'A Hunger Artist,'" *Criticism*,
    IV (Winter 1962), 28-43.

Franz Kafka—
Questions for Comparing the Author's Stories

1. Compare the extreme eccentricity of the protagonist in *A Hunger Artist* with the relatively commonplace
emotions and wishes of Gregor in *The Metamorphosis*.
2. Compare the tones of the two Kafka stories.
3. Which of the two distorts reality more completely?

Ring Lardner   *Haircut* (p. 786)

This story provides an excellent opportunity for discussing the device of the unreliable (biased, or deceived) narrator, for clearly the barber's sympathies
and interpretations do not accord with the facts of the
situation as he presents them. The major discrepancy,
of course, is his admiration for Jim Kendall, who is
clearly a heel of the lowest and meanest sort. Few
readers will misunderstand Kendall's meanness or fail
to grasp how blatantly the author has revealed it, in
spite of his narrator's insistence on the man's value as
an entertainer.

The trick might seem hardly worth pulling if we felt
that the barber was alone in his estimate of Kendall's
worth. But, in fact, he seems to be a spokesman for the
community, and therefore his unshakable misprision expresses the bedrock of malice in the whole social milieu,
where a common vindictiveness is disguised as goodnatured humor. One may even suspect that the narrator
knows he is wrong in his moral interpretations but expresses them anyhow in the conviction that this is what
he is supposed to say. By following this line of conjecture we may come to a glimpse of the black pessimism
in Lardner's view of humanity.

On the surface (or, rather, at the first level below
the barber's prattle) this appears to be a story of
poetic justice. Paul Dickson, who is not as feeble-

minded as folks like to say, blasts Kendall for his many
vicious tricks, particularly for those he pulled on
Julie Gregg. The killing will pass for an accident. A
bad man has been rubbed out. The slate is washed clean.

But if the barber really is a voice which articulates
some residual social malice always ready to join in the
forms of persecution described, then we may suppose the
loss of Kendall will make no real difference in the tone
of community life. If intolerance can pass so readily as
fun, then it is unlikely ever to be ameliorated. A discussion of dark, bitter, and pessimistic comedy might
profitably expand from a consideration of this story.

Questions

1. How do the narrator's prejudices and misunder-
standing obstruct or emphasize the meaning of the events
he relates?
2. What is the character of Jim Kendall? How does it
fit with the general character of the community?
3. What is Doc Stair's feeling about Julie Gregg?
4. Can it be argued that Doc Stair is responsible for
Kendall's death? Or has Kendall brought it on himself?
5. Does the conclusion of the story imply that
justice has been done? If you think it does, do you
agree?

Further Reading

Geismar, Maxwell. *Ring Lardner and the Portrait of
    Folly*. New York, Crowell, 1972, 77-78.
Goldstein, Melvin. "A Note on the Perfect Crime,"
    Literature and Psychology, 11 (1961), 65-67.
Kasten, Margaret C. "The Satire of Ring Lardner,"
    English Journal, 36 (1947), 194-195.
May, Charles E., "Lardner's 'Haircut,'" *Explicator*, 31
    (1973), Item 69.

Margaret Laurence *The Loons* (p. 796)

Most readers will probably conclude that the narrator
is the central and most important character in this
story. In a very real sense the story is a compact summary of her education and the discovery of her place in
life. The melodramatic destiny of Piquette serves as a
pattern to form the imagination and understanding of the
narrator and as a scale by which she can measure her own
stature as she matures.

The summer vacation trip to the cottage by the lake
is an exploratory penetration into nature, but more
specifically into this land with its primal spirits and
voices and its all but vanished Indian legends. These
things tease the imagination of the narrator. She has
read of them in books, but what she has read is flimsy
and superficial, the merest glimpse into the heroic and
terrifying magnitudes of the human and nonhuman domains
of the past. On her realization that Piquette is actually Indian (at least a half-breed), she naively hopes
the sullen girl will serve as "a kind of junior proph-
etess of the wilds, who might impart to me, if I took
the right approach, some of the secrets which she un-
doubtedly knew . . . ."

The path to understanding is not to be that easy. Or,
at any rate, the discovery of the "right approach" to
Piquette will be long delayed. It is the girl's father
who takes her first to hear the loons, and there is no
problem in hearing those birds with her physical ears.
The problem is—as with reading about nature and the
Indian past—to hear within the physical sounds that
core of meaning toward which her imagination yearns.
Father and daughter are not quite deaf to this cry
within the cry of the loons, but neither is able to decipher it, and to all appearances Piquette does not give
"a good goddamn" about what she was supposed to be able
to interpret.

But in the long run, somehow—perhaps by the pathos
of her squalid, heartbreaking, savage doom—Piquette
provides the clues for a deeper (though still imperfect)
interpretation of the voice crying out the secret of the
land. It is by her progress in sympathy for Piquette
that the narrator has come closer to a comprehension of
what the loons declare. The final statement of the story
does not mean that Piquette consciously understood or
"heard" the message of the loons, but that in her fate
she embodied that melancholy signal. Perhaps the

narrator has gone as far as she dares toward a recognition of the despair and longing in the voice of the past.

Questions

1. How is the disappearance of the loons related to the theme of this story?
2. What is the role of the father in developing the narrator's understanding of Piquette?
3. Can you put into words what the narrator has heard in the "half mocking and half plaintive" call of the loons?
4. What is the relation between the narrator and Piquette and how does it change?
5. Why does the narrator surmise that Piquette might be the only one who heard the crying of the loons?

Further Reading

Thomas, Clara. "The Short Stories of Margaret Laurence," *World Literature Written in English*, 11 (1972), 25-33.

D. H. Lawrence *Tickets, Please* (p. 804)

We might well ask whether Annie and John Thomas are lovers or duelists. They are not sure themselves. They move together by compulsion, but whether to kiss or to wound does not seem in their power to determine. Each wants the other, but wants on terms the other will not and finally cannot accept. Once she has begun walking out with John Thomas and is sure of how much he really likes her, Annie's pride convinces her he could not leave her. "The possessive female was roused in Annie. So he left her." Here is the nub of the story, the cruel irony of the passion which can neither be fulfilled nor, after it is roused, suppressed. What began as a "subtle antagonism" between the young man and young woman (antagonism not at all incompatible with sexual interest) ends as a crude brawl that does not so much settle the issues as tear open the wound inflicted by their ill-matched demands on each other.

The wartime (World War I) setting and circumstances have something to do with the course the action follows.

On the home front in wartime there are simply more women
of marriageable age than men and they are working in oc-
cupations they would not have in time of peace. Men and
women meet in an atmosphere of "darkness and lawless-
ness" and the rural tram itself is "perky, jaunty, somewhat daredevil"—an incitement to live recklessly. We
may well conclude that Annie would not have been so open
to John Thomas's advances on the night of the fair if
the circumstances of her job had not made her bold.

Annie's surprise, shock, and outrage at not being
allowed "to take an intelligent interest in him, and to
have an intelligent response" diverts her passion into a
search for revenge, but it is, alas, still the same passion that led her to try to take him over completely,
make him more than a "nocturnal presence." There is a
cruel ambiguity in her determination to "have her own
back"—as the author puts it in words of splendid
dramatic ambiguity. She may tell herself that getting
her own back means getting revenge. Her blind desire is
to possess the man who once made her feel "rich and warm
in herself."

Thus mistaken about her fundamental wishes, she does
precisely the thing that will make it impossible for
them ever to get back together. Of course the attack on
him which she has incited humiliates him as she had expected. But, like her former attempt to take him over,
it goes too far. It goes so far that his humiliation
teaches him exactly how to hurt her most cruelly. She
has exposed more than she realized by the fury she displayed in kneeling on him and slapping him after he is
down. Surely everyone watching is aware that she could
not have showed so much passion if she had not cared
very deeply for him. She has given John Thomas the
opening to repay his humiliation by humiliating her as
badly. He does so by choosing her. She has commanded
him to choose and he is fulfilling the letter of her
instruction at the same time that he reverses the
spirit of it. There can be no reconciliation between
them after this.

"There was the silence of the end," the author tells
us as John Thomas gathers his torn clothes and prepares
to leave. It is the end of a major passion that ought
to have ended otherwise, we feel, and the shock of
watching the man and woman ruin what they might have
had is poignant enough in itself. More poignant still
if we have been convinced that in these lives Lawrence
has discovered a law of contradictions that lies near
the heart of all attempts to approach another human
being in sexual love.

Questions

1. Discuss the significance of the wartime setting
and its effect on the roles and attitudes of women.

2. What are the probabilities that Annie and John
Thomas would have become intimate if they had not met
by accident at the Fair?

3. We are told that John Thomas "hated intelligent
interest." Does such interest necessarily equate with
"possessiveness"?

4. How does Annie get what she wants? Does she get
what she deserves?

5. What is the tone of the story? What devices
contribute to the tone?

6. Could the events described in this story take
place today in any environment you are familiar with?

See Also "Questions for Comparing the Author's
Stories," p. 143 of this *Handbook*.

D. H. Lawrence *The Horse Dealer's Daughter* (p. 815)
(Shorter Edition, p. 337)

The story opens at a moment of business and family
crisis. The three brothers who have failed in the
business passed on to them from their father are
"frightened at the collapse of their lives, and the
sense of disaster in which they were involved left them
no inner freedom." We are told with considerable eloquence in the author's language about their feelings
and their intents. Using the omniscient point of view,
he says about Joe that "he was not master of the situations of life." So we know pretty well that the young
men will accept the loss of their independence and do
whatever they must for mere survival before we get any
inkling of how the sister will respond to the misfortune she shares with them.

The author switches from limited omniscience to a
strictly objective and dramatic presentation as he begins to give her a central place in the story and to
hint that she means to ignore stubbornly the problems
that have now risen. "Well, what in the name of fortune
are you going to do?" one of her exasperated brothers
demands. She does not answer, and he explains to their
visiting friend the doctor, "You could bray her to bits,

and that's all you'd get out of her." The doctor, who is
not much concerned with Mabel Pervin at this point,
merely smiles at this turn in the family bickering.   But
by now the central issue of the story has become what
Mabel will do.

Again there is a shift to limited omniscience as we
are told about Mabel. Mabel is not going to do anything.
She is not going to think about what she might do or
ought to do now. "Mindless and persistent, she endured
from day to day. Why should she think? Why should she
answer anybody. . . . Mindless and persistent, she
seemed in a sort of ecstasy to be coming nearer to her
fulfillment, her own glorification, approaching her dead
mother, who was glorified." The language which declares
the state of her soul is gloomily lyrical, not so much
analytical as evocative. The author, who is skeptical,
anyhow, of the importance of reason, simply omits any
attempt at rational analysis of her motives for silence.
He says she is groping for contact with major reality
and "the life she followed here in the world was far
less real than the world of death she inherited from her
mother." She is intent on death—but no statement is
ever made that she intends to commit suicide. What is
happening in her is happening mindlessly.

Now the fluid point of view switches to that of the
doctor, where it will remain (with some intrusions of
authorial lyricism and omniscience) to the end.   In a
dark landscape, far off he sees a figure whom he barely
identifies as Mabel. (By this device the author is
taking pains to minimize the interest or concern of
person with person in a climax where personality will
count for very little.) When the doctor sees her wade
into the cold, dead pond, of course he rushes to save
her. It is the decent, humane, and practical thing to
do, quite consistent with his ideas of duty.

But what happens to him in the pond where he is almost lost along with the unconscious girl happens without any respect for ideas of duty or any other ideas of
any sort. A transformation takes place that brings them
into a confrontation where he is merely and entirely
male, she merely and entirely female.

After carrying her back to her house, he strips her
naked. No real matter that he does so for the practical
purpose of restoring her to health after her brush with
death. The insuperable fact remains—he undressed her
and looked on her nakedness. She asks the perfectly
natural (but unthinkable, absurd) question: "Do you
love me then?"

The earlier parts of the story have prepared us to understand that she is not playing a trick by asking this. It is completely out of her character to try subtle maneuvers to trap him. The primitive (and surely Lawrence would say the best) part of her has been exposed by her ordeal, and surely it is the shock of this exposure that strips away the young doctor's resistances. She shuffles to embrace him, "clutching him with convulsive certainty . . . as she looked up at him with flaring, humble eyes of transfiguration, triumphant in first possession." He has nothing to oppose against the certainty she has attained.

"He never intended to love her. But now it was over. He had crossed over the gulf to her, and all that he had left behind had shriveled and become void." For fuller and more reliable definitions of the "gulf" and the "all" that the doctor has now abandoned we might look to the whole bulk of Lawrence's writing and thought. The gulf is the false education and civilized manners that separate people from their natural lives. The doctor has given up the superficial definitions of himself as doctor and man, has allowed himself to be redefined (or transfigured) as a primarily physical being. He can know himself truly by his response to the woman and her offer of physical love.

Quickly enough the doctor realizes that in spite of the transfiguration he must go on living in a world that has not been transfigured. "How they would all jeer if they knew! It was agony to him to think they might know." He and the woman may have been reborn in their struggle to come out of the muddy pond alive. It will be terribly hard to hold on to their new lives. Yet the note of the end implies that they mean to cling as well as they can.

If this story does not seem paradoxical to must students, it will mean they are not getting it at all. It is paradoxical that love could be born so contrarily to the intents of the personalities involved. The paradox, at any rate, is only a little more difficult than that in Chekhov's *The Lady with the Pet Dog*, and it might be a good idea to pair the two stories for discussion.

Questions

1. What value does Lawrence seem to place on personality, rational intentions, and civilized ideas of duty?

2. How has the point of view been adapted to the requirements of the material? Couldn't everything essential have been told from Fergusson's point of view?

3. What is the prevailing mood of the story? How
much of this is contributed by the language and the
descriptive passages?

4. Does Mabel purposely misconstrue Fergusson's
motives in undressing her? Does she understand them
better than he does? If you think she does, what gives
her this ability?

5. Is Lawrence trying to picture eccentric characters and a freakish turn of events, or is he trying to
say something that is universally true about men, women,
and love?

6. Does the story struggle against our commonsense
views of reality? In what parts or details?

See also "Questions for Comparing the Author's
Stories," p. 143 of this *Handbook*.

Further Reading

Junkins, Donald. "D. H. Lawrence's 'The Horse Dealer's
    Daughter,'" *Studies in Short Fiction*, VI (Winter
    1969), 210-212.
Phillips, Steven R. "The Double Pattern of D. H.
    Lawrence's 'The Horse Dealer's Daughter,'" *Studies
    in Short Fiction*, 10 (1973), 94-97.

D. H. Lawrence   *The Rocking-Horse Winner* (p. 829)
                 (Shorter Edition, p. 351)

There can hardly be a student who does not recognize
from his own family experience the motivating situation
in this story. *"There must be more money!   There must
be more money!"* This is what children of the modern
world hear from their parents, either aloud or by implication. Either incessantly or on those heartrending
occasions when families are welded together by threats
and trials. Outside the family circle, in academic,
occupational, social, and political groups the anxious
cry is the same. "There must be more money." It is the
fundamental commandment of the modern world—the perverted faith which Lawrence considered to be the worst

poison in modern life. Verging into fantasy from a
realistic initial picture of Paul's family, Lawrence
has written a didactic allegory with a reasonably plain
moral: The wages of the passion for money is death.

The first dialogue shows the mother and son wrestling with a definition of luck. The mother firmly defines it as "what causes you to have money." Paul says,
"I'm a lucky person." We must read this as a declaration
of initial innocence. He is expressing a generalized
childish confidence in himself and life—a confidence
that need not have been fixated as a determination to
get money at any cost except for the mother's perversion
of it. Paul loves his mother and takes her word for
what luck means. The tragedy follows from that.

There is some irreducible difficulty in interpreting
the allegorical significance of the rocking horse itself. Perhaps we can handle it sufficiently with a
"that which" definition. The toy horse is that which
will take the boy "to where there is luck." The horse
might stand for a career in business, the arts, politics
—any of the fields in which the child of the modern
world can gain money if he commits himself to it wildly
and furiously, as Paul does to the riding of his horse.
(After all, the rocking horse of the story is an ap-
proximate synonym of the "hobby horse" which in popular
idiom stands for whatever vehicle people may choose to
pursue success.)

The declaration that Paul has achieved a supernatural
clairvoyance rises out of a perfectly naturalistic conversation among Paul, his mother, and his Uncle Oscar.
"Well, I got there!" Paul says and utters the name of
the horse that won a major race last week. This first
announcement could be taken as the delusion of an over-
excited child. He could have learned the horse's name
from his talks with the gardener. Paul's certainty that
Daffodil will be the winner in the Lincoln—plus the
revelation that he has already won a large sum from
betting on the horses—could still be explained as a
matter of chance, however unusual.

The first major complication of the plot comes when
Paul's mother receives notice, on her birthday, of the
money that she supposes came to her as an inheritance.
Instead of being relieved by this "luck," she simply
wants more. The "whispering" in the house which has so
tormented Paul "suddenly went mad." The acquisition of
money has set loose the mad desire for "more money."
As in a fairy tale, the granting of a wish has had an

unanticipated adverse effect. "It frightened Paul
terribly."

The last section is built on suspense as to whether
Paul can be sure which horse will win in the forth-
coming Derby. It should also be noted that here, for
the first time, the mother's anxiety begins to build.
The point of the story could not be made if the
mother's love for her child were not established. When
Paul falls from his horse, "all her tormented motherhood" floods upon her as she rushes to gather him up.

It is the uncle who, in the last paragraph, pronounces the moral of the story, which may be translated:
Life dominated by the quest for money is not worth
living.

This story, much more than the two others in this
anthology, shows Lawrence as moralist and preacher. For
other examples of his diatribes against the money madness of twentieth-century civilization, look particularly in the volumes of poems called *Pansies* and *More
Pansies*.

Questions

1. What does the rocking horse represent? Is it
significant that at one point it is called a "shining
modern" rocking horse?

2. Why isn't the mother pleased by her birthday
present? Discuss her character and her relation to her
son.

3. What is Uncle Oscar's role in the story? Is his
last comment cynical?

4. How do you interpret the "whispering" of the
house? Is this a reference to something supernatural?

5. The story brings into conflict different meanings
of luck. Discuss.

6. What is the moral of the story? Is the moral more
prominent and important than in other stories you have
read in this text?

See also "Questions for Comparing the Author's
Stories," p. 143 of this *Handbook*.

Further Reading

Beauchamp, Gorman. "Lawrence's 'The Rocking-Horse
    Winner,'" *The Explicator*, 31 (1973), Item 32.

Bloom, Edward A., and Lillian D. *The Variety of Fiction*, pp. 374-377.

Cowan, S. A. "Lawrence's 'The Rocking-Horse Winner,'" *The Explicator*, XXVII (October 1968), Item 9.

Marks, W. S., III. "The Psychology of the Uncanny in Lawrence's 'The Rocking-Horse Winner,'" *Modern Fiction Studies*, XI (Winter 1965-1966), 381-392.

Snodgrass, W. D. "A Rocking-Horse: The Symbol, the Pattern, the Way to Live," *Hudson Review*, XI (Summer 1958), 191-200.

D. H. Lawrence—
Questions for Comparing the Author's Stories

1. Compare the essential motivations in *The Horse Dealer's Daughter* with those in *Tickets, Please*. Is Mabel or Annie more uncertain of what she really wants?

2. Compare tone and use of author's voice in all three Lawrence stories.

3. Compare varying degrees of realism in the three stories.

4. Compare the themes of *The Horse Dealer's Daughter* and *Tickets, Please*.

Stephen Leacock *The Marine Excursion of the Knights of Pythias* (p. 842)

This is hardly fiction at all in the usual sense. Rather, it is one of those warm, delightful exceptions on the borderline where fiction verges over into mirthful reminiscence. There is no central character on whom the action focuses. In fact, such action as there is— the sinking of the Mariposa Belle—turns out to be a commonplace occurrence, the present instance serving little more than to stir up fond recollections of the quality of life on and around Lake Wissanotti. Perhaps it is even a little off the mark to speak of the person recounting the day's events as a narrator. He has no discernible involvement in the excursion and handles character and event as if they were mere color to brighten his exposition of a time and place and happy way of life.

Probably it is not very important how we label it— though to point out the ways in which it diverges from the mainstream of fiction might help clarify for students just what we expect from fiction that is not present in other admirable forms of writing. To consider it as fundamentally reminiscence—a nostalgia piece—permits an emphasis on the author's attitude toward the material and the unifying tone that emerges from devices exploited to express that attitude. There can be little doubt about the author's fondness for the scene and its inhabitants. It is a fondness flavored with astonishment at the incongruity of the heroic (not to say overblown) pomp and solemnity of the excursion and the literal commonplace of the circumstances. The tongue-in-cheek fanfare of the opening passage is indeed a mockery of the great expectations of the excursionists. They are not, after all, setting off to find a new world, but only going for a day's outing on the water. But this mockery of their ceremonial preparations turns out quickly enough to be the kind of joshing derision we direct at people and customs dear to us, an easily decipherable inversion of actual feelings.

The manipulation by which suspense is built about the fate of the sinking boat—before we learn there is neither real danger nor even much novelty in such an occurrence—has the same effect of belittling the fuss it occasions. The perils of the sea? Not at all. Just an additional fringe of entertainment to round out the day of recreation, a touch of spice thrown in when the revelers have grown drowsy from playing in the sun. Of course this belittlement staged by the author is not really intended to ridicule the adventure of the day, only to reveal that in its modest scope there is something as wholesome and precious as it is lacking in heroic scale. The whole is an exercise in rhetorical somersaults undertaken to celebrate the richness of common life, the author's affections for the foibles that are part of it.

Questions

1. Why is no single character given a central role in the action?
2. What is the narrator's relation to the community? His attitude toward it?
3. Why is the reader led to expect the excursion will end in catastrophe?
4. How does the author manipulate the tone of the

story for comic effect? Analyze a few of his devices.

5. Discuss the story as a tribute to a particular way of life.

Further Reading

Cameron, D. A. "The Enchanted Houses: Leacock's Irony," *Canadian Literature*, Winter 1965, 31-44.

Ursula K. Le Guin   *The Ones Who Walk Away from Omelas*
(p. 856)
(Shorter Edition, p. 364)

As the subtitle suggests, this story recapitulates a riddle of the ethical life proposed by William James. Here is James's formulation: ". . . if the hypothesis were offered to us of a world in which . . . utopias should all be outdone, and millions kept permanently happy on the one simple condition that a certain lost soul on the far-off edge of things should lead a life of lonely torment, what except a specific and independent sort of emotion can it be which would make us immediately feel, even though an impulse arose within us to clutch at the happiness so offered, how hideous a thing would be its enjoyment when deliberately accepted as the fruit of such a bargain" (from his essay "The Moral Philosopher and the Moral Life").

In discussing this story it is obviously appropriate to concentrate on the quandary in its starkest form, with an eye for what has been added by its reconstruction in fiction. We note, first, a fundamental limitation: A uniformly happy human society is impossible to imagine. All Utopian visions are incomplete because the contradictions of mortal life are irreconcilable; there are compensating miseries for all joys. This insuperable limitation no doubt accounts for the deliberate vagueness Le Guin chooses in commenting on the patterns and satisfactions of life in Omelas. She is understandably reluctant to try her hand where so many others have failed in trying to render Utopia credibly.

Second, we all know that in every moment of the time in which we are engaged in "the pursuit of happiness," all around us are innumerable children and humans no longer children who have been condemned to perpetual

torment and frustrations of some degree of brutality.
Yet we, as individuals or as a social group, did not
directly or voluntarily choose the formulas that have
condemned them. In a word, we did not design or create
the human condition. We all share, in one degree or
another, the general fate of the most pitiable suf-
ferers. There is not, really, a chance for exemption on
any conditions.

So the conditional nature of the bargain here considered does not apply directly to life as we can know
it. Yet, because we know we accept the fruits of wide-
scale suffering and injustice, we can never completely
escape the shadow of the dreadful enigma posed by our
acceptance of a fractional happiness in a world where
undeserved suffering continues. Does not our mere acceptance of joy represent a voluntary complicity in
this cosmic crime? All sensitive people must be haunted
from time to time with a suspicion that they have
bought a share of happiness by averting their minds
and eyes from the conditions on which it is based, by a
refusal to confront the philosophical enigma James
postulated.

There is, of course, a traditional Christian answer
to this enigma. In Heaven suffering and injustice will
be compensated and the sins of complicity will be
judged and forgiven the contrite sinner. But James and
the author of this story have posed the problem in the
language of secular humanism. Therefore, just as the
picture of the Utopian "city of happiness" must of
necessity be left hazy and incomplete, the author must
refuse to name the destination of those imaginary characters who reject the bargain and walk into the darkness
outside the city. Even the idea that they have a destination is a figurative one, and the indeterminate word
place is an unresolvable metaphor. The imagination of
the reader has been guided to the feeling and belief
that the bargain on which Omelas is founded is an unac-
ceptable one. After such preparation the author has left
it to the reader to choose—by faith, since there can be
no other authority—whether those who walk away have
any alternative except extinction.

Questions

1. Comment on the narrator's assertion that happiness
"is based on a just discrimination of what is necessary."
2. Why is the narrator so uncertain about what Omelas

looks like and the kind of technology it depends on?
Why so tentative about describing the qualities of a
happy community life?

3. Why does the presence of the tormented child and
the attitude of the citizens toward it make the imaginary picture of Omelas more believable?

4. Is the narrator correct in saying "we have a bad
habit . . . of considering happiness as something
rather stupid"?

5. Why is the destination of those who reject Omelas
and walk away "even less imaginable than the city of
happiness"? Can you give a name to this other place?

Further Reading

Jameson, Fredric. "World Reduction in Le Guin: The
    Emergence of Utopian Narrative," *Science-Fiction
    Studies*, 2 (November 1975), 221-230.
Levin, Jeff. "Ursula K. Le Guin: A Select Bibliography,"
    Science-Fiction Studies, 2 (November 1975), 204-208.

Doris Lessing   *To Room Nineteen* (p. 862)
                (Shorter Edition, p. 370)

In the majority of short stories, motivation tends
to be handled rather simply, the success of the design
depending on decisive triggering events presented with
stark simplicity or implied as a moment of confluence
of irresistably determining forces. Rarely does the instructor find a better occasion than is presented here
to examine and discuss the diffuse and indistinct
strands of motivation that may, indeed, be more powerfully operative in most lives than the impact of challenges in crisis situations.

Because of the long span of time evenly observed and
the detached, generalized manner in which the story is
told, it has some of the effect we tend to associate
more with novels than with short stories. The movement
toward the climax of Susan's total abdication and suicide is glacial in its almost imperceptible advance. At
the end, when she feels it doesn't matter whether her
husband will presently marry one woman or another, she
appears to have reached the point where nothing
matters. Turning back from this point to reflect on

what brought her to such a conclusion, the reader is
aware of the great difficulty of defining any particulars or even patterns in her life that "mattered" decisively in draining her will to live.

She has married for love. Her husband is understanding, concerned, unfailingly sympathetic up to the
point that could be reasonably expected, and their com-
patibility is so heavily stressed that we may conclude
the author meant to show the inadequacy of even an ideal
marriage when pitted against the quiet erosions of time.

It may indeed be the point of the story that the
irony of time brings the most favored of mortals to a
realization that all which has appeared to matter—to
make a difference—has been misconstrued by the vanity
of the illusions with which we all start out. The core
of life is a vast emptiness, and even to call it tragic
is to project significance on circumstances whose in-
significance Susan has come to realize. Put this way we
may interpret the outcome as a sort of Schopenhauerian
surrender of the will, and therefore as the achievement
of a type of blessedness beyond the torment of life's
illusions.

But I suspect most students will feel that her life
and its termination are tragic and will almost instinctively try to discern a pattern of causality—i.e.,
will look for susceptibilities in her character and the
motivating turns of events which in their cumulative
effect brought her to despair and death. Some students,
indeed, may try to shortcut this search by a facile explanation that she came to her unhappy end "because she
was a woman," but such a formula is insufficient for
either feminists or antifeminists. At best it evades
the question of whether all women do or must come out
where Susan does—and the fairly obvious response that
they do not.

Even for those who sense that Susan's fate is
typical, hers is a peculiar type, and the progress detailed by the unfolding account of her marriage must
somehow reveal the forces which, ever so slowly, overcome her. Even though the plot line may be obscure,
without those decisive milestones or changes of fortune
by which we habitually identify plot in the midst of
other elements, students should be encouraged to trace
it as imaginatively as they can.

They may be pointed in the right direction by asking
them to consider the adequacy of foresight and realism
to the conduct of a marriage relationship. From the
beginning of the story Lessing highlights these virtues

in both Susan and Matthew, and there is hardly a time when either falls short on such counts. But this may be the author's way of signaling that a disproportionate reliance on foresight and realism can stifle some essential spontaneity. Following from such a hypothesis of original sin or initial flaw, one may see how in each phase of their married life the apparent success is purchased by a further surrender of spontaneity. The foresight which helps them avoid risks ends by narrowing the options in successive increments, so that finally even the remaining options for risk are insufficiently attractive to sustain Susan's appetite for life, and she dies of a sort of spiritual malnutrition. But whatever conclusions are ventured in class discussion, it would seem fair to remind all concerned they cannot quite dispel the ingredient of mystery in the story. Nor should they be expected to. It is the irreducible remnant of mystery that stirs the imagination with intimations of dread at the spectacle of such gradual decline and loss.

Questions

1. Interpret the first sentence in the light of the story as a whole. What ambiguities lie in the words "a failure of intelligence"?

2. Is one partner more to blame than the other for the disappointments of married life? Explain.

3. Does the author seem to favor or oppose any person or social pattern depicted here?

4. Are the husband's adulteries truly decisive in determining the outcome? The timing of the adulteries or his explanation of them?

5. Is there any decisive event in Susan's life or flaw in her character which motivates her to commit suicide?

Further Reading

Brewster, Dorothy. *Doris Lessing*. New York: Twyane, 1965, 94-95.

Gindin, James. "Weary Wives and Lovers," *Saturday Review*, 46 (November 23, 1963), 42.

Markow, Alice B. "The Pathology of Feminine Failure in the Fiction of Doris Lessing," *Critique*, 16 (1974), 95-96.

Carson McCullers   *The Jockey* (p. 890)
                   (Shorter Edition, p. 397)

Very small in scale, hardly more than a vignette,
this story depends for its effect very largely on the
precision with which the author has evoked the milieu.
The single scene is a plush dining room whose luxury
makes an odd—though common—accompaniment to the
physical sport of horse racing. The setting, then,
displays the paradox of professional sports in our
society, the paradoxical association of discipline in
conjunction with indulgence, dissipation, and sensual-
ism. The characters seem chosen to emphasize and, as
it were, personify the discordant elements in this
paradox. The men gorging themselves at the dining
table unattractively represent a type of mindless glut-
tony. The jockey, on the other hand, by temperament as
well as the necessary discipline of his occupation,
seems almost an allegorical figure of asceticism. It
is very interesting that no attempt is made to equate
his asceticism with virtue. The jockey is no more
attractive than the gluttonous diners. He is narrow,
almost pathologically venomous, and as preoccupied with
his resentments as they are with their bellies. His
"dandified courtesy" has no tinge of warmth to it, and
his infantile gesture of spitting half-chewed food on
the floor adds no dignity to the reproaches he levels
at the other men. The confrontation raises no moral
issues—this is merely a matter of the pot calling the
kettle black—but the elegant artistry of observation
wrings from the milieu under scrutiny a certain glamor
of depravity.

Questions

1. What is the tone of this story? How is it
established?
2. In what ways is the jockey's manner of speaking
in keeping with his appearance and his occupation?
3. What accounts for his hysterical hatred of the
three men dining?
4. How does the jockey represent all people set
apart by abnormality or duty?
5. Does the story have any real resolution? Is
there any suggestion of what will happen in the future?
Explain.

James Alan McPherson *Gold Coast* (p. 894)

The developments of action and the changes in Rob
come so quietly they are almost imperceptible. There
appear to be no major events serving as hinges on which
the inward changes pivot—unless the breakup with Jean
is one, and that circumstance is presented so quietly,
offhandedly and with so little explanation that it, too,
seems to make hardly a ripple in the even progress of a
season in Rob's life. The withering changes are handled
so as to be almost as unobtrusive as the calendar
changes marking the passage of summer and arrival of
autumn. Yet the effect of change is felt powerfully,
coloring the end with a sober gloom quite different from
the air of youthful self-confidence that marked the
opening.

For all the attention paid to old Sullivan, his wife,
his dog, his opinions and his pathetic aging, we must
understand that Rob is the central character. What happens to him gives point and unity to the story. To sum
up the overall course of action, we might say that his
pity for the old man makes him vulnerable to a subtle
contagion and that in a figurative sense he has been
afflicted by age, has aged himself immeasurably in a
stunningly brief period. His initial, reckless confidence in his immunity to the contagion carried and
almost personified by Sullivan is the flaw which, as it
were, prematurely traps him in the incapacitating
knowledge of the fatal and inexorable processes he
shares with the beaten older man.

Thus in considering the whole scope of the action,
we will probably conclude that the loss of his precious
and promising relationship with the girl is hardly even
a decisive milestone in a progress to despair, but that
it is a foreshadowing parallel setting the pattern for
what is to come.

The affair with Jean is never presented as perfect.
Jean is ominously proprietary and Rob recognizes in
himself "a great deal of latent hostility" toward her.
But while the temper and mood of the summer remain up-
beat, there is no recognition—no compulsion to recognize—that these deficiencies need spoil the very many
pleasant, brave and hopeful things they share. "In
those days I had forgotten that I was first of all a
black," Rob says. There is a very low-key but nevertheless grim irony in the form of this statement, implying
as it does a later recognition that however he might
wish in youthful euphoria to imagine other aspects of

his being are preeminent, yet, when he is reminded by
time and observation of implacable realities, his black-
ness is the first of his conditioning circumstances.
And from the beginning Sullivan stands there as a re-
minder of those fatal boundaries he has been able,
briefly, to forget.

The reasons for the break with Jean are presented so
obliquely and elliptically that many readers will have
a sense of having been denied something that might well
deserve a more detailed and explanatory dramatization.
We are told that between the hating eyes of white and
black people on the two sides of the subway car, "We
aged . . . and there was nothing left to say." One's
imagination is almost compelled to expand such cryptic
brevity, to envision actions and speech moving toward
the decision to part.

But perhaps everything essential for the functioning
of this element in the whole story is contained in the
laconic words "We aged"—for the underlying subject
McPherson has engaged is the disarray and disenchantment
of aging. Because the true meaning of aging is by nature
so diffuse and hard to state with precision, its significance is best summed up by the emblematic loss of a
lover and the ephemeral hope that thrives until love is
exhausted.

Thus the relationship of Rob and Jean is set into
the story as a kind of touchstone or miniaturized abstraction of all the dreary wisdom Rob takes on too fast
from contemplating Sullivan's bondage and disintegration.

Questions

1. What is the difference between Rob's state of mind
at the beginning and end of the story?

2. What worth is there in Jean's warning to Rob to
give less of himself to Sullivan?

3. What does the story say about the wisdom acquired
by aging?

4. How does Rob's loss of Jean fit into the general
action and meaning of the story?

5. Why does Rob tend to ally himself more with
Sullivan than with the tenants of the building?

6. What does the last paragraph say about Rob's adjustment after the summer in which the main action takes
place?

Bernard Malamud   *The Jewbird* (p. 912)
                   (Shorter Edition, p. 402)

Malamud's master stroke is to transform the stock
character of the poor, dependent relative into a bird.
The poor relation is always a misfit in the family
obliged to take him in, a tax on the charity of his
hosts, something of a nuisance even in his attempts to
pay his own way with small chores. By borrowing from the
devices of the comic strip and cartooning the misfit in
the form of the bird, the author has cut economically to
the heart of the problem, defining it very precisely as
a test of charity for a family group already under pressure from the demands of practical problems and the
competitive routines of daily life.

Of course the bird, Schwartz, is not literally a
relative of the Cohens—he is not literally anything;
he is a symbol created by the author's imagination sent
forth to find his place in ours. But he has been given
mannerisms and characteristic speech patterns—plus a
certain corrosive wit—that incline us to identify him
as an elderly Jew who might well be an immigrant uncle
of the frozen food salesman Cohen. Cohen and his wife
and child have the opportunity and responsibility of
showing what they are made of by their response to the
intruder. Schwartz is only a bird—if that is the way
he is considered. Only a burden if Cohen chooses to
see him so. Cohen makes that choice, fails the test,
misses the opportunity of being either charitable or
just and therefore deserves to be classed by his wife
as one among the Anti-Semites.

Questions

1. Though Schwartz is identified as a bird, he seems
to have a very human personality and a specific role in
relation to the Cohen family. Define his personality
and his role.

2. What is the most important problem he poses for
the Cohens? What are the conflicts within the Cohen
family?

3. Does Schwartz convincingly establish his Jewishness by praying with passion? What does the story say
about the essence of Jewishness?

4. How might Mr. Cohen justify his treatment of the
bird if he were telling the story?

5. To what extent does the story make use of the
devices of a cartoonist?

Thomas Mann *Disorder and Early Sorrow* (p. 920)
(Shorter Edition, p. 409)

The setting is a professor's house in Germany during
the inflation that followed World War I.   The milieu is
characterized by uncertainty of values, a displacement
of habitual roles, and an intellectual chaos in which
mismatched things are flung together in temporary combinations. The story is told in the present tense, perhaps
to emphasize its fleeting contemporaneity. Though the
manner is undeviatingly realistic, it shows some aspects
of allegory. If the characters were not invented to meet
the needs of allegory, still the way they are depicted
and referred to tends to emphasize what is allegorically
representative about them as well as what is individual
—thus Fraülein Plaichinger is tagged as a complacent
worldling, while Ellie is an elfin child, all too pre-
cariously committed to life.

Though Professor Cornelius's family remains an
affectionate one—even a tightly knit one by present
American standards—the surrounding disorders have mani-
fested themselves within its structure. The Professor
would like to see himself as one who continues the
stable traditions of academic humanism, and he consci-
entiously perpetuates the social customs of the middle
class. But beneath his bourgeois exterior he has responded to the postwar chaos with a reactionary escape
into the past, using his academic discipline—history—
as a sort of smokescreen to cover the truth that he
wants to hide himself among the dead who are the subject
of history. More than this, his extravagant love for his
five-year-old daughter is morbidly intermingled, if not
equated, with his antipathy for the present, his
yearning for death, which is "the root of all godliness
and abiding significance." Paradoxical as it may be, his
"devotion to this priceless little morsel of life and
new growth [Ellie] has something to do with death, it
clings to death as against life. . . ."

Such tentative equations of love with death-longing
are typical of Mann—as in *The Magic Mountain* or *Death
in Venice*—but since all speculation on such matters
tends to become abstruse when it is discussed apart from
a text, it might be well to concentrate in class on an
examination of the large paragraph in which the author
traces Cornelius's complex feelings. The paragraph
begins, "But he understood more. He knows, does Dr.
Cornelius, that there is something not quite right about
his feeling. . . ." The civilized part of his mind is

committed to preserving and protecting his child, while
an imperative subconscious wish moves in the other direction, intent on securing her a place in the timeless-
ness of death. Without a good grasp on the conflict
articulated in this paragraph the student is apt to be
more mystified than necessary by the rest of the story.

Though the Professor does not like the music favored
by his children's guests and finds their dancing unin-
terpretable, yet his feelings toward this "unhistoric"
dance of the present are tolerant enough until his
adored Ellie gets carried away by her admiration for
Max Hergesell and grotesquely tries to take him away
from the plump Fraülein Plaichinger. We must suppose
that the Professor is embarrassed by his little daughter's actions, but "uppermost in his heart is hatred
for this party, with its power to intoxicate and es-
trange his darling child." That his hatred is partly
compounded of a jealousy he must not concede only makes
it a more potent ingredient of the explosive combination
being brewed. Even in his own consciousness his hate for
Max Hergesell as rival must be covered over by his rational approval of Hergesell as a "fine lad." He must be
grateful and display gratitude to the young man for
coming to Ellie's room to comfort her in the anguish of
her disappointment.

It is this irremediable disorder in his own feelings
—as in Ellie's—that gives the story its larger dimensions. It is not immensely important that a five-year-
old girl should have lost control of her feelings under
the stimulations of a single evening. She will of course
get over her disappointment. "Tomorrow, beyond all
doubt, young Hegersell will be a pale shadow, powerless
to darken her little heart."

Nevertheless, what has happened to the child is
prophetic and premonitory. "Ellie's suffering is without help or healing . . . just as it is without understanding, so it is also without restraint—and that is
what makes it so horribly painful." Horribly painful
to those, like the Professor, who understand the child
has stumbled on one of the grimmest formulas of life
and that it will be repeated on a larger scale everywhere and forever. The small disorder within the Professor's house is a foreboding premonition of what
Germany—and the modern world—have to undergo. The
protective limits of decorum and of reason itself have
shown how flimsy they are. Like Humpty Dumpty, the Professor's confidence in rational humanism has tumbled
from the wall.

In making a warranted allegorical interpretation of
this story we might well begin by taking Professor
Cornelius as representative of those who believed that
the "Germanic ideal of freedom and individual liberty"
might prevail in Germany after the time of the story—
and developing from Cornelius's premonitions the
pattern of subsequent German (or world) history. The
thematic statement here is close to the beginning lines
of Yeats's *Second Coming:*

> Things fall apart; the center cannot hold;
> Mere anarchy is loosed upon the world. . . .

Questions

1. What special effect is achieved by telling this
story in the present tense? Does this effect have anything to do with the subject and theme?

2. In what sense is there something "not quite
right" about the professor's feeling for his daughter
Ellie? What is not quite right in his feeling about
the subject he teaches? Does the author mean that he is
a bad professor or a bad father?

3. How important to the developing action of the
story are the symptoms of disorder caused by the postwar German inflation? Is the conflict symptomatic of a
general modern crisis?

4. Does the professor over-interpret what is going
on during the party? Does the trouble come simply from
his over-interpretation of inconsequential frictions
and disorders that in themselves are all within the
limits of normality? Since Ellie is certainly not going
to die from her heartbreak, does it make sense to say
that "after all, the effect is the same" as if she were?

5. The atmosphere of the party is called "fatal."
The word as it is used here probably means that fate is
more than usually discernible in the character and
events in the party. In what ways is the party, then,
prophetic of things to come?

Katherine Mansfield   *The Garden Party* (p. 946)

Not infrequently the design of a story can be compre-
hended best by looking back from the moment of resolution. That moment comes in *The Garden Party* when Laura

looks at the face of the dead carter and—surprisingly
—sees him lying there in enviable happiness. While she
and her family and friends at the garden party "were
laughing, and while the band was playing, this marvel
had come to the lane. Happy . . . happy . . ." Confused by this unforeseen "marvel," Laura can only sob,
"Forgive my hat."

Looking back from this moment of confusion and illumination, we see the structure of preparation the
author has made for it from the beginning. First, Laura
is established as a sensitized observer at the center
of the not very important bustle preceding the party.
On the verge of maturity, this girl is ready to take
the imprint of whatever new experience may be thrust on
her by life as, for example, her opinionated mother and
her sister Jose are not. Laura finds her attitudes and
her self changing when she deals with the working men
who have come to set up the marquee for the party. One
of them plucks and smells a sprig of lavender and she
asks herself, "How many men she knew would have done
such a thing?" The warmth among the workmen entices her
away from the social conventions that wall her world.
"She would get on much better with men like these."

Depending little on plot, Mansfield continues to
pattern the story on contrasts between the manners and
circumstances of Laura's family and the life style of
their lower-class neighbors, including the man who dies
—by sheer coincidence—on the day of the party. When
Laura learns of that death, she finds no echo of her
own emotions from her sister or her mother. Her mother,
in fact, chokes off Laura's attempt to acknowledge these
emotions by popping a smart hat on her head, the hat
serving as a symbol of those fripperies that are to be
given precedence over the realities of death. Laura is
by no means yet immune to the authority of her mother's
code, reinforced from within by Laura's conditioning
and natural vanity. When she sees a mirror image of herself in the hat, her previous "extravagant" response to
the news of death is effectively suppressed. "Is mother
right? she thought. And now she hoped her mother was
right."

Yet, because Laura has been prepared for major revelations by her impulses, the trivial errand of carrying
scraps from the party to the dead man's house becomes
an immense journey beyond the boundaries her mother has
set for her. Laura's feeling that she is making a
"mistake" by coming on this errand turns out to be a
thinly disguised apprehension of the knowledge that she

can never truly return to the shelter of the artificial world where hats, "tinkling spoons, laughter [and] the smell of crushed grass" are supreme values. Seeing that these things matter not at all to the dead man, she is smitten with the realization that they can't mean much to her. The incoherence of her statement to her brother Laurie is not at all opaque, since we have been fully shown what she leaves unsaid.

The story is fully dramatized. The author immerses herself completely in Laura's point of view, depending on the natural unfolding of events to deliver the thematic statement. The surface dialogue might easily have been overweighted by the burden of information it must carry if it were not so gracefully managed and artfully broken up into fragments of natural speech.

Questions

1. How have the events of the day changed Laura? Would the same experience have affected her sisters in the same way?
2. Why is the point of view confined so closely to Laura's impressions?
3. Why is the class structure used in the design of the story?
4. Examine the use of minor characters in the development of Laura's awareness. Are all of them useful in directing her attitudes? Are any of them in serious conflict with her?
5. How is Laura surprised by what she sees in the dead man's house? Can you definitely label the change that comes over her?

Further Reading

Robinson, Fred C. "Mansfield's 'The Garden Party,'" *The Explicator*, XXIV (April 1966), Item 66.

W. Somerset Maugham *The Outstation* (p. 958)

This story is built solidly on the conflict between characters who typify the strengths and weaknesses, the values and attitudes of their class background. As the conflict moves to a showdown neither man ever steps out of the character given him by the forces he represents. Warburton embodies the manners and attitudes that go with a life of privilege.   Cooper is a product of the pragmatic, energetic lower classes who assumed a dominant role following the upheavals of the First World War.   "Well, at all events the war has done one good thing for us," Cooper says. "It's smashed up the power of the aristocracy."   Warburton does not disagree—he simply laments what Cooper proclaims with crude satisfaction.   The personal conflict between the two men is overshadowed by the conflict of the principles attributed to each.

Since the story is told from Warburton's point of view, he benefits from the sympathy we almost automatically give to the antagonist we understand most fully. Nevertheless Maugham has made sure that Warburton's snobbery, coldness, ludicrous mannerisms, and intellectual shortcomings are fully displayed. Since Cooper expresses some ugly prejudices, the issue is not finally which character we would like to <u>see</u> victorious as which one <u>will</u> come out on top.

It is testimony to Maugham's extreme skill as a craftsman that he does not seem to pull any tricks in giving the victory to the underdog. Warburton, true to the antiquated principles that have already cost him so much of what he valued in life, even warns Cooper that Abas may kill him—this warning given in spite of his hatred.

But it is just on this point of the warning that the smoothly jointed plot ought to be seized for discussion. It <u>appears</u>, at first glance, that Warburton gave the warning in good faith, in accordance with his duty as an English gentleman, with no regard to his own interest. But it may well be argued that though the <u>form</u> of duty has been scrupulously observed, in truth the warning is a trick played on the younger man. Perhaps Warburton understands the blind spot in Cooper's character that will make him refuse a warning from his enemy—and with ruthless cunning takes advantage of this weakness.

If this interpretation is accepted it will have consequences in our reading of the theme. Perhaps the author intends to say that though the Common Man (represented by Cooper) appears to be moving with the tide of history, the Elite (Warburton) will always come up with a trick to get the better of him. Discussion of this story might well be broadened into a consideration of global political maneuverings of our times.

Questions

1. List the qualities in the characters and attitudes of Warburton and Cooper that make each typical of
his class background. Does either ever step out of character?

2. If the chief concern of the story is the conflict
between English upper classes and the rising lower
classes, is it weakened or strengthened by setting it
far from England, in the jungle of Malaysia? Relate the
small-scale conflict between Warburton and Cooper to
the broad class struggle of modern times.

3. Why does Warburton warn Cooper that his life may
be in danger? Is Warburton acting in his own interest
when he gives the warning?

4. Interpret the last sentence as fully as you can.
What emotion—or mixture of emotions—on Warburton's
part prompts it?

5. When and for what reasons does the author shift
point of view?

Guy de Maupassant   *The Necklace* (p. 983)
                     (Shorter Edition, p. 436)

There is a surprise ending to this story. A certain
quantity of irony is neatly expressed by the revelation
in the last paragraph that the necklace had only a fraction of the value that we supposed, only a fraction of
the value that Mme Loisel paid in money and in hard work
to replace it. Such ironies as this are not very interesting—as surprise endings, in themselves, are not.

But in *The Necklace* the superficial irony is elegantly fitted into other ironies of much greater importance. For instance, when Mme Loisel had to face the
ordeal of poverty in order to redeem the loss of the
supposedly valuable necklace of her friend, she "took
her part . . . with heroism." Perhaps no other happening
in her bourgeois life could have thrust her into a
heroic role. It is ironic that what appears to be a
catastrophe should have had the result of ennobling her,
of making her existence more worthwhile. "How little a
thing is needed for us to be lost or saved!" But while
the necklace was lost, the woman was saved.

There is another, nastier, bit of irony hidden in
the surprise ending. We read that Mme Loisel "smiled

with a joy that was proud and naive at once" while she still assumes that the hard work and sacrifice of her life were necessary. But upon learning that these were unnecessary, she might well lose her joy. That is, the misfortune of truth might cancel out the hard-won bliss of ignorance—as is the case in Henry James's *The Tree of Knowledge.*

Approaching the story from another angle, we find it to be an interesting example of how a very short piece can deal with long stretches of time. The story covers a period of ten years in which major changes take place in the life of the central character. The episode of the loss and replacement of the jewels stands at the beginning of the chronology. The episode in which the revelation is made stands at the end. These two episodes may be visualized as being like the two pylons of a suspension bridge, on which the whole weight of the bridge hangs. The period of Mme Loisel's character transformation is given in very summary form between these two supporting episodes. Yet, summary as it may be, this part of the story may have the greatest import.

Questions

1. What might have been the quality of Mme Loisel's life if she had not lost the necklace?

2. What changes take place in her character during the ten years covered by the story? What irony is there in the kind of changes that take place?

3. To what extent is pride a consistent motive for the heroine?

4. What is the husband's character? Does he have much to do with the outcome of the story?

5. What effect do we expect from the revelation that the lost necklace was made of false stones? Does the story stop short of its natural ending?

6. What does the story tell us about the manners and values of the society in which it is set?

Herman Melville   *Bartleby the Scrivener* (p. 991)
(Shorter Edition, p. 443)

After forewarning us to expect the title character
to be the "strangest" example of his type, the narrator
characterizes himself as a representative of "prudence"
and "method." Thus prepared, we understand not only
that the basic arrangement of the story is to be an examination of eccentricity through the eyes of normal
conventionality but that some part of the conflict will
occur between the values that inhere in each of these
modes of life. The characterizations of Turkey,
Nippers, and Ginger Nut are preparations for the mismatched pairing of the narrator with Bartleby.

That simple comedy of a boss and his trying employees
is given a slight but disturbing twist as soon as
Bartleby crosses the threshold. A kind of hush falls on
the convivial interoffice amusement. At first glance the
narrator seems to recognize what he now must deal with
—"I can see that figure now—pallidly neat, pitiably
respectable, incurably forlorn." That is to say, the
recognition is correct. But what the narrator is not
prepared to guess at this point is how strongly the
incurable forlornness will tug at him, threatening his
presumptions of security, as he tries to keep Bartleby
from sinking. (Imagine a man in the security of a life-
boat, reaching his hand to another struggling in the
water alongside—and then finding that the man he wants
to help to safety has no will to be saved. Shall the
self-appointed savior hold on and be dragged from the
boat himself? At what point—and at what cost to his
image of himself—should he let go and allow the other
to drown? There you have an analogy to the basic situation on which Melville built.)

The discords in the superficial comedy increase
slowly enough. One of the amazing accomplishments of
the story design is that neither reader nor narrator
can be quite sure when he realizes that something
ghastly is going on. At first the narrator finds rationalizations sufficient to suppress what his eye told
him about Bartleby. Bartleby starts his employment with
a burst of diligence that ought to gratify any boss.
"I should have been quite delighted with his applica-
tion, had he been cheerfully industrious," the narrator
confides. Of course everything would come out right had
it been different than it was. The sinister note, still
nondefinitive, cannot be quite ignored. But it is not
only from Bartleby that the signals come of trouble

ahead. We note the dangerous limitations in the expectancy of the narrator. The conventional "safe" man is simply not prepared to accept his own knowledges or contemplate their necessary consequences. By charitably misconstruing Bartleby's character, his boss is undermining the foundations of his own life.

"Imagine my surprise, nay, my consternation, when without moving from his privacy, Bartleby, in a singularly mild, firm voice replied, 'I would prefer not to.'" We must give full value to this surprise. We must also give full value to the word "privacy" in this context and in the general ideological construct of the story. In the exchange from which I have taken this quotation we see that the civilized man—that is, the man whose personality has been shaped by and integrated with the demands of society—cannot reconcile his conceptions of either privacy or preference with those of the nonsocial man (represented by Bartleby). Privacy is a dominant right for Bartleby; for his employer it is only one right among many. Preference is the absolute authority for the truly private man; for the social man, individual preference has no fixed place on hierarchic scale of obligations. For him—for most of us—it is something to be indulged when other duties have been discharged.

The narrator can only regard Bartleby's refusals as lunacy. But, once again, he suppresses his recognition as long as he can. (This suppression may also be regarded as a form of lunacy, a reversed mirror image of Bartleby's. Melville's point is that the two of them are an "odd couple"—complementing each other in a fashion that fits the psychiatric diagnosis of a *folie à deux*, a madness requiring two participants.)

Little by little the suppressed recognitions of Bartleby accumulate and force their way past the "safe," "prudent," and "methodical" denials with which the narrator has been trying to protect himself from the full truth. At last he is forced to the point of reconsideration. He will keep Bartleby, but only as a matter of charity. "To . . . humor him in his strange willfulness, will cost me little or nothing, while I lay up in my soul what will eventually prove to be a sweet morsel for my conscience." But he finds it hard to hold to this resolve and Bartleby forces the issue by retiring more deeply into his privacy and insisting more annoyingly on his preference.

When he learns that Bartleby has become a positive threat to his reputation among other lawyers, the narrator takes the extreme step of moving to another office, since Bartleby declines to leave the old premises. If this seems an extraordinarily delicate bit of charity toward Bartleby—and it is—it is by the same token a measure of the desperation to which the narrator has been reduced in his efforts to save himself from the effects of Bartleby's passive resistance. Surely charity and obedience to the commandment of love will sustain the civilized man if no other bulwark of civilization will.

As Melville tells the story, charity helps no more than fairness, ideas of duty, tolerance, bribes, or other tactics in dealing with the truly private man. The dirty work of hauling Bartleby to the prison is simply passed on to someone else by the narrator's charitable evasion of it.

There is no saving Bartleby within the terms of salvation conceived by the civilized and prudent narrator. Halfway through the story the narrator has experienced a moment in which he has had to recognize Bartleby's "victory" over him. "For the first time in my life a feeling of overpowering stinging melancholy seized me. . . . The bond of a common humanity now drew me irresistibly to gloom. A fraternal melancholy! For both I and Bartleby were sons of Adam." Subsequent events and the narrator's reflections on them simply confirm the gloom that has overcast his initially comic relationship with his employee. His final discovery that Bartleby was once a clerk in the Dead Letter office permits a generalization of this gloom. It is the condition of mankind—"incurably forlorn," as Bartleby, from his first appearance, showed himself to be.

Questions

1. Discuss fully the meaning of Bartleby's "preference."
2. What is the character of the narrator? Is it changed by his association with Bartleby?
3. How does the tone of the narrator's language help to characterize him?
4. What use does Melville make of the setting to develop the theme of the story? What is the theme?
5. Are there any suggestions—either overt or implied—that Bartleby might have been fulfilled by a different occupation?

6. Is the story a satire on the business world? Or on the human condition in general? Explain.

Further Reading

Felheim, Marvin. "Meaning and Structure in 'Bartleby,'" *College English*, XXIII (February 1962), 369-376.

Firchow, Peter E. "Bartleby: Man and Metaphor," *Studies in Short Fiction*, V (Summer 1968), 342-348.

Marcus, Mordecai. "Melville's Bartleby as a Psychological Double," *College English*, XXIII (February 1962), 365-368.

Patrick, Walton R. "Melville's 'Bartleby' and the Doctrine of Necessity," *American Literature*, XLI (March 1969), 39-54.

Springer, Norman. "Bartleby and the Terror of Limitations," *PMLA*, LXXX (September 1965), 410-418.

Widmer, Kingsley. "The Negative Affirmation: Melville's 'Bartleby,'" *Modern Fiction Studies*, VIII (Autumn 1962), 276-286.

Yukio Mishima *Patriotism* (p. 1021)

Much of the effect the story will have comes from the tension between our cultural prejudices—tending to search always for a blend of positive and negative impulses in all human motivation—and the absolutism Mishima attributes to these characters. He does not try particularly to make their undeviating purposes accessible to our sympathy. He does repeatedly stress the purity and intensity of their passions and sensations. We must evaluate purity and intensity as best we can. When these are separated from actions we hold to be admirable, it is not easy to see them as precious in themselves.

It is one of those stories that will neither quite take us in or let us go. It won't do to say, "The Japanese are like that," and stand apart in disinterested curiosity. Because of cultural background, we are different from them, but we are not altogether different. All of us are moved by loyalty and devotion, and we suspect, at least, that life ought not to outlast honor. All of us know, from fantasies if not from literature, that the imminence of death can be an erotic stimulant and can give to erotic passion a semblance of ultimacy that it often lacks in the ordinary course of life. Camus and others have explained that the suicide knows a kind of freedom that most people thirst for vainly. "Was it death he was now waiting for? Or a wild ecstasy of the senses? The two seemed to overlap, almost as if the object of this bodily desire was death itself. But, however that might be, it was certain that never before had the lieutenant tasted such total freedom."

This passage would seem to sum up the tantalizing familiarity of the situation described by the story—and its abiding strangeness.

Questions

1. Which feelings and motivations of the lieutenant and his wife can you share? Do some remain foreign or incomprehensible? Which ones?

2. How is erotic passion related to the decision to commit suicide? Compare the language and amount of detail in the passages devoted to sex with those devoted to the suicides.

3. The author stresses the purity of motive on the part of his main characters. Does "purity" have anything to do with the value of these motives or the acts to which they lead?

4. Is there ever any doubt about the outcome of the story? If not, and if there is no suspense, what compensates for its absence?

5. Does the lieutenant expect to affect his country's policies by his sacrifice? Why does he feel he is "on the front line of the spirit"?

6. Does Reiko kill herself solely out of obedience to her husband's wishes? What does the story say about the proper relation of wives to husbands?

Further Reading

Boardman, Gwenn R.   "Greek Hope and Japanese Samurai: Mishima's New Aesthetic," *Critique*, XII, No. 1 (1970), 103-115.

Lebra, Joyce C.   "Mishima's Last Act," *Literature East & West*, XV (June 1971), 279-298.

Alice Munro   *Royal Beatings* (p. 1041)
              (Second Edition, p. 473)

Seeing that there is something gravely amiss in
Rose's family, students may be inclined to overestimate
the pathos of Rose's situation and see her purely as a
victim of poverty and cruel parents. There is obviously
some truth in such a view, but to take it as the whole
point and excuse for the story would be to miss the
fact that Rose thrives amid her handicaps. Even her
misfortunes and handicaps (including the beatings) feed
her imagination and, by their nourishment, shape her
into the paradoxically triumphant person we see at the
end. The maxim that may resolve the paradox is the old
observation that any suffering which doesn't kill you
strengthens you. Or, in somewhat milder form, that circumstances which don't quite cripple your talents may
fire you with the courage to use them.

The truly horrific story of the Tyde family and the
beating administered to Mr. Tyde by the brutal young
men of the town provide, first of all, a scale of mea-
surement. Compared to what happened to the old man,
Rose's beatings appear well within the limits flesh and
spirit can tolerate without being destroyed. Tyde
really was wiped out. The beating he suffered was
savage enough to deserve the epithet <u>royal</u> though, as
we are told in the second paragraph, her punishments do
not "approach such dignity."

Oddly enough, the same paragraph suggests that her
imagination, at least, is cheated by the beatings as
she actually experiences them. She has imagined something "both savage and splendid" and the romantic anticipation is not matched on either count.

It is only in the extravagant misfortunes of the
Tydes as Rose hears about them from Flo that she is
given the full measure of melodrama that her own suf-
ferings—fortunately—stop short of. The rumors of incest in the Tyde household and Becky Tyde's grotesque
appearance provide images on an extravagant, not to say
heroic, scale. In a very real sense they reveal the
meanings of the muddled hostilities, affections, and
violence in which Rose lives with her family. Her own
experiences, including the unjust beatings (which she
partly provokes), nourish in her a "hard pride and
skepticism." The pride incites her to a recurrent
defiance of Flo, as if Rose were unconsciously asking
for another test which will reinforce both the pride
and skepticism she needs to continue her growth.

Flo obliges her, and the beatings which follow serve as a kind of distorted family communion which all its members lack better means to observe. The father never seems really included in such a communion, only blindly contributing his baffled rage to the drama in which Flo and Rose are the chief participants. There is a fascinating relation between the older and younger woman, which ought to be the primary concern in explicating the story. While they are antagonists, we also see how Rose depends on Flo and converts some of her crude and tentative capacities into something finer for herself. Flo is an ignorant, uncultivated person, but in her primitive style she is something of an artist. "In moments of celebration or emergency she would do tricks." Further, she is a storyteller, though her stories about the Tydes and others are hardly better than lewd gossip.

It is in this role as storyteller that Flo best serves her growing stepdaughter, for surely Rose's progress is that of a young woman coming into possession of her imaginative powers. As her hard pride and skepticism are incorporated as ingredients of her imagination, she moves into position to make something wise and strong of what was handed on by Flo as flagrant gossip. This is probably the chief significance of the last section, which rounds out the Tyde melodrama by flavoring it with irony, tempering it with the mature skepticism which Rose has extracted from her experience.

Surely it is significant that when Rose comes into possession of the information about Hat Nettleton she wishes she could pass it along to Flo. Surely this wish is a recognition of her debt to the woman who, to all appearances, was a poor mother.

To suggest that "Royal Beatings" is a portrait of the artist as a young woman may be to overstep. It may be tactless to go that far. Nevertheless, the true subject seems to be the growth and ripening of an imagination to the point at which it transfigures the raw melodrama of life—the Tydes and the Hat Nettletons —into patterns adequate for literature.

Questions

1. What is Rose's fundamental feeling toward Flo? How does it change over the years and what is it at the end?

2. What is Flo's character and how is it revealed in her actions with Rose?

3. What are the father's motives in administering the beatings to Rose? In what ways can he also be considered a victim?

4. What is the tone of the story and is it consistent with the grimness of the subject matter?

5. What does the story of the Tyde family and Hat Nettleton have to do with the main story of Rose and her family?

Further Reading

Stone, W. B. "Beggar Maid: Stories of Flo and Rose," *Studies in Short Fiction*, 17 (Summer 1980), 353-354.

Vladimir Nabokov *Signs and Symbols* (p. 1059)
(Shorter Edition, p. 492)

Here—as he often does in his major works—Nabokov seems to be playing a game that deliberately defies the reader's attempts to reduce the story to a singular, coherent interpretation. Indeed the main effect comes from the shocking incoherence of images pasted together as the elderly couple makes a fruitless attempt to visit their deranged son. There is no coherent point of view either. Now and again we may suppose we are seeing the present setting and the young man's life history through the eyes and memories of the parents. But their point of view dissolves bewilderingly as we get information, images, and effects of language that are utterly inconsistent with the range of their awareness. It is not only a story about mania—the very form of the narrative is maniacal, disjunctive, hallucinatory.

". . . the patient imagines that everything happening around him is a veiled reference to his personality and existence." Working from this hint, we may go on to say that most of the details in the story seem to be "veiled" references to the lives of the characters. Veiled—and, finally, impossible to interpret. The mother feels "the mounting pressure of tears." She sees an unknown girl weeping. The woman on whose shoulder the girl is weeping resembles someone the mother knew years ago. There seems to be some connection between these things, but as soon as we note their connection the trail fades and is never resumed. On the floor of the old woman's living room lie some playing cards and a photograph or two that she has dropped: "knave of hearts, nine of spades, ace of spades, Elsa and her bestial beau." What has the photo to do with the sequence of cards mentioned immediately before it? Again, we may be led into believing there is a meaningful relationship that might be deciphered. Again we find the author has chosen to leave us with the riddle rather than provide an answer.

Discussion of this story provides a good opportunity to point out that it is among the author's options to create a maze of false clues that fascinate us with mysteries he never chooses to unravel. Not all mystery stories end with neat explanations of the "real" truth. Perhaps it is enough that we have been led into a sinister and bewildering labyrinth. Such stories have, at least, the power to jolt us and involve us emotionally.

Questions

1. Is there any logical explanation for the ringing of the telephone at the end of the story? Suppose that someone is merely calling a wrong number. Is that a meaningful or a meaningless coincidence?

2. Does the story suggest that everything we see has a message for us . . . or that to believe so is a form of insanity?

3. If we take this to be a sort of mystery story, can we find enough clues to decipher and explain the mystery? Or has the author deliberately stopped short of providing the clues we would need? Is a story satisfactory if it presents a riddle and then withholds the means of solving it?

4. Does the story in any way challenge your ideas of what reality is? Discuss.

5. Are the language and imagery uniform throughout? Discuss the effect of any shifts you may note.

Joyce Carol Oates *How I Contemplated the World from
the Detroit House of Correction and
Began My Life Over Again* (p. 1064)
(Shorter Edition, p. 497)

This story imitates the form in which we might find
the preparatory notes assembled by a girl before she
arranges them in a continuous narrative. At some point
in sorting out the memories to be used in her "essay,"
Oates's central character might well list separately the
"EVENTS" and "CHARACTERS" to be accounted for, neglect-
ing the chronology, leaving it to be worked out later in
her determination to approach her task systematically.
Thus the reader is invited—or obliged—to complete the
task of assemblage, straightening out the chronology in
order to make out the plain sense and sequence of things
that have recently befallen the girl and fitting together the qualities of character and milieu that have
given emotional color and significance to these events.
   As in dealing with a complex poem, we might well
begin a critical reading of the story with a paraphrase
that disentangles the elaborately knotted narrative
line. We find that the first paragraph provides an
extraordinary <u>who</u>, <u>where</u>, and <u>what</u> not very different
from what we would find in the most conventional story.
A girl from a wealthy Detroit family is about to steal
some gloves in a department store.
   She is caught in the act. Subsequently her mother
tries to make an adjustment of whatever is wrong by
taking her on a shopping trip. When this inadequate
remedy fails, the girl runs away from home and for two
weeks lives with Clarita and Simon in a depressed area
of the city. Though Simon is repulsive to her, the girl
submits to him sexually, administers drugs to him, and
prostitutes herself to provide him with money. At the
end of the two weeks, irritated by her "hysteria,"
Simon turns her over to the police. In the House of
Correction she is savagely beaten by two girls, one
white, the other black, for no very good reason except
that such things happen in such places. The pain of
being beaten changes the girl's mind about what she
wants. When her father picks her up and drives her
home, she is pathetically grateful for being returned
to a life of comfort. Her present effort to write the
record of her misadventure is an attempt to show her
gratitude for her rescue.
   Certainly there is plenty to fascinate us in the
story reconstructed in this linear, sequential form—

particularly as we note the psychological riddles attending the girl's motivation. As we turn to puzzle them out we will naturally have to take into account images, details, and peculiarities of language scattered with apparent capriciousness through the "NOTES."

The most difficult riddle is her attachment to Simon. He is designated as first among the "CHARACTERS WE ARE ENTWINED WITH FOREVER." This can be partially explained by the fact that he took her virginity, but this explanation obviously only begs the question of how or why such an act begets such an almost metaphysical response or why she put herself in his hands in the first place.

"Simon has a deathly face . . . tender rotting arms . . . he smells of unheated mornings and coffee and too many pills coating his tongue with a faint green-white scum . . . my skin hurt where he rubbed it." Unlike Clarita, for whom the girl can project in fantasy romantic alternative lives, Simon is seen with a terrifying, intensified realism. He is in no way "generous" like the men of her social level, including the father from whom she has fled. We must make what we can of her explanations that Simon's "danger . . . is a way of pressing her against him that is more powerful than any other embrace." "Simon has a deathly face, only desperate people fall in love with it." Certainly the girl is desperate, so we must read this as a declaration of love. "He "breathed gravity into me." The imprecision of such language is certainly convincing as a representation of a sixteen-year-old's floundering attempt to account for experiences she has not been prepared to expect or understand. But it is also the imprecision of poetic metaphor, the necessary ambiguity of language charged by the author's attempt to illuminate experiences we have not been prepared to understand. In the passage that describes the girl's injecting Simon with a drug we find a very artfully contrived parallelism between the release given by the drug and the release given by orgasm. "When the drug hits him she can feel it herself, she feels that magic that is more than any woman can give him, striking the back of his head and making his face stretch as if with the impact of a terrible sun. . . . She tries to embrace him . . ." We may more than faintly suspect that not only would the relatively inexperienced girl be unable to phrase her perception in such language, she would not know the "magic" that "any woman" might give in a sexual encounter.

The discrepancy—surely intentional—between the language and the perceptions that might conceivably find their way into a student's preparatory notes and those of the story can be demonstrated at numerous points. For instance, the end of Section IX can only be read as an intrusion into the story of a point of view that is not the girl's: ". . . revenge on the oppressed minorities of America! revenge on the slaughtered Indians!" etc. Section X develops an apocalyptic image of the end of Detroit, the end of a civilization that plainly does not originate with the fictional writer of the notes. A good guess would be that it is a commentary made by a fictional <u>reader</u> of the notes who has been struck by the horror inadvertently revealed. It comes into the story much like the outcry of a Greek chorus observing the tragedy of the protagonists.

To note this mixture of voices is a good point to begin a consideration of how far and in how many ways the author has departed from adherence to the discipline of the mimetic form we recognized in the beginning. After all, the imitation of a schoolgirl's disorderly attempt at ordering her recollections has been made to serve as excuse or point of departure for a highly sophisticated rearrangement of fictional elements, designed to expose patterns of relevance that would, at best, be subordinated in a chronologically consistent narrative. The apparently erratic shifts from "I" to "the girl" have served as a device for modulating language and point of view not only from objective to subjective and back, but to permit a polyphonic orchestration that includes subtle lyricism mixed with laconic vernacular and the various jargons of urban life.

The product of Oates's experimentation is a highly artificial blend of fictional modes—a gold mine for discussion of technique and just as rich a stimulus for discussions of contemporary values and psychic tensions.

Questions

1. How has the author used the apparent incoherence of preparatory notes to fashion a complete and coherent story? (Identify the basic elements of fiction used here—plot, character, exposition, complication, for example.)
2. Why is the girl submissive to Simon and Clarita?

Is there a personal pathology involved? A social
pathology?

3. What comment does the story make on the phenomenon of "dropping out"?

4. Does the story suggest that corporal punishment—
beatings, etc.—are a better remedy for the problems of
youth than psychiatry? Support your answer.

5. Is the story, as the subtitle suggests, "a revelation of the meaning of life"? In what ways? What is
the theme?

6. Which characters are "generous," which are not?
Is generosity an important value in the story? What has
it to do with the "meaning of life"?

Flannery O'Connor *A Good Man Is Hard to Find* (p. 1077)
(Shorter Edition, p. 509)

In the first several paragraphs a family portrait is
drawn. Details of dialogue, appearance, and action are
all individually credible, but they have been chosen
and combined to emphasize the sour grotesqueness of the
family, which is about to begin a banal vacation trip.
Such purposeful selection gives an effect that does not
correspond with our usual notion of realism. The author
is stacking the cards in a comic distortion so lethal
that it mocks the very idea of humanity. The grandmother's sentimental "niceness" is symmetrical with the
outright brattishness of the children; Bailey is unrelieved surly, his wife a dowdy frump; even the baby,
a presumed innocent, in such a grouping takes on the
corruption of the others. His "bland" face cannot hide
the fact that he is one of them.

The tone of the opening passages betrays no hint of
charity on the part of the author toward her characters.
While she does not picture them committing any crime
against society, the unrelenting exposure of their
grossness suggests that their mere existence is a crime
—as if they had all vandalized themselves. Is this
funny? Yes, it is; but the laughter it provokes may
well be tinged with anxiety and guilt, as if we were
trying to laugh away some radical flaw in human life
that we are afraid to admit consciously. It may be
tinged with malice as we take this journeying family
for scapegoats in whose destruction our corruptions
will be expunged. The humor is, in a word, black humor,
as it was widely called in the Sixties.

The note of disquieting absurdity prevails through
the stop at Red Sammy's. His sign advertises him as
"THE FAT BOY WITH THE HAPPY LAUGH." He turns out to be
anything but happy. In his own view he is perpetually
victimized, by others and by his own better impulses,
and his summary view not only recapitulates the title
but emphasizes a universal decline: "Everything is
getting terrible." Though the grandmother persistently
speaks of a time in which people and the world were
better than they are now, the superficiality of her examples degrades her faith in tradition. (Note, however,
that the grandmother speaks persistently of the "good"
—finding it in Red Sammy's gullibility and even in The
Misfit's impulses. Goodness is surely an important element in the equation on which the story is built; so
we may see the grandmother distinguished from the rest
of her family by the remnant of a piety become meaningless to them.)

But whatever we make of the grandmother's commitment
to goodness, we must acknowledge the fact that it is
her foolish mistake that puts the family on the wrong
road at the time of the accident, thus delivering them
into the hands of The Misfit. The meeting with him cannot be labeled coincidental, though in a realistic
story we could call it nothing else. The encounter is
meaningful and therefore, within O'Connor's terms,
necessary and inevitable. So the grandmother's responsibility for the outcome should not be minimized.
Wanting "good," she is the guide to disaster.

The Misfit himself is the hardest of all to analyze
in a generally enigmatic story. For one thing, we
can't fail to note his kinship with an arry of comic
strip figures to whom extrahuman qualities are attributed. He is the sort of specter that has been codified
in film and television intended for juvenile entertainment, a figure who provokes thrills of terror but can
be laughed off as unreal when the terror he inspires
becomes too intense for pleasure. (Pursuing such an
attempt at placing O'Connor's conception, one can
fairly credit her with borrowing from the popular arts
as many recent painters and film-makers have done,
adapting her borrowings to her own purposes while the
associations appropriate to their origin remain partly
visible.)

The Misfit is also used in the story as a kind of
Grand Inquisitor, a judge unmoved by any appeals his
victims can even conceive of—and as a spokesman for
the grim intuitions of the author. That is, he appears

absurd in two senses of that word: first, as a grotesque fictional invention suitable for entertaining
children, and, second, as an executive power that
transcends human thought, a kind of angel or demon
unmoved by either virtue or wickedness as humans
conceive of them.

It is worth abstracting The Misfit's comments about
Christ and examining them in their own right. There is
at least a fascinating riddle in the idea that Christ
is to blame for bringing uncertainty about death to
men, when they might have been better off if they went
on accepting the inevitability of death.

But, of course, after examining this or any other
part of the story in isolation it is important to see
it as it is given in a fictional combination that, altogether, may not be susceptible to an exhaustive rational analysis. Some stories deliver clear and unam-
biguous themes (or even morals). But this is not one
of them. Held up in various lights, looked at from
various angles, it may seem to have several possible
interpretations, not all of them reconcilable with
each other. More may be gained by comparing it—on the
score of ambiguity—with other O'Connor stories (or
with Kafka's work) than in trying to evaluate the
riddle of interpretation it leaves us with.

Questions

1. Which parts of the story are convincingly realistic and which parts are exaggerated, fanciful, or
improbable? What is accomplished by the mixture of
realistic and unrealistic elements?

2. Do the various weaknesses and shortcomings of
the traveling family have any bearing on their fate?
Would the outcome have been the same if they had acted
differently?

3. What is the significance of their being on the
wrong road at the time of the automobile accident?

4. To what extent does the comedy of the story depend on shock?

5. Explain The Misfit's statement that Jesus
"thrown everything off balance." Is The Misfit a
philosopher or a psychopath?

6. What is the significance of the title?

See also "Questions for Comparing the Author's
Stories," p. 183 of this *Handbook*.

Further Reading

Dowell, Bob. "The Moment of Grace in the Fiction of
    Flannery O'Connor," *College English*, XXVII
    (December 1965), 235-239.
Doxey, William S. "A Dissenting Opinion of Flannery
    O'Connor's 'A Good Man Is Hard to Find,'" *Studies in
    Short Fiction*, 10 (1973), 199-204.
Marks, W. S. "Advertisements for Grace: Flannery
    O'Connor's 'A Good Man Is Hard to Find," *Studies in
    Short Fiction*, IV (Fall 1966), 19-27.
Sister M. Martin, O.P. "O'Connor's 'A Good Man Is Hard
    to Find,'" *The Explicator*, XXIV (October 1965),
    Item 19.
Montgomery, Marion. "Flannery O'Connor's 'Leaden Tract
    Against Complacency and Contraception,'" *Arizona
    Quarterly*, XXIV (Summer 1968), 133-142
Montgomery, Marion. "Miss Flannery's 'Good Man,'"
    Denver Quarterly, III (Spring 1968), 1-19.

Flannery O'Connor   *Everything that Rises Must Converge*
                     (p. 1090)
                     (Shorter Edition, p. 522)

Julian's mother represents and speaks for the older
generation, the status quo, the limited vision, and the
firm moral standards of an epoch that is passing or
already past. At the other side of the generation gap,
Julian embodies the outrage and impatience of the young
with attitudes that seem to him stubbornly blind not
only to actual changes in the power balances of the
world but to the positive values of change.

The author repeatedly suggests, states, or implies
the "innocence" of the aging woman. But innocence, as
Julian knows and as we know, has two faces. While it is
a term of moral approbation, it is also a synonym for
ignorance. When it is maintained by a persistent refusal to look at the evidence of experience, it is a
form of hypocrisy and even of outright dishonesty.

From the beginning of the story it is clear to us
that Julian cares about his mother. Yet we see that his
concern for her is contaminated and undercut by a selfishness he does not even bother to suspect. He wants
her to enjoy the hat <u>as long as</u> it does not provide an
occasion that will embarrass him or call into question

a system of values which he knows to be superior to hers. The hat is a representative emblem or symbol for the whole set of social, racial, and personal values that she refuses to compromise. In fact the hat—her "ridiculous banner"—seems to advertise the quaintness, the grotesquerie, the error of her opionions, and Julian mentally converts it into a confirmation of his own superiority to her.

When, on the bus, they "converge" with a powerful black woman wearing an identical hat, Julian is maliciously pleased by the confrontation, expecting it will help him in his crusade to shame his mother out of her willful blindness, will help him "break her spirit" so she can admit the truths he sees so clearly.

The focus of the story is not on the question of who is to blame for the eruption of violence. Perhaps it is well to emphasize that the incident occurs at a point of inevitable collision between two forces (personalities, races) equally blind to the motivational dynamics of the other. The question is, rather, how will Julian respond to this collision or convergence of historical antitheses? And the answer is that he responds to it in conformity to prejudices that he considers self-evidently correct. Emotionally and intellectually convinced that his mother has been in the wrong, he joins in the assault on her and will not relent in his verbal attack until the shocking strangeness of her speech finally breaks through to him with its revelation of how severely she has been damaged. As long as she merely keeps repeating the monosyllable "Home," he continues in the delusion that only her dignity has been shattered—and this, of course, is what he has hoped for. It is when she says, "Tell Grandpa to come and get me," that he is forced to realize the damage to her mind. (Presumably she is suffering a stroke—a physical consequence that would be consistent with the foreshadowing information about her blood pressure given in the first sentence of the story.)

When this realization strikes him, there is a stunningly swift reversal of relative positions—and, in fact, a reversal of the values that have thus far given him an edge of superiority over his mother. He is precisely in the situation of a man who has been walking confidently on solid ground and now finds there is nothing beneath his feet and nothing to arrest his fall into a bottomless abyss. Even in what are probably her dying moments his "innocent" mother knows where she wants to go—"Home"—while he has not even a notion of where or what his home might be.

In the next to last paragraph the author has very effectively arranged Julian's appeals to the stricken woman to show what is happening to him. "Mother!" he calls first—a still formal, adult fashion of addressing another adult. "Darling, sweetheart, wait!"—a more desperate, abandoned cry of irrepressible emotion bursting through his reversed formality. Then, "Mamma, Mamma!"—the shriek of a lost child. By this swift-paced, dramatic means we come to know how radically he has been stripped of everything on which his self-confidence was built. His vaunted sense of "reality" has been ripped away like gauze and without its defense he must contemplate the magnitude of other layers of reality too grim for him to bear.

Moments before he announced confidently "that the old world is gone." In the swift reversal of the climax we understand—if Julian is too shocked to understand anything—that the "old world" with its moral enigmas and its traps for those blinded by his kind of pride has been biding unchanged in spite of changing appearances and changing social circumstances.

When his mother's eye "raked his face," it "found nothing and closed." This language has the double function of signifying her lapse into unconsciousness and the essential disintegration of a man who has collided with realities he chose to ignore or deny. He is nothing at the end.

Questions

1. List the things that Julian believes in and the things his mother believes in. Are the lists totally dissimilar?

2. Is Julian right when he tells his mother, "the old world is gone"? Does this statement mean what he thinks it means? Is it merely a statement of Julian's prejudices?

3. Why is Julian angry with his mother after she has been knocked down?

4. Interpret the words spoken by Julian's mother after the attack. What has happened to her?

5. Can this story be interpreted without bringing moral judgments into play? Is it possible to decide who is guilty and who is innocent?

See also "Questions for Comparing the Author's Stories," p. 183 of this *Handbook*.

Further Reading

Burke, John J. "Convergence of Flannery O'Connor and
     Chardin," *Renascence*, XIX (Fall 1966), 41-47, 52.
Esch, Robert M. "O'Connor's 'Everything that Rises
     Must Converge,'" *The Explicator* (April 1969),
     Item 58.
Hendin, Josephine. *The World of Flannery O'Connor*.
     Bloomington: Indiana University Press, 1970,
     pp. 102-108.
Kane, Patricia. "Flannery O'Connor's 'Everything that
     Rises Must Converge,'" *Critique*, VIII (Fall 1965),
     89-91.
Martin, Carter W. *The True Country: Themes in the
     Fiction of Flannery O'Connor*, pp. 38-39; 105, 167-
     168; 175; 218.

Flannery O'Connor   *Parker's Back* (p. 1102)

Several critics have pointed out that Flannery
O'Connor's range is not great. This appears to be true
in some senses and not in others. Set her stories in
comparison with those of Chekhov, Joyce, Faulkner, or
Lawrence and you will find that such authors are more
at home in the large world of experience than she.
Their effects of comedy and pathos are more diverse.
Their conceptions of character and situation are more
elaborate and flexible. Even without detailed analysis
one can hardly help being aware of a distinguishing
peculiarity and a certain sameness in Flannery
O'Connor's stories. The world of her fiction is unmistakably her own. In what might be called its surface area it is not large.

But what might seem to one critical reader a
limitation will seem to another a concentration of
forces, and a comparison of the three O'Connor stories
in our text will suggest how many variations she could
ring from her chosen themes, conflicts, and character
patterns. The patterns of complication in all three
may strike us as bizarre, but if the patterns are in
many ways similar they are cut from different cloth.
Probably *Everything that Rises Must Converge* is the
closest to the fabric of life as we know it. The encounter between Julian's mother and the black woman
wearing an identical hat is bizarre—in the unlikeli-

hood of its happening and in the significance revealed
by its consequences—but it is surely not as improbable
as the encounter with The Misfit in *A Good Man Is Hard
to Find* or the collision of the tractor with the tree
in *Parker's Back*. The character of Parker is a truly
astonishing conception and his motives are almost inde-
cipherable—but neither quite so astonishing nor so
inscrutable as The Misfit, while the avenging black
woman who strikes down Julian's mother is reasonably
comprehensible within the terms given us by the history
of racial oppression and class conflict. Each story
moves from a base of earthy and comic realism into
rarified moral and metaphysical quandaries, but probably *Everything that Rises Must Converge* is more
readily explicable in terms of family and social psychology than the other two. At any rate there is a
smaller remnant of mystery after social and psychological analyses are completed.

In all three stories we may feel the author more intent on baffling us with paradoxes than with resolving
them. Again and again we come on instances in which the
language or the story line is twisted just enough to
divert us from the solution we had almost grasped—as
when The Misfit rejects the grandmother's advice to
pray on grounds that "I'm doing all right by myself."
The paradox is that he makes absolutely no distinction
between "doing all right" and "doing all wrong." With
such paradox the human mind cannot deal. The limits of
language and logic have been reached. Led up the garden
path expecting explanation of The Misfit's motivation,
we are stopped by the blank wall of absurdity.

Yet, probably *Parker's Back* is the most consistently
enigmatic of the three stories. Why does Parker pursue
Sarah Ruth and then marry her? Because it is what he
has planned not to do and doesn't want to do? Why, for
that matter, does Sarah Ruth marry him, since she has
no discernible need for such a husband?

We can make an answer—of sorts—by saying that
people sometimes act in a spirit of perversity. Yes,
but when do they act contrarily or perversely rather
than straightforwardly in pursuit of their interests?
Unless that question is answered sufficiently, the
question of motivation remains open, and it is
O'Connor's art to refrain deliberately from attempting
to answer it.

The "evolutionary" series of tattoos that Parker acquires tempts us to read for allegorical meaning. "He
stopped having lifeless [tattoos] like anchors and

crossed rifles." He progresses through animals, ser-
pents, and birds. Then, at least figuratively, these
animate creatures "penetrated his skin and lived inside
him in raging warfare." There is—if we want to take
it up—an allegorical parallel between this progress
and the progress of inanimate matter into animate forms,
which, in turn, become ideas "raging" within the mind
of man (Parker). At the peak of this series is the
image (or idea) of God, which Parker acquires after his
accident (which invites comparison to the conversion of
Paul on the road to Damascus). But the idea (and/or
image) of God acquired by him is no more pleasing to
Sarah Ruth than any of his other adornments.

Looking at the whole map of Parker's progress
through the story, we might see it as an attempt to
learn by trial and error how to please Sarah Ruth—
finding it analogous not only to the grandmother's attempts in *A Good Man Is Hard to Find* to discover an
argument to dissuade The Misfit, but also to man's
attempts to please an inscrutable God. But there is no
clear suggestion that Sarah Ruth *is* God or His surrogate in the scheme of things any more than there is a
suggestion that The Misfit is. If Sarah Ruth and The
Misfit clearly represent anything, it must be The
Principle of Absurdity, the senseless terminus of efforts the mind can make to answer the questions it can
propose. The only answer to the question of what Parker
might do that would please Sarah Ruth is the same as
the answer given by the Book of Job to the question of
what would please God—i.e., "That is indeterminable."

The marvel of such stories is that they can be enjoyed at so many levels of sophistication. Among other
things, *Parker's Back* is an equivalent of a Punch and
Judy show. It gives pleasure (of sorts) just by showing Parker getting baffled or beat up by the Old Woman
for every move he makes. Then it is a comedy of rural
manners; Parker's acquisition of tattoos, like his
courtship, shows us some eccentric folkways. There are
wry and parodistic comments on the meaning and uses of
art in the economy of human life. These levels of edi-
fication and entertainment exist in harmony with the
metaphysical and religious game the author plays with
readers fascinated by abstraction.

Questions

1. What accounts for the ferocity of the struggle between Parker and his wife? Does the author express any attitude toward women by her representation of Sarah Ruth?

2. Discuss Parker's character, paying particular attention to his motives for marrying a woman who gives him so much trouble.

3. What is the symbolism of the burning tractor? How does it serve to motivate Parker?

4. What does it mean that Sarah Ruth raises welts on the image of Christ on Parker's back?

5. Discuss the handling of chronology. What is added to the story by including glimpses of Parker's life before he met Sarah Ruth?

6. What serious comments does the story make about idolatry and true religion?

See also "Questions for Comparing the Author's Stories," below.

Further Reading

Browning, Preston, Jr. "'Parker's Back': Flannery O'Connor's Iconography of Salvation by Profanity," *Studies in Short Fiction*, VI (Fall 1969), 525-535.

Fahey, William A. "Flannery O'Connor's 'Parker's Back,'" *Renascence*, XI (Spring 1968), 162-164; 165.

Hendin, Josephine. *The World of Flannery O'Connor*. Bloomington: Indiana University Press, 1970, pp. 154-155.

Flannery O'Connor—
Questions for Comparing the Author's Stories

1. Which of O'Connor's stories depends most on improbable circumstances? Which is closest to real problems of people of our time? Do her exaggerations all focus on metaphysical riddles beneath the surface of commonplace lives?

2. Compare the use of religious questions in *A Good Man Is Hard to Find* and *Parker's Back*.

3. Compare the uses of comedy in these three stories.

4. Is the Southern setting or background equally important in the three stories?

Frank O'Connor   *Guests of the Nation* (p. 1119)
                  (Shorter Edition, p. 535)

The story is effectively divided into numbered sections. The purpose of the first section is essentially expository. Here the full cast of characters and those qualities in them that will signify in the story's progress are presented. The action has already begun, but it is choked back to a low level of tension and suspense until the business of exposition is sufficiently accomplished.

Since the narrator is one of the characters committed to the action, we do not expect detachment in his reportage. Therefore the author has used him, and conveyed information through his limited, <u>interested</u> perceptions in a fashion that is emphatically dramatic (dramatized). In the first paragraph we find O'Connor exploiting the possibilities of such a narrator. A we-they relationship—which will prove fateful in the unfolding of events—between the Irish military and their "guests" is signaled through the language of perfunctory reporting—"(for we had picked up some of their curious observations)." In the same offhand way the narrator speaks of his "natural feeling of responsibility" for the prisoners. At this early point in the story there is no sense of the awesome in the idea of responsibility—but it is a key word in the building of the story structure, for at the end it will be his undeniable responsibility for the dead men that shatters him.

This oblique use of expressions perfectly commonplace to the actors in the drama culminates in the curious fulminations of the old woman of the house. Her cranky, superficially foolish explanation of how the war began ends the first section on a comic note. But her observation that "nothing but sorrow and want can follow the people that disturb the hidden powers" will reverberate with oracular power and truth when we have learned all that is to happen. Thus, without disturbing the perfectly naturalistic surface of his presentation, O'Connor has made the old woman function like the Chorus in a Sophoclean tragedy, or like the witches in *Macbeth*.

The pace of action is hastened and the central
crisis prepared for by the shaping of the second section. Here the terrifying potential of the previously
established we-they relationship is sprung into the
open when the label "hostages" is used for the first
time. The terror of the word rings in the ear of the
narrator and is made to ring in the ear of the reader
by the narrator's easily comprehensible protests to
Jeremiah Donovan. Of course the conversation that follows the pronouncement of this word makes us linger on
the word until its implications begin to soak in. The
"gab" of Hawkins is being loaded with theological,
eschatological concerns—disguised and made comic as
they are in the old woman's prophecy, to be sure, but
henceforward incorporated as part of the concerns to be
accepted by those responsible for the death of their
guests. "It would be great cruelty to put the wind up
them now," says Noble. His comment gives us a measure
of the way the young men are shrinking from the enormity that is now a visible possibility.

It is impossible to overstress the importance of the
pace at which the third section begins. The very
abruptness with which we learn that Belcher and Hawkins
<u>will</u> die works more on our emotional responses than the
announcement of fact. The facts are brutal enough. The
English have executed four "of our lads." Primitive and
fundamental passions for justice call for some response
to this deed of the English—indicated by the narrator's
perfectly natural, naturally understated "That's bad."

Of course it is Jeremiah Donovan who has brought the
news and who passes it on to the hostages. These actions
are appropriate to both his character and his role in
the paramilitary chain of command. Yet, certainly, it
would be a mistake to read him as the villain of the
story. He is not the source of evil but only its instrument, only more hardened than the narrator—neither
more nor less responsible for what happens. Note that
at the end of this section the word "responsibility" is
again flashed before our reading eyes, this time with
an altered and heavier significance, still short of
what it will mean when we have finished reading.

We have been prepared by the first three sections of
the story to anticipate some peripety of the action in
Section IV, some surprise ending that <u>might</u> allow an
evasion of the full horror menacing all the characters
involved. O'Connor's choice was to surprise us by not
surprising us. As far as the action goes, it bears
straight on to the predestined end. The reader who has

not flinched is not so much surprised, perhaps, as astonished at the recklessness of this exposure of what it means to kill a friend.

There is more to be said about this last section than that the killings take place. The author's management of this climaxing scene in the bog is consistent with the preparations that have been made for it and with its importance. In the previous sections time has been compressed and telescoped by a mixing of scenic snippets with narrative passages in which hours are passed over quickly. Here we find O'Connor using purely scenic means, in which the time of the telling is slowed to something close to the time it would take for such an action to be completed. Here no detail, no fragment of conversation can be omitted from the grim concentration of the moment.

The doomed men, Hawkins and Belcher, are both revealed in sharper distinction from the background than they have been previously. Belcher, typed as the strong, silent man, has quite a bit to say. His eloquence at the brink does not amount to a change in character, of course; what he says is perfectly consistent with and even provides an explanation for the reserve and reticence that have been stressed earlier. Hawkins does not exactly plead for his life—that would be out of character—but he puts the matter in terms that make his execution as costly as possible for his captors. After he speaks they know what they are doing. They move out beyond the shelter of that prayer which asks forgiveness for them "for they know not what they do."

It is also to be noted that it is the narrator who puts the last shot into Hawkins' body. Whatever may be said about his motives, the insuperable fact remains that it is his hand that has killed his friend.

The story is rounded off with the very brief encounter between the executioners and the old woman of the house, she "with all her cantankerousness gone." In the exchange of questions and answers the words death and kill are not used. The communication among them does not require those words. This might be cited as an example of understatement which carries a higher charge of emotion than open declarations or inflamed rhetoric. A similar observation can be made about the colloquial simplicity of the last sentence. Its eloquence resides in its candor. Its impact depends on the utter purity of its earnestness. The quiet force of the last words is set against the shock of silence following a swiftly hushed turbulence.

Questions

1. List some of the reasons why their friends kill
Hawkins and Belcher. Is there any one of these reasons
so important that, if you took it away, the others
would not have brought matters to such a conclusion?

2. Are the arguments about religion conducted in
terms that make them merely ridiculous? Why are they
included instead of—say—arguments about women or
sports?

3. Discuss Donovan's character and his role in the
action.

4. How are we to take the old woman's explanation of
what started the war?

5. How has the author handled the flow of time in
each of the numbered sections?

6. Is it out of character for Belcher to become
talkative in the last section?

7. How does the use of first-person narrative
contribute to the effect of the whole?

See also "Questions for Comparing the Author's
Stories," p. 190 of this *Handbook*.

Frank O'Connor   *My Oedipus Complex* (p. 1129)

A good deal of the charm and force in the story is
generated by the way it skims blithely past the solemn
bugaboos commonly associated with the Oedipus complex.
The inflations of popular psychology have made it seem
as if every male child who loved his mother were a
wretch afflicted with a loathsome ailment, particularly
if there were any tint of sexuality in his love. The
common experience of family life ought to have kept
clear the fact that there are always random currents of
sexuality meandering through family relationships,
coloring both the hostilities and the devotions that
bind families together. How could it be otherwise,
since the family is primarily a sexual unit? Still we
rejoice in O'Connor's comic deftness in disposing of
the impediments to candor and, most of all, in the way
he restores proportion to a subject usually either
overblown or denied.

This triumph of sanguine common sense appears to be
achieved largely from the tone of the story—a tone

which implies that of course little boys would like to turn their fathers out of their mothers' beds and sleep there themselves, and what's wrong with that if it leads to vigorous manhood, as it usually does? This tone of unshadowed confidence is generated largely from the narrator's present, adult attitude toward what he remembers of his childhood misconceptions and their consequences.

In this attitude there is nothing at all of remorse, nor is there any apparent impulse to repudiate the absurdities of childhood by derision, excuse, or denial. If anything, there is a note of pride in recollecting the wit and spunk of childish days, however misguided these may have been, based as they were on false assumptions about the nature of marriage. The implication is surely that we come to truth by resolutely following paths of error. It takes time to clarify the family roles of parents and children, but it takes only time. The cool and confident tone of the present narration suggests that a hullabaloo of anxiety about the Oedipal problem is generally a painful redundancy, at best duplicating nature's corrections.

To give full value to the implications of tone, it was incumbent on the writer to make a clear distinction between the narrator as a child and the narrator as a poised and reflective adult. At the same time, much would be lost of verisimilitude and comic suspense if the adult's superior sophistication were to be obtrusive from the beginning or were to override the mistaken assurances of the child's mind at any point. How O'Connor manages this balancing act may well be studied in the first two paragraphs. The distinction between "the war" and "the first war" is a definitive but unobtrusive signal of the lapse of time between the events to be narrated and the actual narration. So, perhaps, are certain minuscule stylistic touches added to the following exposition: the "In fact" which begins the second paragraph or the wry adjective "astounding" which qualifies the interest inherent in the process of shaving. "There was a bit of the magpie about Father, he expected everything to come in handy." Here we also discern, faintly but positively, the wry amusement of the observer securely detached from the web of emotions spun by the far-off circumstances. Nevertheless, aside from these restrained touches, the circumstances themselves are reported just as they would have appeared to the unsophisticated child. Now and then the straightforward account of childhood

perception is touched delicately by reminders of afterthought: "Little, indeed, did I know what I was praying
for!" Yet very few such touches are required. Mostly
the author counts on the reader's recognition of the
constant degree of error in the child's interpretations
to keep them disentangled from the parallel assessment
made in recollection. Choice of diction reinforces the
crucial distinction between the way it seemed and the
way it was? ". . . The sheer indignity of being struck
at all by a stranger, a total stranger who had cajoled
his way back from the war into our big bed as a result
of my innocent intercession, made me completely dotty."
This is unmistakably the voice of an adult—and a
quietly amused adult—though the substance being reported is perfectly recognizable as a child's outrage
at apparent injustice. Thus on to the end O'Connor
holds his impressive balance, achieving not only comedy
by the incongruity between childish and adult interpretation, but also a depth of wisdom in reconciling
errors within the benevolent tolerances of experience
ripening with the passage of years.

Questions

1. Does the boy seem to be undergoing a major psychological crisis? Relate your answer to the title. Is it
seriously intended or facetious?
2. What devices are used to characterize the mother
and father?
3. Does the action provide any signs that the boy is
maturing? Is there a decisive point at which he
changes?
4. Are there significant changes in the character of
the narrator from childhood to the time at which he
recollects these childhood events?
5. What is the narrator's attitude toward his
behavior as a child? How does this attitude affect the
tone of the story?

See Also "Questions for Comparing the Author's
Stories," p. 190 of this *Handbook*.

Further Reading

Weiss, Daniel. "Freudian Criticism: Frank O'Connor as
Paradigm," *Northwest Review*, Spring 1959, pp. 5-14.

Frank O'Connor—
Questions for Comparing the Author's Stories

1. Note that both stories are told in the first person. Is it possible to make a clearer distinction between the author and the narrator in one than in the other? In which of the two stories is such a discrimination most necessary?
2. Is the author equally effective in comedy and tragedy?
3. Discuss the importance of setting and background situation in each story. Does the author use his characters in each to dramatize the essentials of the milieu?
4. Which of the stories is more tightly structured? Does difference in subject matter account for differences in story design?

Tillie Olsen   *Tell Me a Riddle* (p. 1138)

The "riddle" has a multitude of forms. It is the riddle of life, the masquerade of love as anger, of anger as love, the lovers' quarrel with the world that torments and confronts us, the nearness of distant things and times, the distance between ourselves and our real lives, the discrepancy between what we say and what we want. These protean forms of the riddle are projected here in the story of a long marriage and the death of the wife.

The first two sentences practically equate marriage with quarrel. The children of the elderly couple cannot understand how the quarreling can go on after many of the issues have vanished with the passage of time. Surely the habit of quarreling has come to be the substitute for all the other ways married people might communicate with each other, and—rather miraculously, though still painfully—the man and wife have learned to express a wide range of feelings through the vocabulary of anger. They still mean to pay each other back for remembered wrongs, but the memories, after all, are of things they shared and endured, so what divides them is paradoxically also a bond.

The chief questions they now have to quarrel about have to do with how they will spend their old age. Go to an old people's home or remain in their house? Find

new interests? Visit the children and grandchildren?
Soon enough the question of the wife's health appears
and gradually pushes all others into the background.
After surgery discloses the presence of cancer and the
approach of death, there is a change in the tonality of
the quarreling. Now, of necessity, the husband's object
must be to protect and deceive the dying woman. The
real significance of the quarrel, too, is altered and
expanded. Now we see it as a lover's quarrel with life
reaching beyond the marital relationship. Husband and
wife shared a past of revolutionary sentiments before
they immigrated to America. Their quarrel then was with
the oppressive darkness of religion, as later it became
a quarrel with the oppressions of poverty, child-
bearing, the economic and social roles assigned to men
and women. The old woman cannot bear to touch her infant grandchild because the baby reminds her too
strongly of what has drunk up and wasted her own life.
To the unbending strictness of her mind, the grateful
recollections of her children seem hypocrisies.

In section 3 of the story the husband and wife run
into a Mrs. Mays who had been their neighbor thirty
years before—"a friend of *hers*, not his." They go with
her to a community sing. The wife becomes ill during
the singing and Mrs. Mays offers to take them to her
place nearby. The sight and smell of this room conjure
up a terrible vision of unused life in all the people
who are moving toward death. "She in this poor room
with her pictures. Max You The Children Everywhere
unused the life And who has meaning? Century after
century still all in us not to grow?" This vision
of waste culminates in her realization "that she was
dying." More is meant here than that she at last
understood the doctor's prognosis. It is a realization
of the whole ghastliness in the wastage of unused life,
desires and potentials never to be achieved however
much agony and hope has been paid for their sake.
"*That* nightmare thought."

In the fourth part the woman who has always suppressed so much of her thought while she tended to the
needs of others begins to talk. Her words touch on
reminiscences of her youth in Russia and particularly
of her friend Lisa, who gave her the love of books
that was never to be gratified—"To her, life was holy,
knowledge was holy, and she taught me to read. They
hung her. Everything that happens one must try to
understand why." But what happens is incomprehensible,
as we see when her drifting thoughts and words turn to

Hiroshima: *"78,000 in one minute* (whisper of a scream)
78,000 human beings   we'll destroy ourselves?"

The story ends with riddles unanswered, enigmas un-
resolved. The granddaughter Jeannie perceives something
majestic and triumphant in the elderly people. She
makes a drawing in which they are united, "their hands
. . . clasped, feeding each other."

But Jeannie does not have the last word in the story.
The resolution, if there is any, is not so confident as
she. If there is a positive theme, it has been stated
almost in passing some time before we come to the last
passages and dedication: "life may be hated or wearied
of, but never despised."

The frequent shifts into stream of consciousness will
probably not present a real difficulty for most readers.
There appears to be no formula for such shifts; they are
made to heighten the immediacy and emotional impact of
the material, and since the emotional line is the powerful center of the narration, minor jolts of grammatical
disjunction can hardly break the continuity.

Questions

1. What is contributed to the effect and meaning by
the use of stream-of-consciousness passages?

2. Why doesn't the approaching death of the wife put
a stop to the quarreling? How does the nature of the
quarreling change as the story progresses?

3. Of what importance are the revolutionary sentiments of the dying woman in the whole context of the
story? What has the fate of the revolutionary Lisa to
do with the meaning of present events?

4. Are there any clear notes of optimism? From what
do they come?

5. Is Jeannie's interpretation of the situation adequate to the riddle it presents? In the last paragraph
she says "it is all right." Is it?

6. What, in the view of the dying woman, is the
worst thing about death?

Grace Paley   *The Used-Boy Raisers* (p. 1168)

Very few stories, even of much greater length,
demonstrate so impressively how public and historic
conflicts are built into private lives. The breakfast
scene turns out to be a crossroads at which converge
not only the personal pathways of three lives but also
the major determinants of the historic times we are
living through. In the suppressed emotion of their
early morning conversation we hear the conflict of: the
roles of men and women, religion against religion,
religion and apostasy, parental rights embroiled with
parental feelings and obligations, the benefits and
handicaps of marriage, sexual liberty against sexual
stability, nationalism and individualism. These are not
merely the topics for restrained argument. The story
lives so vividly because these limitless contentions
and conflicts are inherent (and partly recognized) in
the relationships of the characters.

The terse, ironic style is well suited to display
the profundities that intrude into random banalities of
our daily routines. Thus, even the first sentence plays
with the comic, tragic correspondence of minor and
major disappointment. The "eggs" that disappoint the
husbands are not only the viands on the table—they
also stand for all the disappointed wife can offer in
marriage. The narrator's tone of amusement is also a
tone of despair and awe at the discovery of huge
destinies reduced to trivial squabbles.

Questions

1. Is Faith better matched with her present husband
than with her former one? If not, what does this seem
to say about the source of her marital problems?

2. Is either man the "real" father of the boys?
What does the story say about the role of fathers or
the nature of fatherhood?

3. What is the narrator's fundamental attitude
toward both husbands?

4. Do the boys play any decisive part in the encounter between their parents?

5. If you conclude that the story is, in whole or
part, satiric, what is being satirized?

6. What does the story say about the forces that
shape personality and destiny?

Dorothy Parker   *Big Blonde* (p. 1173)

This is an example of what used to be called "a slice of life." The slice is cut the long way of the loaf. We see enough elapsed time to understand the pathetic downward drift of a woman's life, achieving no resolution, revelation, or significant change even when she attempts suicide. The story suggests no remedy for the necessarily accelerating deterioration, nor will the reader find a redeeming principle to compensate for the torpid waste, as there is in Chekhov's *The Darling*.

Hazel Morse is as much a type as an individual. We may feel that the author has concentrated on what is typical in such a woman's life, but we would probably not, in any case, expect much individuality in someone caught as Hazel is in the slowly grinding mill of her own mediocrities and the expectations of her admirers. "She was not a woman given to recollections." Her pride in her small feet, the self-inflicted punishment of always buying shoes that are too tight are signs of her submission to a social stereotyping that might be too formidable for even a shrewder woman to challenge. Her successes in life are, in themselves, part of the trap. She succeeds by her sexual attractiveness and availability—and by being a "good sport." Her alcoholism is hardly even a personal affliction, let alone a choice. It is simply there, part of the course for women life her. Only her hands—mentioned at the beginning of the story and never again—are "curious" as, we suppose, every living person ought to be, protruding like the hands of a living women entombed in the corpse of her life. (Note that the author intrudes to comment, "She should not have disfigured them with little jewels.")

The narration is evenly noncommittal, as though the author had been unable to find an occasion for anger, regret, or sympathy. Yet the very drabness of the tone works to suggest a pity as strong as it is vague. When we read that Hazel "prayed without addressing a God, without knowing a God," we sense in the understatement a wish that there might be a God to intervene in such hopelessness.

Questions

1. Is Hazel Morse anything but the "type" defined in the first sentence? Is the whole story merely an extension of that definition?

2. What is the tone of the narration? What gives an indication of where the author's sympathies lie?

3. Can you determine the causes of Hazel's alcoholism? Is there any suggestion that she is curable? That alcohol is the only possible consolation for her hopeless life?

4. What is the significance of her "curious" hands and her small feet?

5. Is her attempt at suicide consistent with the rest of her life and with her character? In what ways?

6. Could this story be interpreted as protest against the condition of women? If so, at whom might the protest be directed and what remedies does it demand?

William Peden   *A Boone County Parable* (p. 1192)

The author calls this work a "mini-fiction" and for teaching purposes that may be a better label for it than a "short-short" story, for we will want to see how many of the essential components of a story have been retained through the miniaturizing process and how they have been adapted to a very small unit.

The story is structured on two contrasting encounters made in the course of a day's casual shopping trip. First the narrator is engaged in conversation by the cross-eyed countryman. Though he is diffident, polite and clumsy in his address, he has a grief to tell of, and when he eventually communicates it there is a flash of genuine sympathy between the two men, a glimpse of the human solidarity that makes the occasions of grief into celebrations of our ability to endure the worst.

The second encounter is depersonalized—perhaps only by the technological circumstance that puts the "dough-face" woman behind the wheel of an expensive car. Whatever the reason, her absorption in the power of the machine leads her to ignore the basic rights—indeed, almost the existence— of the narrator on his bicycle. His anger springs not from the fact that he has been slightly injured when his ankle scraped the curb, but by the woman's reckless violation of the bond affirmed in his exchange with the bereaved father.

There is no resolution in the action, but we perceive that here, as in more extended stories, something has happened to change our narrator, a slight but irreversible shift in the cosmos.

Questions

1. Why is the story called a parable? What moral
proposition does it illustrate?
2. How many of the basic elements of fiction are retained in this miniaturized work?
3. What is the character of the narrator and how is
it modified or opened by the encounters with the cross-
eyed man and red-haired woman?
4. What is the narrator's feeling toward the man who
lost his daughter?

Jayne Anne Phillips   *Souvenir* (p. 1193)

As a hedge against apathetic or superficial reading,
it is often appropriate to ask students to measure a
fictional situation by the patterns of their personal
experience. In few cases could it be more appropriate
than in this instance, for the story is structured from
the anxieties and obligations generated by the evolution of roles in a changing family situation. However
much families may differ, everyone is aware that roles
do evolve with the passage of time and under the pressure of crises.

Though "Souvenir" focuses chiefly on the brief
period of crisis brought on by the mother's illness, we
are given enough background of family history to see
that the pattern has changed in ways that force Kate
into reconsiderations when obligations of a different
complexion and magnitude come to rest on her. Of the
cardinal past events, the earliest was the occasion of
Robert's flunking out of college. At that point Kate,
still a child at home, tried "in vain" to comfort her
mother. The only compensatory move she can make is the
indirect and largely symbolic one of studying frantic-
ally when her own turn comes to leave home for college.
At the death of the father, "Robert became, always and
forever, the man of the house." It is Robert who stays
near his mother, handling those practical concerns incumbent on the surviving male, while Kate's destiny
carries her farther and farther away on an independent
course. At the most extreme point of her trajectory,
Kate is still bound to her mother by tethers of affection, though this emotional bond ripens into something
like a sisterly camaraderie, as we see when they

jokingly discuss the men in their lives and the hypothetical prospects of marriage for either of them. In
this phase of family evolution they communicate as
equals, equally independent even of each other. The
Valentine cards are a token of this matured relationship. When Kate at last forgets the habitual card, we
may read this as a sign that the diverging paths of
their lives will continue to widen their separation.
Their argument of the previous summer presages just such
a future.

But when her mother's terrifying illness calls her
home, Kate returns to find that the affection of independent equals is insufficient for the magnitude of the
demand. A woman at the threshold of death can no longer
be an independent woman. Robert, whatever his intention,
simply cannot anchor a situation so grave. When Kate
says to him, "'I'll stay. Go home,'" we hear her intention of taking on the full responsibility herself for
seeing her mother through what is coming. In a real
sense she moves to assume the role her mother is necessarily vacating, claiming the weight of grief as well
as the practical obligation of keeping up her mother's
spirits by small attentions and by withholding information about the seriousness of her condition.

It is a role her mother will not abdicate, and in
the final contention between them lies the supreme
pathos and power of the story. The final episode may
seem inconclusive, something of an irrelevant substitute for the resolution we have been led to expect. To
point out that the ride on the ferris wheel is symbolic
is not in itself sufficient to make up for the disappointment we may almost instinctively feel when the
story ends here. When the issue is life or death,
haven't we the right to expect an answer as to which it
will be?

Fortunately, the symbolic ride is the kind of
symbolism that is absolutely consistent with the concreteness and objectivity of the rest of the story. It
is a symbolism chosen by the characters themselves—
not merely laid on by the author—in the tension of a
situation that cannot be directly articulated by either
mother or daughter. As they vie for the responsibility
of shouldering the secret, it is unthinkable that
either should let it out into the open. Yet part of the
paradox is that they must communicate about it as each
asserts her claim. The natural compromise is that they
choose the wheel and their ride on it as the ciphers
in a code suitable for the transaction.

It should suffice for an interpretation to note that
the little car in which they are riding stops almost at
the top of the wheel. They are suspended in a precarious
balance where they share equally the roles of protector
and protected, mother and child. The mother, whom we
know to be sick, asks, "You're sick aren't you?" Of
course Kate is sick—with her mother's impending death.

We have been forewarned that the little park in
which the ferris wheel sits is "magic." This should
prompt us to surmise that there is a magic reconciliation of opposite and discrete roles of mother and
daughter as each yields to the other.

Questions

1. What does the information about the Valentine
cards tell us about Kate's evolving relation with her
mother?
2. What is Robert's character and the significance
of his behavior?
3. How satisfying to Kate are her attempts to establish an independent life?
4. How does the present crisis clarify Kate's role
in the family?
5. Does the story end without a real resolution.
What do you still want to know?

Further Reading

Peterson, M. Review of *Black Tickets*. *North American
Review*, Winter 1979, pp. 77-78.

Edgar Allan Poe   *The Fall of the House of Usher*
                   (p. 1206)
                   (Shorter Edition, p. 545)

This story might be approached as an example of the
Romantic imagination—the doomed, hypersensitive hero
with his unworldly *angst* is kin to many of the figures
populating the literature of the early part of the
nineteenth century. Gothic elements could be pointed
out—the lugubrious setting in an old castle beset by
storms that produce a fantastic illumination, the sub-

terranean passages, and the noise of groaning hinges.
Or it could be discussed as an example of Poe's special
methods and his theories of the short story. He saw a
story's success dependent on its singleness of effect.
His first priority was to work directly on the sensi-
bilities and susceptibilities of the reader, subordinating to that end the objectives of developing a
coherent and responsible account of human behavior or
constructing a moral overview of human conduct.

He is not, in this tale, trying to portray the
mental pathology of Roderick Usher nor tell us about
the responsibilities, guilts, or existential plight of
being such a man. The author is, purely and simply,
piling on as many extravagances of language, circumstance, and uncanny stage business as he can assemble
to make the reader feel a crescendoing wave of (presumably pleasurable) terror. The style does not aim at
precision but at morbid excess. The events are chosen
for shock value and not to exhibit character. Working
toward the same end as the film director Alfred
Hitchcock, Poe neglects the history and inner life of
his protagonists to bear down consistently on the
reader's vulnerability to disturbing spectacles. Thus,
when we try to examine the meaning of the subject matter, we are severely circumscribed by the realization
that it has only the meaning of stage properties in a
horror show. It means that people are made upset by
dark places, storms, mysterious noises, subterranean
confinement, walking corpses, and the sight of blood.

Yet by subordinating the usual responsibilities of
an author to his subject matter, Poe and those who work
in his tradition perform a trick of displacement that
we can properly admire. They make our own fears and
superstitions serve in the place of subject matter. The
horror show becomes a mirror of the dark crannies of
the reader's psyche. For example, it seems to have very
little to do with the action or the outcome of the
story that Madeline is Roderick Usher's twin. We are
certainly given no explanation of how this fact might
have worked throughout his life to shape his destiny.
Rather, it is the kind of detail that plays on the
widespread superstition that each of us has a double,
a second self, whose fate we must magically share.
Like all ghost stories—of which this is an example as
elegant as it is famous—it is an index of the un-
credited but persistent parts of the common psyche.

Questions·

1. Identify some of the means used by Poe to achieve the mood of this story.
2. In what ways is Roderick Usher a picture of the artistic personality? A psychotic?
3. How is Usher's ballad related to the story as a whole?
4. In what ways is his sister a mirror image of Usher and his afflictions? What evidence is there that she has an independent existence?
5. What suggestions are there that Poe considers the imagination, in itself, to be a disease?
6. In what ways does the story conform to modern psychological ideas? Is psychological analysis of Usher possible on the basis of evidence given in the story?

See also "Questions for Comparing the Author's Stories," p. 202 of this *Handbook*.

Further Reading

Bailey, J. O. "What Happens in 'The Fall of the House of Usher'?" *American Literature*, XXXV (January 1964), 445-466.

Howarth, William L., ed. *Twentieth Century Interpretations of Poe Tales*. Englewood Cliffs: Prentice Hall, Inc., 1971, pp. 47-62.

Pollin, Burton R. "Poe's Pen of Iron," *American Transcendental Quarterly*, II (2nd Quarter 1969), 16-18.

Stein, William Bysshe. "The Twin Motif in 'The Fall of the House of Usher,'" *Modern Language Notes*, LXXV (February 1960), 109-110.

Wilson, James D. "Incest and American Romantic Fiction," *Studies in Literary Imagination*, 7 (Spring 1974), 42-46.

Edgar Allan Poe   *The Purloined Letter* (p. 1222)

Here is Poe in a playful mood, relinquishing his effects of horror and gloom, delighting in an intellectual conundrum as he builds his detective story around the type of super-sleuth who was later to receive his greatest celebrity in the person of Sherlock

Holmes. From the outset Dupin is supremely—almost arrogantly—confident of his ability to solve the mystery
that has baffled the best efforts of the Paris police.
Their methods are, he says, very good of their kind,
and they have an abundance of practical resources unavailable to him as an individual. But he has a trick
which is, perhaps, never at the disposal of a bureauc-
racy as such. He will proceed by "an identification of
the reasoner's intellect with that of his opponent."
Thus by a species of mental jujitsu he briskly retrieves the missing letter from D—— and leaves that
nefarious gentleman where he is sure to be punished in
full measure for his theft.

In part, the satisfaction we get from the story is
in seeing the confounder confounded and in relishing
the triumph of the individual over the fruitless collective efforts of the police force. Our sympathies
always go with the individual rather than with the com-
mittee. But the retrieval of the letter is only part of
the story as Poe tells it. A very large proportion of
the narrative is given to Dupin's account of how he
proceeded to identify his intellect with D——'s, and
in the course of this disquisition he has occasion to
disparage the mathematical intellect in favor of the
poetic. In sum, the mathematical intellect is the
prisoner of its own exacting methodology, while the
poetic intellect embraces all possibilities, the lax
as well as the strict, the obvious as well as the rec-
ondite. That refinements of procedure and technique are
not always appropriate is the theme of Dupin's sermon.

From this praise of the superiority of the poetic
intellect it may go without saying that the author has
constructed Dupin as his own alter ego, putting words
in Dupin's mouth that will rather transparently extoll
the superiority of the author over mere scientists and
mathematicians.

Questions

1. What is the relationship between the narrator
and Dupin? What aspects in the character of each is it
based on?

2. Since the rightful owner of the letter knows who
stole it, why can't she simply demand its return?

3. How does Dupin define and take advantage of the
blind spots in the best of institutional methods? What
does he say about the importance of the individual
intellect?

4. How has Dupin assured the punishment of the thief? Was there any other option for insuring punishment?

5. What does the story say about the role of games in the management of human affairs?

See also "Questions for Comparing the Author's Stories," below.

Further Reading

Babener, Liahna K., "The Shadow's Shadow: The Motif of the Double in Edgar Allan Poe's 'The Purloined Letter,'" *Mystery and Detection Annual*, 1 (1972), 21-32.

Hoffman, Daniel G. *Poe*. Garden City: Doubleday, 1972, pp. 106-125.

Kennedy, J. Gerald. "The Limits of Reason: Poe's Deluded Detectives," *American Literature*, 4 (1975), 194-195.

Levine, Stuart. *Edgar Allan Poe: Seer and Craftsman*. Deland: Everett/Edwards, 1972, pp. 162-168.

Shulman, Robert. "Poe and the Power of the Mind," *Journal of English Literary History*, 31 (1970), 254-256.

Edgar Allan Poe— Questions for Comparing the Author's Stories

1. How does an interest in psychology link these two stories? Are Poe's psychological views acceptable today?

2. Do the stories play equally on the reader's emotions? What differences in technique account for any different emotional effects?

3. Discuss Poe's preoccupations with the dark side of life.

4. Are both stories designed more to entertain than to instruct?

Katherine Anne Porter   *Theft* (p. 1237)
                         (Shorter Edition, p. 560)

Starting where the story starts, we find that
Camilo's hat is a possession he uses to project an
image of cavalier gallantry. It is of a color impracti-
cal for ordinary wear in the dirt of a city, and by
wearing it in the rain he poses as a man disdainful of
material things when the demands of courtesy lay a
greater claim on him. He reminds us of Sir Walter
Raleigh throwing his cloak down for a lady to walk on
so she will not wet her feet—until the girl sees him
try to save the hat by putting it under his coat as
soon as he supposes he is unobserved. "She felt she
had betrayed him by seeing," we are told. Actually,
this serves as the first instance in which she is betrayed by the false pretenses of those with whom she
has to deal. Instead of truly sustaining her by self-
sacrificing gallantry, the phoniness of that gallantry
lays demands on her tolerance.

We see her throughout as a young woman living so
marginally that she has little to spare. She is a
struggling young writer trying to stay afloat in New
York. The mention of a letter in which someone has
evidently pulled the rug out from under her and her
encounter with Bill, who weasels out of his obligation
to pay her the fifty dollars he owes her (and which
she so badly needs), complete the preparation for the
climactic action in which her purse is stolen. In her
first response to that theft we see a repetition of
her characteristic response to those who have robbed
her: she refuses the role of victim by the irrational
but understandable device of denying there was any
crime—or any crime worth her notice—as she told Bill
to "Let it go then," rather than demean herself by
arguing over the money he refuses to pay her.

Understanding the story depends on understanding
the rather convoluted psychology of such a maneuver, so
it is worth the teacher's while to concentrate on a
full explication of the paragraph beginning, "She remembered how she had never locked a door in her life
. . . ." In summary we may say it depicts a person who
has immunized herself against loss or betrayal by dis-
claiming all ownership of things, by such immunization
conditioning herself to the brave and precarious life
she has undertaken as a woman and writer on her own.

The following paragraph enlarges the significance
of the theft of the purse by its strong implication

that this immunity has been taken from her. Too heavily
taxed for too long by the losses she has, in fact, endured, her definition of herself is shattered when she
finds that, contrary to her intentions, she is truly
disturbed by loss of the purse. Suddenly all the losses
she has been able to ignore come cascading down on her.
Her will no longer sustains her. The "murderous anger"
in her blood can no longer be mastered, and when her
will is fractured, it is as if the tightrope she had
been walking above all the risks and disappointments of
her life had been jerked out from under her, and she
falls.

She makes one last attempt to redefine herself and
reclaim her necessary immunity when she tries to force
the janitress to keep the purse. It is, of course, too
late, and therein lies the tragic weight of the story.
Having lost control, having seen herself lose control,
she can no longer reclaim something all-important in
her image of herself. She knows now that she is not
immune to the dominance of material things over her
spirit, and therefore she is truly in great peril. The
losses that did not matter while she could consider
herself above them and indifferent to them now return
to plague her when the illusion of her indifference is
stolen from her. The purse itself is of course unim-
portant. How she handles its loss is crucial. She
fumbles, and loses immeasurably important parts of her
system of defenses.

Questions

1. Enumerate the kinds of theft (or cheating) touched
on by the story.
2. How are the shortcomings of Camilo and Bill related to the theme?
3. By what details do we learn about the kind of
life led by the central character? Why is her name
never given.
4. To what extent and in what ways does she bring
her troubles on herself?
5. Comment on the thematic relation between material
possessions and the integrity of self.

See also "Questions for Comparing the Author's
Stories," p. 207 of this *Handbook*.

Further Reading

Givner, Joan.   "A Rereading of Katherine Anne Porter's
   'Theft,'" *Studies in Short Fiction*, VI, 463-465.

Katherine Anne Porter   *Flowering Judas* (p. 1243)
                          (Shorter Edition, p. 565)

Students may have some difficulty simply in ab-
sorbing the basic data of this story, particularly on
a first reading. This is understandable because of the
story's special qualities, which make it altogether one
of the master works of twentieth-century American fiction. The present scene (which in actual chronology may
take place in one hour, more or less) tends to be dissolved almost indistinguishably with the persisting
situation of the present weeks or months, and even with
this whole phase of Laura's life in Mexico, by an extraordinary use of the present tense. This fluidity of
time may be discerned in the first paragraph, so it
might be worthwhile to examine it in isolation, perhaps
even at the time the reading assignment is made. Note
that the first two words "Braggioni sits . . ." and the
whole first sentence refer to the specific evening of
the present scene, while the rest of the paragraph expands the moment until its boundaries are lost in a
succession of evenings through what has become an
habitual situation. "He waits . . .," the last words of
the paragraph, represent what the maid announces every
evening on Laura's return to her dwelling.

Once grasped it will be perceived that the fluidity
of temporal consciousness, plus a richly melodic and
rhetorical prose, represent the quality of Laura's
experience with a touching fidelity. In Mexico she is
adrift amid the alien, deep and brutal colors of what
is for her an exotic society in the chaos of a continuing revolution. The repugnant Braggioni is, if anything
can be, an element of stability in the flux of swirling
demands on her emotions and political commitments. By
intent Laura is as much a revolutionary as Braggioni,
but he is a powerful and cunning exploiter of revolutionary forces while she is young, vulnerable, lovely,
idealistic and a foreigner to boot, unable to sort
practical considerations and necessities from the
kaleidoscopic swirl of events and the range of emotional

demands on her feminine resources.

She is obliged to tolerate Braggioni's courtship because she must suppose that his influence will help
some of the comrades who are faring badly—in prison or
in danger from the revolutionary processes profitable
to him. But while she tolerates him she also contrives
to keep him at arm's length by a strategy of what we
finally understand to be self-immolation. Her security
lies in a terrible frigidity of spirit, a precarious
balance in the eye of the storm, which leads her to
utter a convincing "No" not only to Braggioni but also
to all the appeals which might liberate her to either
life or death. Her present crisis has been brought on
(as we learn very late in the narrative) by finding one
of her dependent comrades, Eugenio, dying by suicide in
prison from an overdose of the drugs she has brought
him to relieve the boredom of incarceration. The dream
which concludes the story shows her wrestling with the
temptation to follow Eugenio. At least he has found a
way out of the labyrinth of pointless and tormenting
anarchy.

The temptation is powerful. The dream figure of
Eugenio first seems to offer her salvation when he
proposes that she follow him to "a new country," but
then, when she refuses, he reproaches her for being a
"Cannibal" who has perpetuated her life at the expense
of his. Her last terrified and spontaneous "No" rejects
the escape he offers, but returns her to the terrifying
and frozen immobility which seems to be her destiny.
She can share neither life nor death with the rest of
humanity. It is an ultimate alienation.

Questions

1. What advantages and disadvantages does Laura get
from her friendship with Braggioni?
2. What sets Laura apart from all the people she
habitually deals with?
3. How has the author related past times and events
to the present action of a single evening?
4. In what ways has Laura's Catholic background prepared her present attitudes as a revolutionary?
5. In what ways is the dream at the end a resolution
of the conflicts of the story? Can there be a resolution for a person like Laura?

See also "Questions for Comparing the Author's Stories," below.

Further Reading

Bluefarb, Sam. "Loss of Innocence in 'Flowering Judas,'" *College Language Association Journal*, VII, 256-262.

Bride, Sister Mary. "Laura and the Unlit Lamp," *Studies in Short Fiction*, Fall 1967, 61-63.

Redden, Dorothy. "'Flowering Judas,' Two Voices," *Studies in Short Fiction*, VI, 194-204.

Katherine Anne Porter— Questions for Comparing the Author's Stories

1. What are the similarities in character and situation of the young women in the two stories? Is there sufficient similarity to support a conjecture that the stories may be autobiographical?

2. Does the revolutionary setting of "Flowering Judas" carry a greater threat of inherent danger than the urban setting of "Theft"?

3. Since one story is told in the present tense and the other in the past, discuss the differences in effect and meaning obtained by the author's use of each tense.

4. What do the stories say about the isolation and independence of young women on their own?

J. F. Powers   *The Valiant Woman* (p. 1253)
(Shorter Edition, p. 576)

The author has chosen to begin near the end of an occasion which is itself near the end of a lifetime and a long relationship between Father Firman and Mrs. Stoner, the "valiant woman" of the mocking title. To strike in at such a point is a shrewd and simple authorial tactic if the point is to sum up the comic and painful meaning of the priest's living with a domineering woman in a state resembling wedlock.

The penultimate scenes at the dinner table and card

table are broken open for flashbacks that reveal how Mrs. Stoner has cunningly (though not deliberately; she is too stupid for deliberate cunning) transformed her position in the household into something that makes Father Firman a laughingstock to his friends and a ridiculous figure in his own eyes. The scenes serve to lay on the last straw that breaks his tolerance of her, and his reading has discovered that according to "the letter of the law" he has a right to get rid of her. (She does not conform precisely to the prescription that a priest's female housekeeper should be of "*advanced age*.") But almost as quickly as he discovers the means for his deliverance, he comes upon a Catch-22: though the letter of the law permits him to get rid of her, the spirit of the law does not. The mere fact that he is intelligent and scrupulous enough to distinguish between letter and spirit completes the trap in which he must continue to squirm.

The episode with the mosquito at the end is, in a real sense, anticlimactic, but it is by no means irrelevant. It is a symbolic reenactment of the priest's futile efforts to be rid of his human tormentor, Mrs. Stoner. The cunning of the mosquito in taking sanctuary in St. Joseph's beard is the fairly transparent equivalent of Mrs. Stoner's security within the spirit of the laws governing her presence in the house. Powers's sly and nimble tactics of comedy show up particularly well in this play with symbols, and in the fact that "murdering" is only mentioned in connection with the fracas involving the mosquito, though we are meant to understand that the woman is figuratively murdering the priest, just as she has "skunked" him at cards.

Questions

1. How much of Father Firman's life is summed up in the short span of the evening's action?

2. Is Mrs. Stoner alone responsible for having made his life a "shambles"?

3. Is Mrs. Stoner aware of how she has distorted her position in the household? Is her relative ignorance the same as relative innocence? Does the story suggest that intelligence may be a handicap in dealing with stupid people?

4. Why, precisely, can't Father Firman get rid of Mrs. Stoner? What has this to do with his inability to swat the mosquito that is tormenting him?

5. What does Father Firman mean by "the perverted decency of the times"?

Further Reading

Burgess, C. F.   "The Case of the Hen-Pecked Priest in J. F. Powers's 'The Valiant Woman,'" *Cithara*, IX (November 1969), 67-71.

Philip Roth   *The Conversion of the Jews* (p. 1261)

The question Ozzie Freedman raises is serious enough —after all, religious wars and persecutions have resulted from differing answers to it—but the circumstances in which it is raised would appear to minimize its gravity.   It can be taken as merely the sign of a small boy's obstinacy and impertinence. The rabbi and his mother choose to take it that way.

It is not in Ozzie's character to expand the issue, though it is in his character to be the one among this group of students who has the habit of wanting to understand the sense of what he is required to read aloud. The bullying to which he is subjected by the rabbi is the mild authoritarianism that usually provokes no major explosions in classrooms. The bloodying of Ozzie's nose may be accidental, and Ozzie's insulting response may stem from hysteria at the sight of his own blood. Further, Ozzie has no conscious intention of heading for the roof when he bolts from the classroom.

From such coincidences great conflagrations ensue. Once Ozzie is on the roof, he begins to realize that he has made a move of staggering significance. The author takes time to emphasize the transformation by comparing Ozzie's situation to that of a thief and bridegroom, both of whom are changed utterly from one instant to the next. Now Ozzie has power over the adult world. The extent of that power is impossible to measure, but it is in itself so intoxicating that he can not resist testing it.

He uses it to force his mother and the bullying rabbi into a "conversion"—at least into making statements contrary to their religious faith. But the power has no effect on his peers. They go on wildly encouraging him to jump and kill himself. He realizes the "strangeness of what these people, his friends, were asking. . . . If there was a question to be asked now it was not 'Is it me?' but rather 'Is it us? . . . Is it us?'"

The nature and the uses of power are, in a word, ultimately inscrutable. The story is not perfectly clear about whether he finally compels his young classmates to say they believe in Jesus. We are told that they "all" declared their belief, but this may refer only to the adults.

And, of course, it is not clear, either, what happens when Ozzie hits the yellow net being held for him by the firemen. All we can say for sure is that such jumps are very dangerous. People can be killed in making them. The author chose to end by leaving us in uncertainty beyond our knowledge that the achievement of such power as Ozzie found is to enter the terrain of maximum danger.

Questions

1. What distinguishes this story from a mere anecdote? How has the author revealed the truly important issues built into the conflict?

2. What is Yakov Blotnik's role? Why is Ozzie insistent on converting him?

3. What brings on Ozzie's uncertainty about who he is?

4. Is there any implication that a real and irreversible conversion has taken place? Or are all the statements of belief in Christ made to deceive Ozzie until he is safe on the ground?

5. Why does Ozzie jump from the roof when he could have gone back down the stairs? Does he safely reach the ground? How do you know?

Further Reading

Waldhorn, Arthur and Hilda. *The Right of Becoming.* New York: World Publishing Company, 1966.

Saki (H. H. Munro)   *The Open Window* (p. 1274)

It will hardly do to load a story so clearly intended as entertainment with too many heavy psychological or metaphysical interpretations. The little
girl's inventions have a macabre ring to them, and all
we can be sure of is that in Framton she has encountered
a young man whose mental balance is so precarious that
he will be particularly susceptible to the morbid
fantasy she weaves to explain why the French window has
been left open on an October afternoon. Surely the girl
could not have the clairvoyance to foresee that the
hunters will actually return in a manner that precisely
dovetails with the misinformation she has spilled out
to the guest. That dovetailing—including Mrs.
Sappleton's cry "Here they are at last!"—is unmistakably a contrivance of the author's, a management of
the story accomplished to give it a neat comic twist.
Or, if we want to consider it as something more than
author manipulation, we might say that it is pure coincidence that the return of the hunters should, on this
one occasion, fit so neatly with the little girl's
romantic make-believe.

Yet it must be said that there is something witch-
like about the child. Calling the outcome coincidence
or author's contrivance will not entirely dispell the
suspicion that the girl has a monstrous knack for
sniffing out the psychic flaws in people like Framton
and exploiting them mercilessly, turning the most mun-
dane circumstances into instruments of psychic
destruction. And even though we can see exactly how
the pieces have been fitted together to make the plot
come out as neatly as it does, we may suspect that the
plot may represent a malevolent design in the nature of
things, a malevolence to which this child has the key.
It would appear that the story works as well as it does
on our imagination because it hits us with a sly
secondary shock just as we are laughing off the relatively harmless first jolt of surprise at how things
have worked out. It is as if a magician or other
master of illusion gave a thorough explanation of his
tricks . . . and left us smelling brimstone while we
wondered if the explanation itself was not intended to
compound the tricks played on our eyes and understanding. This is the kind of comic play with the
possibilities of storytelling which sets up disturbing
resonances.

Questions

1. Is the tone of the story purely lighthearted, or is it touched with malevolence?

2. In what ways is Framton the ideal victim for the child's make-believe?

3. At the end of the story is the girl manipulating her family in the same way she manipulated Framton? If so, why?

4. Are we to believe she is diabolically malicious or is she merely a child with a hyperactive imagination? How sure can you be of her character and her motives?

Further Reading

Peltzie, Bernard E. "Teaching Meaning Through Struc-
    ture in the Short Story," *English Journal*, 55
    (September 1966), 703-709.

Max Schott   *The Horsebreaker* (p. 1277)

The character of Clyde is the preeminent focus of interest here. The younger horsebreaker merely serves to provide the circumstances from which the central action proceeds, action that serves as a test in which the aspects of Clyde's character—late in his life— can be demonstrated. These aspects can be tested and demonstrated for Clyde as well as for the reader, since Clyde at the threshold of old age has encountered a distressing quandary about who he really is. After a long, successful and adventurous life he has attempted to settle down with the fruits of his accomplishments. He is old and rich . . . but what has become of the harvest from his active years? Only the husks remain. "The stories he told about himself began to ring false even to his own not unsympathetic ear."

His situation is comparable to that of Ulysses, his adventures done, as we see him in Tennyson's poem, finding "How dull it is to pause, to make an end," in search of one more challenge worthy of his name and the man he has been. And like the prototypical Ulysses, Clyde counts on the cunning and experience of his years to accomplish what the younger horsebreaker has failed

to do. Hornet seems almost supernatural in his unpredictable frenzy, being thereby a fit antagonist for
the ultimate conflict between him and Clyde. The spirit
of the man must summon every remaining resource to
master the negative and resistant tricks of the de-
mented animal.

Clyde almost succeeds in his task by the routine
measures of subjugation to which he submits the horse
before beginning the ride. It is only the chance appearance of the coyote—and a momentary lapse of caution on
the rider's part, a lapse into pride and overconfidence
—that almost costs him his victory.

After the incredible battering he takes while the
horse is dragging him, Clyde is understandably tempted
to finish off the combat in the easiest possible way:
to lead the horse in or leave him on the spot. But we
understand that the purpose of what he has endured would
be lost if he did not see it through in the right way by
riding back into town. It is not merely that he must
keep his image intact in the eyes of others. In any
event, he refuses to lie about what has happened and the
townspeople discover he has been thrown. The point appears to be that he must do things the right way to
retain the identity of which age tried to rob him. At
the price of bruises, sprains and some lost teeth he has
earned the assurance that bodily decrepitude cannot defeat him.

For all its echoes of heroic myth and tall-tale
extravagance, the story operates easily within a realistic discipline, and the wry comedy of the narration
provides a counterweight to balance the potential
solemnity of Clyde's predicament.

Questions

1. Is the relationship between Clyde and the young
horsebreaker more competitive than cooperative? Explain.

2. What changes in motivation explain Clyde's actions
as the story progresses?

3. Is the main conflict between Clyde and the horse,
or between Clyde and something or someone else? Specify.

4. In what ways does the character of the horse
Hornet complement Clyde's? Can you define Clyde's
feelings toward the horse?

5. What does the story say about pride and determination? About the resources an aging man can call on?

Irwin Shaw *The Girls in Their Summer Dresses* (p. 1290)

Shaw's precise little story may say very little
about what people will do under the pressure of this
temptation or that, but it states with touching exact-
ness how they will feel. We see only part of one Sunday
in the lives of Michael and Frances. We learn very
little about where they have come from and can hardly
guess where they will go from here. But here they are,
stirred by the promise of spring in the air, stirred by
the desire to make the most of the day before it passes
swiftly and is gone forever. And—cruelly enough—they
want different things. The woman wants them to "hang
around with each other." The man wants at least to
savor the daydreams of changing his life that are inspired by glimpses of pretty girls passing on the
street. "I casually inspect the universe," he says, and
testifies further that his inspection of other women
has been casual. Perhaps it will not always be. He
doesn't know; his wife wants him to say, at least, that
he will never act on the temptation to be free of her.
So the possibility of buying tranquility with a hypocritical declaration of fidelity is brought in to
further exacerbate the rawness of the stratches they
have given each other.

The story does not say that love dies at such moments of candor as these young married people have come
to. It does say that when we press, as Frances does,
for certainty, the answer is very apt to be a distressing one. When Michael says, "I'll keep it to myself,"
he seems to be threatening as well as promising not to
share with Frances some vital fraction of his life and
spirit that he would have liked to open further if
there were any way left to do so. Neither is at fault.
Neither, in the nature of things, can be blamed for
wasting the promise of the day.

To an extent this story echoes Hemingway's *Hills
Like White Elephants* in manner as in theme. The search
for parallels and differences between the two should
make both of them come more vividly to life.

Questions

1. How important is the setting to the meaning of
the story?
2. Does this small story fairly represent a major
incompatibility between the desires of men and women?

Or is it a conflict of transient whims?

3. In what sense are the women on the streets a fair representation of the city's glamor?

4. Is anything lost except one day that might have gone better? How does the author suggest that one day's loss is important in the pattern of lifetimes?

5. This story deals with manners and attitudes of the 1930s. How would it have to be modified to deal with those of the 1970s?

Further Reading

Baird, Joe L. and Ralph Grajeda. "A Shaw Story and Brooks and Warren," *CEA Critic*, XXVIII (February 1966), 1-4.

Isaac Bashevis Singer *The Spinoza of Market Street*
(p. 1294)

The charm of this story no doubt comes from its primitive simplicity. The Warsaw setting is described at some length, but the images have the predictable sturdy crudeness of folk art. In this regard, note particularly the description of the street below Dr. Fischelson's attic study. For purposes of the story it is enough that the noisy, swarming street should contrast with the firmament overhead—the other of the "two worlds" into which we can see. The lack of sophistication in this contrast suggests slyly that Fischelson is a very unsophisticated man for all his lifelong study of philosophy. He has retained only a few simple precepts of conduct from Spinoza and these seem to do him little good, being at odds with the barrenness of his external life and the weird tumult of his dream. So probably we are supposed to see him as a special sort of fool. And after the miracle of his wedding night when both he and Dobbe are transformed by an unexplained and inexplicable bliss, he seems crankily determined not to admit his good luck. There is not much to be gained by rational analysis of a story so steadfastly whimsical, but it offers a fine opportunity to consider the effects of tone, setting, and the story-teller's play with the reader's expectations. The miracle will resist most attempts to explain its causes or state its meaning. Take it or leave it.

Questions

1. Has the author developed clear lines of motivation that lead Dr. Fischelson and Dobbe to marry? Is
motivation in the ordinary sense necessary for the
success of the story? If not, what makes up for its
absence?

2. Why does the author emphasize the physical un-
attractiveness of bride and groom?

3. Is it meaningful that the story takes place at
the outbreak of World War I?

4. Why label Fischelson the "Spinoza" of his shabby
milieu? Is the old man a philosopher or a crank? Does
he become a fool? Remain a fool?

5. What general names might be given the "two
worlds" that Fischelson sees from his study? In what
sense and to what extent are these worlds reconciled
by the marriage?

Jean Stafford   *In the Zoo* (p. 1309)

Among the associations that will be stirred up by
this story are memories of Aesop's fables, comic strips
with animal characters, and the multitudinous allego-
ries in which human conflicts are worked out in the
destinies of beasts. (See, for example, Thurber's *The
Owl Who Was God* and Balzac's *A Passion in the Desert*.)
For in Stafford's virtuoso performance not only are
major metaphors drawn from the animals, the animals
also serve as proxies for the terrible, indeclarable
warfare of the humans. She has married the dreamlike
persuasiveness of fairy tale and fable with a realistic
account of the way two young sisters were warped by the
perverted charity of the woman who sheltered them. The
dialogue and circumstances of the present scene and of
times past are perfectly credible throughout—and yet
the sense of something uncanny moves in the shadows of
reminiscence. The rather extravagantly rhetorical style
contributes to our sense that behind the foreground
action an unforgiveable crime is being enacted. Among
the signs pointing to the larger and darker dimensions
of the story is the comment of the "edgy" millionaire:
"That girl gives me the cold shivers. One would think
she had just seen a murder," and the narrator's comment, "Well, I had." The reference here is certainly

to more than the deaths of monkey and dog. Something as
abstract but important as good faith has been murdered
in the orphans' world, and they themselves are
corrupted by its extinction.

The dominating character is Mrs. Placer—a comic but
utterly sinister woman from whose hypocrisies neither
human nor animal is immune. Gran is the tyrant of her
boarding house. She presides over ugliness and dis-
penses it to her boarders, who seem weirdly but believably grateful to be a part of her entourage. Many people
like to lick boots in return for the feeling of power
they get from association with a successful bully of
Mrs. Placer's sort. And there is not much to suggest to
the little girls that they have any choice other than
to conform like the boarders to Gran's ingenious bullying. Like many bullies, Gran accomplishes part of her
evil enchantment by portraying herself as a permanent
victim. (Most students will be able to draw parallels
to her tactics from their family or social experiences.)
The false and corrupting image of herself as a victim
is abetted by her fraud of righteousness in the face of
an unrelieved surrounding corruption. "There was no
stratum of society not reeking with the effluvium of
fraud and pettifoggery"—according to this woman, and
she succeeds in indoctrinating the girls with this view
in spite of their instinctive struggles to find an
alternative.

Mr. Murphy, the "gentle, alcoholic ne'er-do-well"—
a sort of secular St. Francis—seems to offer such an
alternative. Though we are given no glimpse of his
thoughts, he seems to understand what the children are
up against with Mrs. Placer, and he seems to think he
has found at least a partial antidote to her influence
when he gives them the dog, on whom they can expend
their impulse to love. Mrs. Placer counters his move,
almost effortlessly—and that ease is the bottom line
of horror as Stafford sees it—by corrupting the dog.
It seems easier for dogs as well as humans to accommodate themselves to the routines of the bully than to
act out the more devious and contradictory roles of
love. The change of the dog's name from *Laddy* to *Caesar*
is a token of the changes to be wrought in his character by Mrs. Placer's influence and training. The somewhat satiric language is here again used to suggest a
kind of superhuman power emanating from the woman:
"There was between these two such preternatural rap-
port, such an impressive conjugation of suspicion, that
he, sensing the approach of a policeman, could convey

instantly to her the immediate necessity of clapping his nose cage on." That is, their very compliance with the law is a means of treacherously superseding it.

With their dog alienated from them, "Daisy and I wished we were dead," the narrator declares, preparing for the worst. The worst comes tumbling on them when, in their sorrow, they make another appeal for Mr. Murphy's aid. There is gallantry in the parade the three of them make through the dizzying heat to confront Mrs. Placer. "Here we were on a high moral mission, two draggle-tailed gumptionless girls and a toper whom no one could take seriously. . . ." What happens when the confrontation takes place <u>can</u> be read in a way that leaves Mrs. Placer blameless. She does nothing more than open the door to let the-dog-who-has-become-Caesar out. She expresses formal regret when she sees that he has killed Murphy's monkey. But to read it without understanding her total culpability for having <u>prepared</u> just such an outcome is to miss most of what the story has to tell us about the ways of evil and the locus of guilt. This is the high point of the story, the resolution of the main plot line, and the intensification of language marks it. "We stood aghast in the dark-red sunset, killed by our horror and our grief for Shannon and our unforgivable disgrace. We stood upright in a dead faint, and an eon passed before Mr. Murphy picked up Shannon's body and wove away sobbing, 'I don't believe it! I don't *believe it*!'" This is the cry of a man who has supposed that he has taken the measure of the power of evil but who learns in a flash that it is far vaster than he had guessed. His response of poisoning the dog may suggest that he too has become an agent of Mrs. Placer's power. At any rate he is finished as an effective force for goodness.

Though the plot of the story-within-the-story is concluded at this point, the full revelation of what Mrs. Placer's victory means is still to be given in the summary made by the narrator of her life after that time. In this summary and in the compulsive suspiciousness she displays in her last conversation with her sister (and later on the train) we see that she too has been corrupted into one of Mrs. Placer's allies against the natural goodness of the world and against the trusting faith that might vindicate human existence.

Questions

1. What ways of life are represented by Gran and by Mr. Murphy? To what extent is the story a conflict between them for the souls of the children? Who wins the conflict?

2. How are human problems worked out or clarified by the actions and destinies of various animals?

3. How do style and point of view contribute to the meaning of the action?

4. How is the present meeting between the sisters a suitable occasion for sorting out events of the fairly remote past? What would be lost if there were no perspective of time on those events?

5. What does the story say about the cooperation of victims with their oppressor?

John Steinbeck   *The Chrysanthemums* (p. 1326)

Few spectacles are more inherently poignant than that of a person gifted, strong, and good caught in a situation where her capacities are trapped and her virtues become their own jailers. Though we see Elisa Allen objectively, everything about her suggests vigor not used up by her life on the ranch as Henry's wife. The imagery that describes her "terrier fingers" suggests an animality deliberately suppressed by her energetic devotion to housewifely duties.

The appearance of the vagabond tinker inevitably suggests to her the possibility of taking to the road herself in search of broader horizons. "I wish women could do such things," she says when her conversation with him brings out how "nice" it is to be footloose. (So many conflicting connotations of the word <u>nice</u> are played with that its ambiguity must be examined as it relates to the theme of the story. Escape and self-reliance are nice, but nice women resist the temptations of what would be <u>nice</u>. Note that Elisa herself, struggling to complete the awareness sparked by the tinker's visit, challenges her husband to tell her what he means when he says "nice.")

Something more than her sales resistance is broken down when the visitor takes an interest in his flowers. There is an embarrassing moment when she reaches to touch his trousers. Then she "crouched low" like a fawning dog." She can only be shamed by this near destruction of her dignity and her defenses. Perhaps the ruthless scrubbing she gives herself in her bath a little later represents an attempt to purge herself of the soiling impulse she felt as she reached for the man.

To be sure, we can only guess at the tinker's motives for throwing away the chrysanthemum sprouts she gave him in good faith. Just as surely Elisa must interpret their presence in the road as evidence that the man took her in with a shoddy trick, that his interest in her passion was only feigned. Now she is more deeply shamed than before, but we know that shame does not, by itself, eradicate libidinous impulses once they are roused. It is more likely to convert them into anger, and probably her vision of prize fights in which "the gloves get heavy and soggy with blood" is the expression of her wish for revenge against all men, men who undervalue and misuse her offerings of eagerness and strength.

The ultimate pathos of the story consists in the fact that it is she, not her husband, who denies herself even the tawdry satisfaction of watching men get the punishment her feelings tell her they deserve. This woman who has felt the yearnings of a sort of giantess stir in her says it will be "enough" if she gets some wine with her dinner. It is _nice_, no doubt, to be as agreeable as this, but the implied price is that she must be old before her time.

Some of these comments certainly make the story sound more melodramatic than it seems in Steinbeck's language. That should lead us to observe how he has deliberately muted the melodrama by a scrupulously objective presentation and by adherence in dialogue to the restricted vocabulary of his characters.

Comparison of theme and structure might profitably be made with Joyce's _A Little Cloud_.

Questions

1. What details of imagery and physical description serve as evidence of Elisa's frustration in her role as housewife? Of what importance is it that she and the stranger share laughter at the beginning of their conversation?

2. What ironies are contained in the frequent but contradictory uses of the word "nice"? How do these

ironies fit with the ironies of Elisa's situation?

3. Explain the significance of the scene in which Elisa bathes.

4. Why does Elisa finally imagine the prize fights to be so gory? Why does she decide against going after her husband offers to take her?

5. Who or what is ultimately responsible for Elisa's troubles?

Further Reading

Marcus, Mordecai. "The Lost Dream of Sex and Children in 'The Chrysanthemums,'" *Modern Fiction Studies*, XI (Spring 1965), 54-58.

McMahan, Elizabeth. "'The Chrysanthemums': Study of a Woman's Sexuality," *Modern Fiction Studies*, XIV (Winter 1968-1969), 453-458.

Sweet, Charles A. "Ms. Elisa Allen and Steinbeck's 'The Chrysanthemums,'" *Modern Fiction Stories*, 20 (1974), 210-214.

Peter Taylor   *Dean of Men* (p. 1335)

In Taylor's story the fictional convention represents a man talking (or perhaps writing a letter) to his son. The character of the listener is implied, and though he is never actually brought into view, we realize that his personality, his memories, as well as his age are influencing the shape of the account his father gives. This account actually consists of several stories or instances, linked together as family history but also similar in that each records the betrayal of a man who trusted too much in what others promised. Therefore in our interpretation we will have to confront the major question of what the narrator hopes to convey to the young man by his illustrations. He must be trying to make a point at some critical moment in his son's life. And, in fact, it is easy enough to isolate the sentence in which he formulates his point as an axiom: "A man must somehow go on living among men, Jack."

Yet it is not just the vagueness of that "somehow" which leaves the moral so nebulous once we have come to it. In his character as mature scholar and adminis-

trator the narrator is well equipped to assemble and
order his thoughts, to articulate them with eloquence
and precision. Like other good fathers he no doubt
wishes to offer what he has distilled from the wisdom
of the world. But "the wisdom of this world is folly,"
the sages tell us—and Taylor has left us latitude to
believe, if we choose, that his narrator is not so much
revealing the strength he has gained from experience as
rationalizing the weakness that led him to conspire at
his own defeat.

The launching point for the series of episodes that
make up the story is the occasion in which the narrator's wife repeats the exact words he once heard his
mother address to his father. The coincidence becomes
immensely important in the design of the story because
the narrator is sharp enough to see it as an emblem of
the cruel subtlety with which history repeats itself in
generation after generation despite superficial differences in circumstance or character and despite all the
learned strategms by which we attempt to evade its implacable recurrences. The coincidental repetition of
words—"I would be ashamed of myself if I were you"—
sets the pattern for the stories of grandfather, father,
and narrator, each a story of betrayal followed by a
withdrawal from wholehearted commitment to the struggles of a man with the world of his chosen endeavor.

The narrator tells of going to his office (just as
his father had done on another day) after the banal,
prophetic, recurrent words were spoken. In his office
he thinks first that his books, paper, and pictures
have betrayed him—that is to say, the things he has
loved and trusted most have made him an idealist unfit
for the ugly rough and tumble of academic politics as
they are actually perpetrated. His second thought is
even more painful. The books, papers, pictures—the
life of the mind he loved and thought secure—are
"dead—murdered" by the self-serving treachery of his
colleagues. To decipher this fanciful metaphor of
murdered books, one must assume that they spelled out
a code of honor which, the narrator has now been
taught, he must abandon if he wants to survive. This
code of honor is an adequate equivalent of the code of
political honor from which his grandfather withdrew
and the business honor abandoned by his father in the
equivalent crises of their lives.

The abandonment of a code of honor and the image of
the self it sustained while it was intact does not mean
for these men of successive generations a collapse into

cynicism or acquiescence in merely practical expedients
for survival. Each is still bound by moral obligations
and love though he has lost his guiding star. Each must
"somehow" do his best though his idea of the good has
been shattered. The narrator seems to be well aware of
the logical dilemma in such a situation. (One assumes
that as a scholar the narrator has read as much as any
of us has about the crisis of faith that frightens our
age.)

Ultimately he has nothing to oppose against the absurdity of his dilemma except a stubborn refusal to let
his defeats minimize him one iota more than they must.
This heroic, Sisyphean persistence in spite of frustration might well be more impressive to his son than any
moral intellectually deduced from the instances he cites
—it might also complement or clarify the vagueness of
the "somehow" in the advice he is trying to pass on to
the younger man. His actions expand the meaning of what
he wishes to say—as is always the case in fiction. It
is not at all necessary that those actions should exactly reiterate his thought.

The story abounds in ironies. Injustice that brings
husband and wife closer together brings them so close
that the marriage is destroyed. The father's anxiety for
his daughter's happiness leads him to destroy the delicate balance of her romance. Bad luck clears the way
for good luck to come. Good intentions lead to good results just as often as to heartbreaking ones. This
profusion of ironies may well make the story more
comprehensible to readers the age of the narrator than
to younger people. It should be fascinating to ask
young readers to see themselves in the role of the son
Jack who is being addressed and to respond by imagining
his responses.

Questions

1. What is the common denominator of the stories
told by the narrator of his grandfather, his father,
and himself?

2. The form of the story implies a particular
listener—the son of the narrator, being advised by his
father. Can you imagine the occasion for this advice?
Is it generally applicable to members of his son's
generation?

3. What does the narrator mean when he says that he
found the books, pictures, and papers in his office

"murdered"? What, specifically, ended for him on the morning of this discovery? He goes out of his way to emphasize the success of his second marriage and the "happy, active life" he subsequently led. Does this mean he has resurrected whatever was murdered by the treachery of those he trusted?

4. There are several patterns of betrayal in the story. Does the narrator betray himself or abet his own betrayal?

James Thurber   *The Secret Life of Walter Mitty*
                 (p. 1359)
                 (Shorter Edition, p. 587)

Let's face this from the beginning: Thurber was, at least professionally, a misogynist. One of his favorite targets in cartoon and story was the American wife. She appears again and again as a comic but nonetheless frightful ogre. Crass and domineering, as pitiless as she is unattractive, she figures at her worst in this brief farce that has added an eponym to the American vocabulary.

The means by which she gained the upper hand in the marriage are not even suggested by the scope of the drama we witness. We may infer that Mitty was too feeble from the start to have put up much resistance. Be that as it may, from the instant she first speaks until the end we see her tyranny as unassailable by any means at her husband's disposal. She finds fault with everything he does and cuts the ground from under his feet by her undeniable predictions of failure in anything that might mitigate her oppression. She allies herself with his infirmities—"You're not a young man any longer"—and dismisses even his attempt to find sanctuary in compensatory fantasies as mere illness—"I'm going to take your temperature when I get you home"—and defies him to deny it.

Yet, by the skin of his teeth, with nothing to support him, he does deny it. However ludicrous his final posture as a hero scornful of the firing squad, there is some saving remnant in his (perhaps unconscious) choice of this pretense when the more attractice ones have all failed him.

As we know, Thurber wrote many fables, most of them with some embittered modern twist to old moralities and assurances. Perhaps it is appropriate to see this story as fundamentally a fable, and to see its moral in the path by which our hero comes to an unassailable redoubt within himself when all else has failed. In rather mocking language we are told he is "inscrutable to the last," and from what we have seen of his attempts to shed his own inadequate personality in favor of something he imagines to be nobler we may assume that he was inscrutable to himself. That is, he himself did not know what he could call up in extremity until he was reduced to that extremity by absolute tyranny. However farcical his ultimate parody of heroic refusal of circumstantial defeat, surely his name and image would not have stuck in the collective imagination if the real thing did not show through the outrageous parody. He is the extreme, sublimated archetype of the anti-hero who has replaced the traditional hero in much contemporary literature.

Questions

1. For what circumstances in his real life do Mitty's fantasies compensate?

2. Enumerate the details that link the fantasies with what is really happening.

3. In what sense may it be said that Mitty's fantasies reveal his character more truly than his behavior?

4. From what sources are the fantasies drawn?

5. What is the relationship between the last fantasy and all that has gone before? How does this fantasy shape the theme of the story?

Further Reading

Elias, Robert. "James Thurber: The Primitive, the Innocent, and the Individual," *American Scholar*, 27 (1958), 362.

Ellis, James. "The Allusion in 'The Secret Life of Walter Mitty,'" *English Journal*, 54 (1965), 310-313.

Holmes, Charles S. *The Clock of Columbus: The Literary Career of James Thurber*. New York: Atheneum, 1972, 216-219.

Lindner, Carl M. "Thurber's Walter Mitty—The Underground American Hero," *Georgia Review*, 28 (1974), 283-289.

Satterfield, Leon. "Thurber's 'The Secret Life of
    Walter Mitty,'" *Explicator*, 27 (1969), Item 57.
Sundell, Carl. "The Architecture of Walter Mitty's
    Secret Life," *English Journal*, 56 (1967), 1284-1287.

Leo Tolstoy   *God Sees the Truth, but Waits* (p. 1364)

There could hardly be an example of greater purity
and simplicity in storytelling than this. The characterization is limited to essentials. The circumstances
are laid out as they occurred, the accompanying emotions declared without any attempt to color them or
involve the sympathies of the reader.

It is a story of justice delayed—delayed so long
that it becomes inconsequential in worldly terms. Perhaps to most of us it will seem a story of the way
injustice prevails. Our idea of justice is very powerfully attached to ideas of equivalence—if something is
taken from a man, something of equal value must be returned to restore the balance of the scales of justice.
But here nothing is given to Aksënov for the years of
freedom and family happiness wrongfully taken from him
except that his "heart grew light and the longing for
home left him." Surely that longing might have been
worn away by mere despair. Are we to believe that
liberation from desire is sufficient compensation for
all that life has denied us?

Tolstoy says it is. Surely the whole point of the
story is to "justify God's ways to Man." No doubt in
class discussions there will be considerable argument
about whether he has done so.

Questions

1. What compensation does Aksënov get for all he has
lost? What does the form of compensation say about the
meaning of the title?

2. Could this story be classified a protest against
injustice? Could it be classified as religious propa-
ganda?

3. Would the point of the story be lost if, after
Makar's confession, Askënov returned to spend his last
years happily with his family?

4. How does the relatively sparse and generalized characterization of Aksënov and others fit the purposes of the story?

See also "Questions for Comparing the Author's Stories," p. 230 of this *Handbook*.

Leo Tolstoy   *The Death of Ivan Ilych* (p. 1370)
              (Shorter Edition, p. 591)

La Rochefoucauld said that no man can truly face the fact of his death any more than he can stare with open eyes at the sun. Tolstoy apparently agrees with this, maintaining only a slight reservation to be incorporated at the very end of his relentless exposition of the degrading terror with which an average man approaches his end. With his legalistic mind Ivan has learned the syllogism: "Caius is a man, men are mortal, therefore Caius is mortal." He does not dispute the syllogism. Simply, because there is a dissociation between the compartments of his mind, he has never understood and cannot truly understand how it applies to him. While he dreads increasingly that his body and his unique self are approaching extinction, he has no means to reconcile himself to the insuperable fact.

The main part of the story has to do with his flailing attempts to deny, evade and postpone the inevitable horror. And what makes this fiction so potent is the prolonged and unremitting treatment of a progressive decline, with every new phase accompanied by increasing desperation. Only the attentions of Gerasim provide a measure of comfort or distraction from what the dying man must face alone, and these seem trivial in comparison to the enormity of approaching death and to the increasingly perceptible failure to find any justification for the life Ivan has led.

It has not been, by usual standards, a bad or unpleasant life. He has had a measure of success and good luck. He has enjoyed at least some parts of his existence—though playing bridge is the only pleasure that he has found durable, and that in itself comments on the vanity of his earthly term. The gratifications are mockingly transient and insignificant in scale when stacked against the magnitude of approaching death. This is a point that Tolstoy belabors with brutal and unswerving

insistence: "Ivan Ilych's life had been most simple,
most ordinary, and therefore most terrible." There is
no mincing the horror. At the height of his career as
a judge he has sensed his power with some satisfaction:
"Ivan Ilych never abused his power; he tried on the
contrary to soften its expression, but the consciousness of it and of the possibility of softening its
effect supplied the chief interest and attractiveness
of his office." Now he is in the grip of a power which
has no means or inclination to soften the effect of the
universal sentence, and all the bourgeois gratifications
are trivialized by its intransigence.

The slight accident which leads to his fatal illness
occurs when fortune (as he conceives it) is smiling on
him. He has survived certain disappointments in family
life, and, being a man of strength and ambition, he is
preparing what he conceives as an expansion suitable to
his attainments when he gets a minor bump in the side.
From then on, of course, the long decline continues as
even the memories of past success grow vapid or bitter.
That he is correct in his last bitter assessments is
established by the opening sections of the story. There
we see that his friends and even his family are relieved
to be free of the burden he has become. Surely such an
aftermath clinches the argument. His life has been truly
terrible, truly worthless.

The one gleam of comfort in this seamless pessimism
is peculiarly Tolstoyan in its ruthless logic: Since
life has been terrible, what a blessing that it is
finished! "What joy!" What joy to realize that in relinquishing life one has overcome death and the terrors
it spread through what was at best an equivocal existence, shot through with vanities, disappointments, and
bad faith. Good riddance of bad rubbish, Ivan says joy-
fully when he dies.

He has been guided to this redemptive wisdom by
only one of the other characters encountered in the
story. The young man Gerasim, still in the prime of
health, tends to the whims of the sufferer with constant
good cheer. But beyond this his matter-of-fact kindli-
ness nurtures the germ of an idea which finally blossoms
in Ivan's soul and in the conclusion of the story. It is
the idea that, since death and suffering are part of the
tissue of mortal existence, goodness consists of treat-
ing them as unexceptional. This attitude, and this
alone, enables Ivan to extricate himself from the "mesh
of falsity" in which his life and suffering have both
been trapped.

For most of us it will be very hard to accept the proffered resolution to the most terrifying of enigmas. But that is all Tolstoy will grant us. He meant it to be hard, hard as life and death are in his stern view.

Questions

1. How do his colleagues, friends, and family respond to Ivan Ilych's death? How does the presentation of their response set the stage for an account of his life?
2. What guided him in choosing the course his life would follow? What options did he neglect?
3. How does he deal with the difficulties of marriage and fatherhood?
4. Is there significance in the timing of the accident that leads to his death?
5. What are his feelings about the power given him as a magistrate?
6. What does the author suggest about the value of doctors?
7. Why does Ivan Ilych find no consolation in philosophizing about death?
8. Discuss the role of Gerasim in the last phases of Ivan Ilych's suffering. Is there a particular lesson in the young man's attitude, behavior, or character?
9. Interpret the sentence: "Ivan Ilych's life had been most simple, most ordinary, and therefore most terrible." Why "therefore . . ."?
10. What is his final attitude toward what his life has been? Does this attitude console him to dying?

See also "Questions for Comparing the Author's Stories," p. 230 of this *Handbook*.

Further Reading

Christian, R. F. *Tolstoy, a Critical Introduction*. Cambridge: Cambridge University Press, 1969, 236-238.
Dayananda, Y. J. "'The Death of Ivan Ilyich': A Psychological Study on Death and Dying," *Literature and Psychology*, 22 (1972), 191-198.
Forster, E. M. *Two Cheers for Democracy*. New York: Harcourt Brace, 1951, pp. 210-211.
Friedman, Norman. "What Makes a Short Story Short?" *Modern Fiction Studies*, 4 (1958), 103-117.

Hirschberg, W. R. "Tolstoy's 'The Death of Ivan
    Ilyich,'" *Explicator*, 28 (1969), Item 26.
Olney, James. "Experience, Metaphor, and Meaning: 'The
    Death of Ivan Ilych,'" *Journal of Aesthetics & Art
    Criticism*, 31 (1972), 101-114.
Rahv, Philip. "The Death of Ivan Ilyich and Joseph K.,"
    Southern Review, 5 (1939), 174-185; reprinted in his
    Image and Idea. New York: New Directions, 1949,
    pp. 111-127.
Trilling, Lionel. *The Experience of Literature*. New
    York: Holt, Rinehart & Winston, 1967, pp. 525-527.
Wasiolek, Edward. "Tolstoy's 'The Death of Ivan Ilyich'
    and Jamesian Fictional Imperatives," *Modern Fiction
    Studies*, 6 (1960), 318-321.

Leo Tolstoy—
Questions for Comparing the Author's Stories

1. How do Tolstoy's views about the nature of God and
His ways appear in the two stories?
2. What do the stories say about the form of the good
life? What values does the author consider preeminent?
3. Contrast the personalities of the central characters. Do they come to the same attitudes in the end?
4. Does either story offer consolation in a form you
can recognize?

John Updike   *A & P* (p. 1416)
(Shorter Edition, p. 637)

Gestures of protest are commonplace in our time. As
ordinarily reported by the journalistic media, they are
routinely made to protest a clearcut injustice or in
support of a cause easily labeled. Since *A & P* is primarily the story of an individual's gesture of protest
on an issue that is extremely hard to define with precision, our main interest will be in Sammy's motives.

Motives take the shape of the character in whom they
gather force. Sammy is certainly neither an ideologue
nor a grouch waiting for an excuse to take a stand
against his employer. He is a goodnatured, average boy,
not even particularly restless in his boring job. He
manages to find amusement in his work by making sarcastic observations of customers, by exchanging irrev-

erent banter with Stokesie, his fellow worker, by trans-
lating the sounds of his cash register into song, and
by ogling girls. When the three girls in bathing suits
come into the store, the slack potentials of his character are hooked by them in the most natural way. He is
stirred by the beauty of the girl he calls Queenie, by
her air of class and by the "sweet disorder of her
dress"—i.e., by the lowered straps of her bathing suit
and the exposure of untanned skin on her breasts.

He wants to attract her attention. Her little fuss
with the manager Lengel gives Sammy a chance to appear
to her (and the other girls) as "their unsuspected
hero." So he makes his first declaration that he will
quit. But the girls have already gone. There can be no
profit in persisting with his gesture. He thinks
"once you begin a gesture it's fatal not to go through
with it." But this seems to be a brand new realization
on his part, crystalizing at the same time his latent
motives for siding against "policy," though he knows he
will feel the consequences of his act for the rest of
his life and the world is going to be "hard" for him
hereafter. At this moment, the bow is strung. Everything in the boy's character that gave him a vague
preference for beauty, liberty, youth, and recklessness as against the stultifying cant of a stodgy civilization has been formed into a commitment that he must
honor, at whatever cost. It would, we see, be "fatal"
to his honor not to carry through with his gesture.

To be sure, he does not understand what has happened
as fully as the reader can. The tactic of the story is
to show the reader the ingredients of motivation and
their convergence to a point of fusion while leaving
the narrator unaware of how he came to act as he did.
No doubt Sammy would reject the notion that "honor"
forced him to make his gesture and stick to it. The
word, after all, is perhaps part of the cant against
which he has taken a stand, has become part of the vocabulary of "policy" made by those who see everything
that is not policy as "juvenile delinquency."

Nevertheless we can see that whatever has happened
to the term, the compulsions of honor rise from the
same sources as always. Beauty in distress compels a
young man to declare who he is by coming to its defense.

One promising line of discussion might start from
pointing out the way in which this story parallels the
myth of the Judgment of Paris. In the myth a sleepy,
unformed boy is wakened by the appearance of three
goddesses. He makes the judgment required of him—and

from it comes all the turmoil of the Trojan War. As
Sammy foresees in his own case, the world becomes a
harder place.

Questions

1. Does Sammy understand why he sticks to his decision to quit? Is it "in character" for him to quit?
What does the reader know about Sammy that he doesn't
realize himself? Has something new emerged out of the
ingredients of his character?

2. What is the importance of the fact that the girls
are wearing bathing suits. Of calling one of the girls
"Queenie"? Of the fact that there are three girls
together?

3. To what extent does the conflict depend on different interpretations of such concepts as decency and
policy?

4. Do you think the girls meant to cause trouble by
coming to the store in bathing suits? If so, what has
this to do with the theme of the story and any mythic
allusions called up by the situation itself?

5. Is Sammy right in thinking the world will be a
harder place for him hereafter? If it is, will this be
a gain or a loss for him?

Further Reading

Gilbert, Porter A. "John Updike's 'A & P': The Estab-
    lishment and an Emersonian Cashier," *English Journal*,
    LXI (November 1972), 1155-1158.
Rupp, Richard H. "John Updike: Style in Search of a
    Center," *Sewanee Review*, 75 (Autumn 1967), 693-709.
Ward, J. A. "John Updike's Fiction," *Critique: Studies
    in Modern Fiction*, 5 (1962), 27-49.

Alice Walker   *Everyday Use* (p. 1421)
              (Shorter Edition, p. 643)

The conflict in this story has been structured so
that, instead of being primarily between individuals,
it is a conflict between the value systems of older and
newer generations of American blacks. Though Maggie and

her sister Dee are of the same generation, Maggie clearly abides in the genuine tradition of her kin, in which objects of beauty like the churn dasher and the quilts are treasured as objects of "everyday use." The dasher handle, while it has been made of "beautiful light yellow wood," is more beautiful because from use it has taken the indentation made by the hands that have used it over the years. Dee does not fail to appreciate its beauty, but she means to retire it from use. "I'll think of something artistic to do with the dasher," she says—meaning that she will convert it to something purely ornamental. The same is true of the quilts fabricated from garments worn by family members over the years. Dee considers them "priceless" and wants to hang them up for display, to save them from being worn out, as no doubt they will be when Maggie uses them for her marriage bed. "Maggie can't appreciate these quilts," Dee argues, defining appreciation as the nonutilitarian contemplation by people educated to recognize purely aesthetic merit.

The thematic argument is very clearcut in this distinction, and there is little doubt as to the side chosen by the author. Through the narrator we perceive the shortcomings in Dee's acquired values. "She washed us in a river of make-believe, burned us with a lot of knowledge we didn't necessarily need to know. Pressed us to her with the serious way she read, to shove us away at just the moment, like dimwits, we seemed about to understand."

There is something fortuitous and shallow about all of Dee's bright attitudes, and though she proclaims a new day, she has forfeited the heart of the tradition in which her mother and Maggie choose to persist. The price of Dee's rejection may be measured by Maggie's quiet—and not vindictive—question, "Mama, when did Dee ever <u>have</u> any friends?"

Questions

1. What is the mother's feeling toward Dee? How is it changed in the course of the story?

2. Why has Dee rarely had friends? Does she want friends or expect to have them?

3. How does Maggie feel in the presence of her sister?

4. What does Dee's attitude toward the quilts say about her sense of her family and her roots?

5. Is the conflict of the story between two equally justifiable views of life? Can these views be reconciled?

6. What is implied by the subtitle in the form of a dedication?

Further Reading

Callahan, John. "Reconsideration: The Higher Ground of Alice Walker," *New Republic*, 14 (September 1974), 21-22.

Fowler, Carolyn. "Solid at the Core," *Freedomways*, 14 (1974), 59-62.

Nyabongo, V. S. *Books Abroad*, 48 (Autumn 1974), 787.

Eudora Welty   *Powerhouse* (p. 1429)

A voice—as much entranced as excited—chants the opening passages of this story, fades back to let us hear the dialogue preceding and during intermission, and then reasserts itself in the closing paragraphs. It is impossible to specify the source of this voice. Actually it seems to combine a number of voices, harmonized as various notes are harmonized in a chord. It celebrates the musician Powerhouse, emphasizing his charismatic hold on his fellow musicians and on the audience. It contains notes that seem to resist the enchantment of his power, yet when it labels him "monstrous" or "obscene" these do not seem to be terms of derogation. Rather they grope to define the more than human range of his performance, the sense that he draws on resources beyond the grasp of ordinary imagination. He is beyond "any known discipline." He is in a trance. He is like a man caught in a whirlpool and the whirlpool must be the demonic spirit of the music whose servant and prophet he becomes.

After the incantatory exposition, the whole perspective changes. Powerhouse begins to compose his hallucinatory story about his wife and someone named Uranus Knockwood. Now the mode of narration is much more objective. Powerhouse speaks—his fellow musicians respond, very much as their instruments would respond to the lead he provides with his in their musical performance. The improvised story of Gypsy's suicide is absurd and yet persuasive. The facts are not straight, but the mood and the image of a pursuing nemesis (who might as well be called Knockwood as anything else) have the authority of a vision. We see the birth of tragedy out of the spirit of music (to borrow a Nietzschean phrase). The grim vision is true whether or not it can be literally verified. Its power to convince is demonstrated by its effect on the waitress in the bar to which the musicians adjourn during intermission.

There the mood of the off-duty musicians relaxes from the pitch it achieved in their performance. But now we see that a man who has cast himself into the "whirlpool" of composition, of art, cannot escape its momentum. The true compulsion comes from within. Having made himself the instrument of the demonic knowledge that speaks through him, Powerhouse can only relax momentarily before resuming his testimony about Knockwood the nemesis.

Some of his listeners beg him to soften his message. "Hush about her brains. Hush about her insides." Nevertheless, at the peak of his testimony, his fellows support him, affirming that they do indeed share his vision —and however dark it may be, "Everybody in the room moans with pleasure." This specification again underlines that the author is showing us the nature of tragic art—while it rouses pity and terror, it also delights.

The waitress is so caught up by the power of invention that she says, "It must be the real truth." Powerhouse denies it at last. "Truth is something worse, I ain't said what yet." Here again the author echoes Nietzsche, who said that man had invented tragedy to serve as a curtain shutting off the glimpse of the truths of existence too terrible to be borne. The artist alone confronts those truths and, in a sense, defies them by his art or by primal human stubbornness.

The voice that began the story ends it. Again we have moved back from the close dramatic perspective. We are in a position to understand how much the intrusive voice functions like the chorus in a classic tragedy, celebrating the struggle in which it has no direct part.

Questions

1. What is the relation between his music and the story Powerhouse tells about his wife and Uranus Knockwood? What does Knockwood represent?

2. What leads the waitress to believe Powerhouse's story is true? Why does he deny that it is? What might be "worse" than the story he has told?

3. What does the story say about charisma and its sources? Why do all the listeners in the bar "moan with pleasure" while listening to Powerhouse's tales?

4. How are point of view and the use of the present tense suited to the material of the story?

See also "Questions for Comparing the Author's Stories, p. 237 of this *Handbook*.

Further Reading

Appel, Alfred. "Powerhouse's Blues," *Studies in Short Fiction*, II (Spring 1965), 221-234.

Griffith, Benjamin W. "'Powerhouse' as a Showcase of Eudora Welty's Methods and Themes," *Mississippi Quarterly*, XIX (Spring 1966), 79-84.

Kirkpatrick, Smith. "The Anointed Powerhouse," *Sewanee Review*, LXXVII (Winter 1969), 94-108.

Stone, William B. "Eudora Welty's Hydrodynamic 'Powerhouse,'" *Studies in Short Fiction*, 11 (1974), 93-96.

Eudora Welty   *A Worn Path* (p. 1439)
(Shorter Edition, p. 651)

This is a story without a plot, and the dramatic interaction of characters has little importance. Everything depends on the representation and evocation of the old woman and the world she sees through her oncoming blindness. It is a world in which ordinary things— hills, brush, animals, scarecrows, and people—are all partially transformed, all appearing to have the same degree of personality and the same degree of manageable opposition to Phoenix Jackson. She knows them all from the long experience of her life. They have been worn by the passage of time as she has been worn until there is an extraordinary smoothness in the way she can pass among them. The man with the gun is neither more nor less to her than the bush that catches her dress or the lady who ties her shoes when she gets to town.

The representation of Phoenix herself is the main focus of interest. We note how the author's prose, sometimes objective and concrete, is sometimes hardly distinguishable from the quaint remarks Phoenix directs to

her dim and yet familiar environment. The absence of
any note of complaint from her is as eloquent as any
positive statement in the story in the rendition of her
dignity.

Questions

1. How does the point of view help in characterizing
Phoenix? Cite examples showing how point of view is
managed.
2. What is the significance of the title? Of
Phoenix's name?
3. Why does the hunter point his gun at Phoenix?
4. What does the story say about human dignity and
what is required to maintain it? Does it in any way
protest against the conditions in which Phoenix lives?

See also "Questions for Comparing the Author's
Stories," below.

Further Reading

Apel, Alfred, Jr. *A Season of Dreams: The Fiction of
    Eudora Welty*. Baton Rouge: Louisiana State Univer-
    sity Press, 1965.
Daly, Saralyn. "A Worn Path Retrod," *Studies in Short
    Fiction*, I (Winter 1964), 133-139.
Trefman, Sara. "Welty's 'A Worn Path,'" *The Explicator*,
    XXIV (February 1966), Item 56.

Eudora Welty—
Questions for Comparing the Author's Stories

1. Compare the use of storyteller's voice in the two
Welty stories.
2. What adaptations of point of view are noteworthy
in these two stories?
3. Examine the effects of tone and their importance
in the two stories.

Edith Wharton   *The Muse's Tragedy* (p. 1446)
                (Shorter Edition, p. 658)

The aim of this story is to summarize a slowly unfolding tragedy that encompasses Mrs. Anerton's entire
life, not merely a tragedy that befalls her at a certain
juncture. It is, we think, one of those stories that
might have been a novel because of the long span of
time through which the knots of action are tightened
before the revelation is fully prepared and because of
the major complications which intertwine a past relationship with a present one. Therefore the devices
Wharton has used to compress the tale within the compact form of a short story are of particular interest,
as they are of particular effectiveness in structuring
a pattern that will skimp none of the essential components in the tragic equation.

We note that Mrs. Anterton's long relationship with
the poet Rendle is, first, sketched in its main outlines by sifting it through Danyers' impassioned but
still somewhat impersonal concern with the mystery of
the private life of a man of letters. Then the story
of her devotion to the poet is reinterpreted and ampli-
fied by her double-purpose letter which comprises the
third and last section of the story.

In the meantime, Danyers' romantic enthusiasm for
all that pertains to Rendle provides the momentum to
sweep him into a romantic attachment and an interlude
in Venice with the woman who was the Sylvia of the
poet's all-too-literary infatuation. That part of the
present action in which the younger man and the woman
cheated by an unreciprocated love come to a recognition of their feelings for each other is not directly
rendered. At first glance this seems to be a most
surprising omission, and many readers will feel—as
they are no doubt supposed to—a rather breathless
surprise that what has been foreshadowed as a development to climax the opening maneuvers is only recounted when it is already over and has ended in various painful ironies.

But then we will reflect that what really and significantly links past with present is not that Danyers
and Mrs. Anterton should be brought together by their
unequal interests in the poet and fall in love, but is
what Mrs. Anerton makes of this development.

Speaking in the first person in her heartbroken
letter, she is the one best placed to distill and
clearly articulate what the new love has meant and why

it is more hurtful to her than her disappointments from
Rendle. The happy month in Venice was supposed to be a
compensation for what she had missed in her previous life,
and perhaps to an extent it was. But the price of the
compensation was to show her with a final and ineradicable
clarity just what she had missed and how irretrievable
were the losses of her years as Rendle's unrequited lover.

So the economies of the short story—the ellipsis of
time and the compression natural to a letter that not
only summarizes the past but is a decisive termination of
the present action—turn out to be the means by which the
power and meaning of the interlocking complications are
so elegantly clarified. But though the story parts have
been so artfully jigsawed, there are still in the leisurely obliqueness of the opening and in the shift to an
unguarded first-person confession of the concluding
letter opportunities made by the author to develop tones
and nuances of character with the profoundest implications. For example, we see in the scrupulousness of Mrs.
Anerton's renunciation of her new love the fineness that
has been wasted by the tragic ironies of time.

Questions

1. Is Mrs. Anerton being selfishly cruel in rejecting
Danyers? Is he also a victim of Rendle's eccentricities?
2. Is her separation from Danyers a second tragedy or
the culmination of a single tragic pattern?
3. What does the story say about the entanglement of
public images with private lives?
4. What do you suppose Danyers' feelings to be when he
gets Mrs. Anerton's letter?
5. Do you understand Rendle's treatment of Mrs.
Anerton? What further kinds of information would make his
character and motivation more comprehensible?

Further Reading

Lewis, R. W. B. *Edith Wharton: A Biography*. New York:
Harper & Row, 1977.
Wolff, Cynthia Griffin. *A Feast of Words: The Triumph
of Edith Wharton*. New York: Oxford University Press,
1977.

Richard Wilbur   *A Game of Catch* (p. 1458)

Like William Carlos Williams' "The Use of Force" (which
is comparably brief), Wilbur's story explores a question
that appears to be fundamental in human affairs of any
given magnitude, from the squabbles of children to the
struggles of nations at war: What is the nature of power
and what kind of power triumphs in the long run?

Clearly Monk and Glennie outclass Scho in the power
that comes from skill and physical strength. Outclassing
him, they thoughtlessly and cruelly use their power to
humiliate him and finally injure him (however slightly)
by forcing his fall from the tree, Completely unable to
respond in kind to their bullying, Scho falls back on
what may appear to be the absurdly ineffective expedient
of taunting them. It is the peculiar form of his taunt
which gives the story its philosophical base. When Scho
says "I can make you guys do anything I want," he is pro-
claiming his alliance with powers unarguably superior to
the prowess of the stronger boys—with the powers of an
inscrutable destiny to which their wills are blindly and
hopelessly subordinate. His claim that he has achieved
the alliance he claims cannot be demonstrated by him,
but by the same token it cannot be refuted by them. It
is, in a literal sense, an irrefutable argument, dependent for its verification on faith alone. Against the
power of faith in things unseen the faith in visible
strength must, at the least, be shaken into an acknowl-
edgment of its limitations. Military men as well as
theologians and philosophers have long acknowledged that
to shake the faith of the adversary while one's own
faith remains intact is to triumph.

It is on this philosophical conundrum that the story
is built—or perhaps it might be better to say that the
author found this philosophical formula embodied in a
trivial and transient episode, an utterly commonplace
playground squabble. Better, for it is always important
to emphasize that, in the making of fiction, ideas are
found or developed by the growth of the story out of
observation and rarely serve very well as the basis from
which the design of a story is elaborated.

In any case, as a minimum, it ought to be recognized
by students that though the circumstances are banal and
trivial, some far-ranging or even ultimate principles
are illustrated here. The last words in the battle are
Scho's. He utters them "in triumph and misery." The
pairing of these words is important. They should be
understood to be inseparable, for in claiming a

<u>transcendent</u> victory, Scho (or anyone) must pay for it by relinquishing all claims to the happiness of a physical victory. This is the old story of the martyr figure who claims his triumph over his persecutors by yielding his body as victim to their torments.

Questions

1. What does the story say about the cruelty and vengefulness of children?
2. Discuss Scho's claim that he "makes" the other boys do what they do. In your discussion consider the various meanings of the verb "to make." (As, for example in the expression "two and two make four"; obviously two and two do not <u>compel</u> four to come into existence.)
3. Who finally has the upper hand in the conflict between Scho and the other boys?
4. Note any parallels you can see between the situation of this story and historic instances of confrontation between "strong" and "weak" nations.

Further Reading

Hills, L. Rust, and Penney C. Hills. *How We Live*. New York: Macmillan, 1968, pp. 987-988.

William Carlos Williams   *The Use of Force* (p. 1461)
(Shorter Edition, p. 670)

We know absolutely nothing about the characters of this story except what we learn in the brief action depicted and what we can infer about the doctor from his sparse interpretive comments. There are not even any proper names. Characterization is thus reduced to elemental—one might say subpersonal—traits and roles. There are three adults and one child. Two males and two females. The doctor's role is strictly defined by his professional obligations. The two parents are bound almost as strictly by their concern over the child's illness. Only the child has essential freedom in her choice of responses.

However commonplace the little girl's refusal to cooperate may seem to us, it is undeniably perverse—

according to the social and technical rules to which the
adults are committed. The essential conflict in the story
rises from their attempt to overcome this perversity—for
the unarguably good end of saving the girl's life.

The genuine surprise that emerges from the very
limited action is not at all in what is done or how the
action ends. Its end has been predetermined. The surprise
is that in carrying through a necessary and benign action,
the doctor's motives have been monstrously changed, something awesome and terrifying has been unleashed that will
not in any way change the practical outcome of his efforts
but must radically change his understanding of himself. At
the moment of forcing the girl's mouth open the doctor's
motives are not simple adherence to professional ethics:
they are those of an adult ravisher violating a child.
Without fracturing civilized routines—without needing to
—the monstrous and perverse power of the irrational has
revealed its superior authority.

The shock of this revelation is mainly intellectual.
There is no superficial melodrama here, no dying child,
no unmasked villain shamed in his crime. But if we realize
the social, political, moral implications of the small-
scale demonstration, the shock will be powerful enough.
Reading this story is a bit like watching the laboratory
discovery of a reaction that will sometime, somewhere,
devastate all that we call civilization.

Questions

1. Since we know nothing of the past history of these
characters, what means does the author rely on to make
us understand them?

2. Does the sick girl's physical beauty have anything
to do with the outcome and the meaning of this encounter?

3. Can you find any fault with the doctor's behavior?
Has he done something that is simultaneously good and
evil? Was the component of evil avoidable?

4. Since the use of force seems a necessity in preserving orderly civilizations, what does the story say
about civilized life in general?

5. What has the straightforward simplicity of the
narration to do with the emotional effect of the story?

Virginia Woolf   *Kew Gardens* (p. 1465)
(Shorter Edition, p. 673)

Technique and conception are extraordinarily well coordinated here to produce a revision of conventional notions of character. Technically speaking, the point of view is so dissolved or capriciously fragmented that the shapes defined by the light falling through the flower bed are given a prominence equal to the thoughts, recollections, and emotions of the passersby—and their histories are dissolved into a series of random images. Thus the author expresses her conception of lives as being far less solid or continuous than our ordinary parlance credits them with being. What is reality? "For me, a square silver shoe buckle and a dragonfly . . .," says the man named Simon. The past has been reduced to details that seem to float indistinguishably among the leaves, clouds, flowers, and human or insect creatures adrift in the weather of a summer's day. The snail on the ground is as much a part of the web of life as the inarticulate young lovers or the elderly eccentric.

The author has assumed some of the prerogatives of omniscient narration. She moves in and out of the consciousness of a number of people and even speculates on realities imperceptible to the senses. But it remains a strange sort of omniscience. Instead of being used to weave the story tightly together, as is usually the case, the omniscient technique contributes to dissolving everything into a flickering play of colored lights. The imagery is noticeably fluid throughout. "The ponderous woman looked through *the pattern of falling words* at the flowers. . . ." (My italics.) "She saw them as a sleeper waking from a heavy sleep sees a brass candlestick reflecting the light in an unfamiliar way. . . ." Who is making the association between the appearance of the flowers and that of a brass candlestick? We cannot say. It is not evident that the ponderous woman ever stared at a candlestick as the "sleeper" is said to do. Nor is there any suggested personality of a narrator to whom we can attribute the simile.

It might be helpful to students to suggest to them that this fluid play of imagery has some kinship with impressionism in painting or in music. Certainly any of them who respond strongly to the story will be moved to admit that the boundaries between character and environment are less stable and definable than we generally suppose.

Questions

1. Why is there little more information about the
people in the story than about the flowers and insects?
What happens to point of view in such a statement as
this? What happens to human values?
2. What, if anything, relates the various passersby
to each other?
3. Discuss the importance of style and imagery in
establishing the tone and meaning of the story. Is
there a theme?
4. Can you locate any devices of personification?
What do they contribute to the meaning of the whole?
5. Is the personality of the author rendered or
implied by the manner in which the story is told?

Richard Wright   *The Man Who Was Almost a Man* (p. 1470)
               (Shorter Edition, p. 678)

The setting and the race of the characters are important components of this story. Dave and his family
are black; therefore their poverty is extreme enough to
add special complications to both the acquisition of
the gun and the magnitude of the disaster when the mule
is accidentally killed. The outlay of two dollars for
the gun means that the tight economic discipline by
which they live has to be breached; the prospect of
having to pay fifty dollars for the dead mule means an
enormous handicap for an adolescent black farm laborer.
The rural setting conditions the operative values of
all the characters, white and black—for example, the
significance of possessing a gun is both more innocent
and imperative for a farm boy than it might be for an
urban youth.
But the firm, straightforward, tragicomic plot is
Wright's main resource in showing the ironies in this
essentially American rite of passage. Dave's initial
motivation is his unexamined conviction that owning a
gun will make him a man. The catalogue—his poor substitute for tales of chivalry—adds fuel to the fire of
his conviction that he must at all costs own a weapon.
"If he had a gun like that he would polish it and keep
it shining so it would never rust." To his fervid
adolescent imagination it has become a symbol of what
is most precious in himself—of the "manhood" so hard

to define in the cultural vocabulary available to him from his environment.

After the gun is bought, the second main phase of the plot action leads to the death of the mule Jenny. Because he is still partly a child, Dave is so befuddled in his excitement at owning the gun that he simply cannot see the mule at which he shoots. The passage in which he chases the wounded animal and tries to stanch the flow of blood by plugging the bullet hole with dirt fully reveals the magnitude of the emotions that are sweeping him along.

The result of the accident—the exorbitant debt he has contracted and his subsequent flight from it into an unknown and hazardous future—is an ironic fulfillment of the wish that set the action in motion: that is, in the end he is _forced_ to accept the role of a man, entirely dependent on himself.

This outcome of the plot, this ironic correction of his expectations, is hardly to be construed as an unhappy ending. It is merely a sharp jolt that expresses the shock of wakening into reality, the archetypal announcement that the dreaming child must, willy-nilly, become a man when he is called upon to pay for his dreams.

Probably many contemporary students will have difficulty in properly assessing—or sympathizing with— Dave's wish to own a gun, and a misinterpretation of that wish can be an impediment to understanding character and the statement of the plot. Discussion of gun-ownership as an American tradition may help to dampen excessive psychological interpretations of the gun as phallic symbol—or as an indication of criminal propensities in Dave.

Questions

1. What is the importance of the social setting in shaping Dave's motives and course of action?

2. How do the dialogue and limited point of view help reveal the meaning of local social pressures?

3. To what extent is the accidental shooting of the mule crucial to Dave's departure from home? Does it merely hasten him on a course he would in any case have followed?

4. What sort of future for Dave is implied by the last paragraphs?

5. Discuss the role of the minor characters in shaping Dave's character and in determining his actions.

Further Reading

Burgun, Edwin Berry. "The Art of Richard Wright's Short Stories," *Quarterly Review of Literature*, I (Spring 1944), 198-211.